T5-DIE-111
3 2711 00086 4011

COLUMBIA COLLEGE LIBRARY
600 S. MICHIGAN AVENUE
CHICAGO, IL 60605

R A F A E L   O E I

riding
the
b a n d w i d t h

Producing
for Digital
Radio

Marshall Cavendish
Academic

ENTERED JUL 2 9 2005

© 2005 Marshall Cavendish International
(Singapore) Private Limited

Published 2005 by Marshall Cavendish Academic
An imprint of Marshall Cavendish International
(Singapore) Private Limited
A member of Times Publishing Limited

Times Centre, 1 New Industrial Road,
Singapore 536196
Tel:(65) 6213 9288
Fax: (65) 6284 9772
E-mail: mca@sg.marshallcavendish.com
Website:
http://www.marshallcavendish.com/academic

All rights reserved. No part of this publication may
be reproduced, stored in a retrieval system, or
transmitted, in any form or by any means, electronic,
mechanical, photocopying, recording or otherwise,
without the prior permission of the publishers.

ISBN: 981-210-415-1

A CIP catalogue record for this book is available from
the National Library Board (Singapore).

Printed by Times Graphics Pte Ltd, Singapore
on non-acidic paper

**London • New York • Beijing • Shanghai
• Bangkok • Kuala Lumpur • Singapore**

International Board
of Advisors

Dr. Abdul Rashid Moten, Professor
International Islamic University, Malaysia

Dr. Amitav Acharya, Professor
*Institute of Defence & Strategic Studies
Nanyang Technological University, Singapore*

Dr. Anne Pakir, Associate Professor
National University of Singapore, Singapore

Arun Mahizhnan, Deputy Director,
The Institute of Policy Studies, Singapore

Dr. Ban Kah Choon, Professor
Mahidol University, Thailand

**Dr. Chua Beng Huat, Professor
(Current Chair of Board of Advisors)**
National University of Singapore, Singapore

Dr. Eddie C. Y. Kuo, Professor
Nanyang Technological University, Singapore

Dr. Gerald Tan, Associate Professor
Flinders University, Australia

Dr. Hong Hai, Professor
*Nanyang Business School
Nanyang Technological University, Singapore*

Dr. Jason Tan, Associate Professor
*National Institute of Education
Nanyang Technological University, Singapore*

Dr. Jon Quah, Professor
National University of Singapore, Singapore

Dr. Josephine Smart, Professor
University of Calgary, Canada

Dr. Lee Lai To, Associate Professor
National University of Singapore, Singapore

Dr. Leo Suryadinata, Professor
Institute of Southeast Asian Studies, Singapore

Dr. Lim Hua Sing, Professor
Waseda University, Japan

Dr. M. Sornarajah, Professor
National University of Singapore, Singapore

Dr. Ramadhar Singh, Professor
National University of Singapore, Singapore

Dr. Roxanna Waterson, Associate Professor
National University of Singapore, Singapore

Dr. S. Vasoo, Associate Professorial Fellow
National University of Singapore, Singapore

Dr. Tan Tai Yong, Associate Professor
National University of Singapore, Singapore

Ten Chin Liew, Professor
National University of Singapore, Singapore

Dr. Victor Savage, Associate Professor
National University of Singapore, Singapore

Dr. Wang Gungwu, Professor
National University of Singapore, Singapore

Dr. Wang Ning, Professor
Tsinghua University, Beijing, China

Yu Xintian, Professor
*Shanghai Institute for International Studies
Shanghai, China*

Contents

Content

Acknowledgements

Heartfelt thanks and gratitude go to the Director of the School of Film & Media Studies, Dr Victor Valbuena and Deputy Director, Ms Gurcharn Kaur at Ngee Ann Polytechnic, Singapore. They have been very encouraging and supportive of my research, seminar and workshop engagements, and management of the radio section in the Mass Communication Diploma programme.

Gratitude and thanks also to a great team: Mr Kwek Chin Ling, Ms Anita Kuan and Mr Yokanathan Ramakrishnan. It has been a pleasure sharing the vision; lighting the spark in our young broadcasters. To the cutting edge research team headed by Mr Chua Beng Koon and Mr Darran Nathan; thank you so much for the sharing and collaboration. You have kept our radio students at the forefront and abreast of the digital broadcast revolution through your research and in allowing our students to experiment on your DAB setup.

To the committee and staff of the Broadcast Education Asociation, USA—especially Prof Frank Chorba and Prof Michael Keith who are so inspiring. Thank you for being so supportive and patient with me. Thank you, for also giving me the opportunity to share a little bit of Asia at the BEA Convention through the Asian Digital Broadcast panels, three years in a row. It was a very rewarding experience getting the experts together and prepared.

To all my friends at the various radio stations around the world that have been patient with my queries and hypothesis about the state of radio in our time, I appreciate your contributions and advice.

For the years of experience, development and support, thanks to the people, past and present, at the Caldecott Broadcast Centre. I owe a debt of gratitude to so many people from both the radio and television industries locally and abroad. Special mention goes to Ms Pearl Samuel, Mr Brian Richmond, Mr J T Koh, Mr Norman Lim and the late Mr Steven Lee, Singapore's first television news presenter. I appreciate your mentoring and advice. Thank you.

To my classmate and now Singapore radio programmer and personality Colin Gomez and his tireless passion for radio, I appreciate all the long hours of sharing and discussions. I admire you as much as you do me. Dreams do come true. You will make a great educator.

To my students who went through the exercises in this volume: you made teaching a joy for me. Thank you for allowing me the privilege of sharing my experiences with you.

To the editorial staff at Marshall Cavendish Academic and Katherine Krummert for their expertise in publishing this book.

Lastly, to Dr Jackie Cook, my supervisor, Prof Claire Woods and Nigel Starck: you were all so encouraging. You provided the inspiration that fuelled my quest in digital radio research. There is so much to know and learn.

List of Figures

List of Tables

Introduction

> Yet radio as an invention, and a cultural force, is regarded as mattering very little now in the grand scheme of things, especially in the face of cable TV, blockbuster movies, and the Internet. It is low-tech, unglamorous, and taken for granted. (Douglas 1999, p. 9)

Douglas, making an observation and statement in a study and chronicle of American radio titled *Listening in: Radio and the American Imagination, from Amos 'n' Andy and Edward R. Murrow to Wolfman Jack and Howard Stern*. In that one sentence, she pays tribute to radio as an innovation of the past and its influence on shaping societies and adding to the culture of communities. With the emergence of Internet radio and the streaming of radio programmes through mobile cellular phones, we see traditional radio listening slowly fading into the woodwork. This, despite the development of Eureka 147: Digital Audio Broadcasting (DAB) in 1987 that was intended to optimise the frequency bandwidth available to radio. A comprehensive introduction to the structure of the DAB transmission process is available in my first book, *Borderless Bandwidth: DNA of Digital Radio*. The book also discusses the importance of approaching the business and organisation of radio differently, given the structure of the system and encoding available to DAB. While *Borderless Bandwidth* explores possible solutions to the approach of programming and structuring the radio organisation in a digital environment, this book will explore traditional content generation for conventional radio broadcasts and discuss possible formats and enhanced content that can be broadcast on digital radio.

As the media landscape evolves with increased cable television programming, wireless digital communication systems, and broadband Internet access, all of which enable interactive communication, on-demand information, and entertainment, Douglas' observation that radio matters very little to the present generation resonates like a death knell. However, listener surveys and radio ratings seem to indicate that traditional radio continues to command a steady, avid following in spite of the dazzling array of impressive communication and media services that are available. Radio still holds the listener's ear in a unique way that none of the other media can. Is it the on-air personality? Is it the music, programming and news content?

Working from the premise that radio is accepted as an integral part of daily life, this book explores the methods, techniques and approaches taken in producing, presenting, creating and writing for radio. Beginning from a historical perspective to lay the foundation for later discussions, these practical issues are eventually juxtaposed with the technological challenges that face broadcasters who want to operate and function effectively in an interactive digital environment. Both traditional analogue and digital technologies employed in radio broadcasting already negate the latter half of the Douglas' statement quoted above. To the listener, radio seems ostensibly low-tech and unglamorous, a "noise-box" that can easily fade into the woodwork and be taken for granted. Curiously, that point of view contradicts the technological deterministic attitude of "media prophet" Marshall McLuhan.

Conventional radio technology is hardly "low-tech," whether it is the transmission, presentation or production process. The complexity of radio production and presentation may not be apparent in the first instance. Packaged documentaries, talk shows, news bulletins and interviews seem effortless when well constructed and produced. More "criminal" is the association, by some listeners, of regarding radio listening as nothing more than the mere spinning of one's favourite tunes like a disembodied jukebox. This, as history already witnessed, was the intended purpose of radio, the popularity of which had already been foreseen in the early 1920s by David Sarnoff, head of the Radio Corporation of America. Radio as a source of news, information, discussion, music and entertainment involves extensive preparation, research, production and presentation—processes which are far from "low-tech."

With the onslaught of the digital revolution that began with the advent of the personal computer and the connection of individuals and communities through the World Wide Web in the early 1990s, the throes of the "next wave" of radio broadcasting—widely proclaimed since the mid-1990s—are still hovering in a holding pattern with radio broadcasters uncertain how to proceed with the potential available to them through digital technologies. There have been pockets of activity and innovation in the development of Internet radio and free-to-air wireless digital radio. The question is how would a radio "jock," journalist or presenter prepare and produce content that contributes to an enhanced radio-listening experience streamed through a digital interface? And as producers and managers, what relevant services would be required to attract and retain listeners through enhanced digital radio receivers?

The reference to "relevant services" as a tangible deliverable, within the context of this book, functions on two levels. The first refers to relevance as the mode and structure of programming that conforms and is appropriate to the architecture of the digital broadcast technology being adopted and utilised in any given radio station. The second, and what many may consider the more important of the two, is the relevance of programme content and services for the listener.

While radio may be considered a consumable product, history has shown that radio broadcasting as a service resonates more with the listener than as a product to be consumed. Radio as life, or radio as an essential part of one's daily routine, has sustained its relevance in the home or in the car. This underscores radio's impact and influence on society and communities, evidenced in its history.

Undoubtedly, radio production processes have moved far beyond the simple voice to music that is transmitted over the airwaves. Today, listeners are familiar with digital technology and regard it as an essential tool in many areas of their professional and domestic lives. Personal computers, mobile telephones, digital receivers in cars, or portable digital MP3 players are more than appendages to the consumer. While many may not have considered its importance, broadcasters will increasingly need to grapple with digital systems such as Eureka 147, to understand its potential and design programming that optimises its multidimensional nature. This will enable the lone presenter to be armed with digital tools that will deliver enhanced content and services that now go beyond mere aural broadcasts. The presenter is now able to formulate that same content in a visual form as well. Packaging for both the ear and the eye enables digital radio to deliver more to the listener.

Digital radio architecture allows the broadcast of interactive content, compressed data and audio (WorldDAB Forum and Eureka 147 Project Newsletters, Blair 1999, Dambacher 1996, Hoeg & Lauterbach 2001). This implies that a host of audio and visual information services can now be provided through digital radio. Within an organised and systemic structural context, consideration must be given to production value chains and the ability to install processes that will address daily radio production, programming and scheduling. Debates on the integrity of radio as an audio medium distract from developing operations that enable the seamless inclusion of data and information services for digital radio. The years of debate within the radio industry have allowed the telecommunications industry to leapfrog into bringing consumers some of the most innovative digital cellular phones for that industry. After all, telecoms did not have the baggage of conforming to accepted perceptions of what constitutes good radio. It is no longer a question of who will dictate the direction, shape and form of digital broadcast services. That is done. Having said that, the relevance of what will be discussed in this book is still essential. Radio as a medium will be enhanced with digital interactive broadcast technology. Conceptualising and delivering content through integrated digital radio services presented holistically to listeners must permeate the creative mind of the digital radio broadcaster.

In *Borderless Bandwidth: DNA of Digital Radio* (Oei 2002), I gave the example of a radio organisation that, rather than adapting and preparing adequately for the change, operated largely as an institutional radio of the 1950s and 1960s; not providing ample resources to support and educate its personnel to operate within a commercial structure and then, launching onto a digital platform without first installing adequate infrastructure to ensure its personnel were attuned to all the implications of providing digital radio services. In fact, the mechanism that may have facilitated the maintenance of an active reading of the broadcast environment, reviewing it and responding to it by equipping the station's producers and presenters with the necessary tools and education—the radio training school— was discontinued and dismantled by this radio organisation during its restructuring exercise in the 1990s. Maintaining an active learning environment within an organisation ensures innovation and sustained growth in spite of market influences because of its ability to constantly redefine itself to remain relevant to its consumers. To dismantle a "training school" brings the need, then, for leaders within the organisation to be able to develop and motivate their team while monitoring the competition and industry developments.

Mobile telecommunications have developed by leaps and bounds within just a few years. This is fact. While this may have been a concern within the broadcast industry, the truth is the consumer/listener is not concerned about backend operations or the petty wrangling about control and succession between service providers, operators, or broadcast and telecommunication magnates. All they care about is that they receive services that satisfy their needs.

Douglas explains it this way:

> Radio is an especially rich example of such technological insurgency, in which the design and use of inventions is fought over, contested, and reimagined by a host of actors, including consumers, despite the power of corporate control. (Douglas 1999, p. 15)

And consumers have been open about their preferences, enthusiastically purchasing cellular phones that connect to the Internet, send emails and faxes, and receive radio signals. Similarly, with the publication of books like *Borderless Bandwidth* (Oei 2002), broadcasters and academia have openly discussed the implications of the emergence of digital radio for the radio broadcast industry and consumer expectations.

Reiterating the stance I took in *Borderless Bandwidth* (ibid.), I strongly believe that modification to programming paradigms is imperative. Mobile telecommunication services and the Internet, today, provide similar entertainment and information services over cellular phones once only broadcast through the radio and television, using an "on demand" model and the ability to access the Internet through their mobile phones anytime, anywhere. With this service model, consumers are able to access the news, stock prices, information and the weather just by *uplinking* to an Internet provider through what was once a simple mobile communication device. To see how far down the line telecommunication research has gone, I relate the following:

> In June 2002, Dr Lawrence Rabiner, retired vice president of research from AT&T Labs, Florham Park, New Jersey presented keynote lectures for the *Communication and Media Forum* organised by the National University of Singapore and the Nanyang Technological University of Singapore as part of their Summer School series. Over three days, Dr Rabiner highlighted the technological trends in three areas: telecommunications, media technologies and wireless technologies. In his final lecture on wireless technologies, Dr Rabiner presented an outline of the history of telephony services and shared some research data from AT&T on the direction that wireless telephony is headed.
>
> His suggestions to improve wireless performance included the use of Orthogonal Frequency Division Multiplex (OFDM) architecture, or what is now known as 4G, fourth generation wireless technology that utilises "wide-OFDM" (WOFDM). Amongst the initiatives that

are underway, he cited the need to create services for the "4G" environment that will be compelling to the wireless user. This includes creating a compelling set of wireless location-based, personalised services that will make the wireless web ubiquitous and part of everyday life. The buffet of services includes mobile commerce, time-critical services such as news, financial and market updates; data services that include weather, traffic, flight details and entertainment; and media streaming that includes web radio, web television and a jukebox-type music service. (Rabiner 2002)

The intention of my book *Borderless Bandwidth* (Oei 2002) and of my various presentations—besides sharing knowledge—was to rally the radio broadcast community in Singapore into action to spearhead digital services on broadband DAB. I listened to Dr Rabiner's declaration that 4G-WOFDM will be the standard for the next generation of cellular telephones with interest. As described in the chapter on DAB technology (Oei 2002, pp. 11–22), OFDM is the backbone of the DAB-Eureka 147 transmission process, developed for radio to address the problem of spectrum limitations in FM transmission back in 1987 (WorldDAB Forum and Eureka 147 Project Newsletters, Blair 1999, Dambacher 1996, Hoeg & Lauterbach 2001). After all, Eureka 147 was developed for mobile transmission with inbuilt redundancies that ensure clear reception at all times, whether the user is stationary or in motion. This robust technology, not optimally used by radio sooner, has now been utilised and modified for mobile telecommunication services.

Innovations in telecommunications have enabled more mobility, more data services and more access to information, adding new dimensions to the use of the telephone. Similarly, innovations in broadcast technology allow more than just video or audio to be streamed to the masses. We are looking at new creatures in broadcasting that can no longer be categorised into merely radio or television.

Having outlined the debate and development of radio onto a digital platform, the fundamental principles of conceptualising, writing, producing and presenting in radio remain largely the same. These attributes and skills reside in radio personalities who are able to tap these resources instinctively through years of practise. Even at an enhanced level, conceptualising and delivering radio content will begin from the point that it is largely an audio medium. And so, delivery of the value in programming will be in the experience and in the concise manner in which information and entertainment are packaged.

This little volume presents some of the basic approaches to radio production and presentation. These are notes, summaries and material that have served me well during my career as a radio and television broadcaster. The principles of writing, producing and presenting for radio have also helped me in managerial tasks. These include being able to approach my tasks systematically, and writing and communicating clearly and succinctly with my peers and subordinates.

The benefits of having the good fortune of working in radio have been manifold in my subsequent and parallel careers. Having taught radio production, presentation and management, being a mentor to my presenters during my years in radio, and the value of using radio principles in other areas of my working life has been immeasurable. While there are books on radio production, writing and presenting, as well as on radio station management and programming, few mention the usefulness in applying these to oneself. Incredibly, the craft of radio in recent years has also been misunderstood by aspiring deejays.

While the reality is we are now operating within a digital realm, it does not detract from the importance of laying a firm foundation in the fundamentals of audio production, script writing and presentation skills. These would include grounding the acolyte with skills in splice and dub editing using analogue tape, if available, and in providing a basic introduction to phonetics—a system that, strangely, even some media professors consider archaic. In practise, phonetics is useful, effective and still required knowledge by many broadcast stations.

Having the broadcast student go through such skills as those above may not be considered essential in the minds of those who believe firmly that these are unnecessary in a digital world. Based on sound pedagogical principles, my stance in this matter is that the student must first progress from the tangible to the intangible, from physically manipulating analogue tape to manipulating audio regions within a virtual digital audio editing environment. To guide the young broadcaster through this provides the historical significance that may be overlooked by the uninitiated. It provides a basis for understanding how some production and presentation processes have become institutionalised in the medium. Looking at available audio editing software, the look and feel of multi-track consoles and recorders have been recreated so that some of these aesthetics remain even in a technologically more advanced medium. These issues, however, will not be argued in this book. What is presented are some of the fundamentals that can be built upon.

This book will begin with a summary of how radio evolved as a service, how radio productions can be conceived, some approaches to radio presentation and how these may be applied to developing content for digital transmission.

Chapter One focuses on institutional radio and the question "How did we get here"? Against the backdrop of radio history, you will be introduced to some of the events that shaped radio as an industry. Why is radio news the way it is today? I will trace the emergence of Public Service Broadcasting and Commercial Radio, the events that formed them, and how radio in the community evolved. This chapter will also explain traditional approaches to radio programming through its many phases.

Chapter Two covers the notion that radio listeners of today are now consumers/users. The radio listener of today is more sophisticated than the radio listener of the 1950s. Listeners are now familiar with functioning within a digital environment, accessing the information and may be considered co-producers. The chapter explores some of the listening habits of these listeners and suggests that institutional radio, which is still functioning in an organisational model from the 1950s, will need to acknowledge the change in the listener profile and update itself.

Chapter Three addresses the approach to conceptualising for and "thinking radio." Based on the attributes of radio, how do you develop an idea for radio and script it? How does one write for an audio medium?

Chapter Four then covers the various production and editing processes that go into producing a radio programme. I include dub and splice editing techniques through to discussions on using digital editing software and the concept of stereo productions.

Chapter Five looks at the architecture of a DAB receiver and the process of putting together text and graphics for digital radio transmission. This reinforces the fact that radio broadcasters are faced with the need to expand their perception and production skills to take advantage of the enhanced potential of digital radio.

Chapter Six concludes by emphasizing that though mastery of digital media concepts is essential, producers and presenters must have a firm foundation in the essential elements of radio as a medium of communication. Digital technology remains a tool to efficiently deliver the message. Crafting the message transcends the novelty. Content and sevices are still key to reinforce the credibility of the medium. Although consumer uptake is languid, producing for digital radio transmission now will avoid a mad scramble to deliver when the curve finally turns.

CHAPTER 1

The Radio Journey

This chapter traces the evolution of radio through its popular history, including its application and relevance to the listening community in Singapore. Singapore is included because it was one of the first markets in the world to adopt and deliver digital radio services using Eureka 147-DAB.

The focus in this journey is to reflect on and illustrate how technological and social demands in the past redefined radio and how radio services adapted to each phase to remain relevant to the listening community. These events contributed to forming the processes that make up "institutional radio." To focus on some of its core components, my approach will centre on the milestones in radio history from three perspectives: the assumptions of the programmer, the producer and the presenter.

The intention here is to define what constituted the "radio experience" as it progressed through the years, evolving as "institutional radio" developed its foundations. The importance of looking at the radio experience as a whole is also to identify components that have become essential to the experience. This is important, as the radio experience itself is an intangible phenomenon that is a composite result of systems and processes. O'Connor and McDermott (1997) define a system as "an entity that maintains its existence and functions as a whole through the interaction of its parts" (O'Connor et al. 1997, p. 2). When the system functions as a whole, the result is an "emergent property" (ibid., p. 6).

> You could study acoustics and the physics of sound for years without suspecting the beauty and emotional power of music. Put two eyes together and you do not simply get a bigger picture but three-dimensional vision. Two ears do not simply give you the ability to hear twice as well, they give you the ability to hear in stereo. ... Put an eye by itself on the table and it would see nothing. You cannot find sight, hearing, touch, taste or smell in any of the parts of a body. Your life is dependent on your parts working together. When the parts are isolated from the body, they die. Post mortems do not discover the secret of life, but death (O'Connor et al., pp. 6–7).

FIGURE 1.1   Broadcaster/Listener Forces of Influence

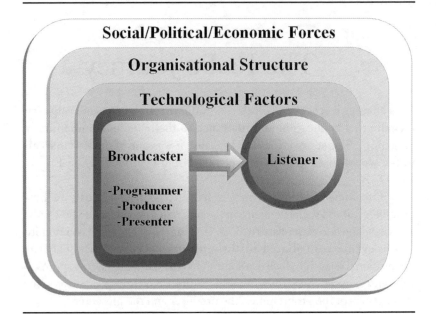

Rafael Oei 2002

Similarly, it is not the presentation style, the music, the news, the way the weather report is delivered, nor is it the FM, AM or audio technology, the gramophone, the compact disc player or the computer and web-streaming that individually possess the secret of the "radio experience." If you met Howard Stern, Rick Dees and Casey Kasem and had a conversation with them, that itself is not a "radio experience" although to listen to them delivering their programme over the radio is. Consequently, while this chapter traces the development of each of the components mentioned above that make up the total experience, I do not pretend to "understand the whole system properties by breaking the system into its constituent parts" (O'Connor et al., p. 11). Instead I will address key components in respect to how together they may function to create the enhanced experience of digital radio as will be proposed in a later chapter. With this, I hope it will serve to explain approaches, practices and expectations currently held by broadcasters and listeners about the current business of radio broadcasting. This brief outline serves my purpose in setting the tone for subsequent chapters on production and presentation in this book.

As Figure 1.1 represents, it is the sum total of the above and a variety of forces that directly or indirectly influence the listening or production experience.

To maintain focus, I will limit my discussion to three key and distinct components in the radio broadcast system—the programmer, the producer and the presenter—to concentrate on how these key processes shaped and will shape the radio listening experience within the constraints of an organisational structure influenced by social, political, economic and technological determinants. Confining the boundaries of radio technology, I will simplify technological milestones and divide them into the periods before and after the introduction of digital broadcast systems, though Castells (2000), Crook (1999), Fang (1997) and Richardson (2001) have different views.

For the purpose of consistency and clarity, my terms of reference are as follows. The "programmer" is the person or team responsible for the daily broadcast schedule. By "producer," I mean the person or team responsible for creating, constructing, preparing or packaging content for transmission. The "presenter" is the person who delivers announcements, narration, commentary or verbal presentations in a production or radio broadcast. Figure 1.2 serves as a visual representation of the production-broadcast value chain that delivers the "radio experience." Two-way arrows denote two-way communication.

In relation to the evolution of role-assumptions for the radio programmer, producer and presenter through the radio-history continuum, we will see a pattern of behaviour in the adoption, innovation and re-innovation of technologies and applications. Castells (2000) expresses a useful theoretical perspective that may be applied to this pattern. In describing the process of generating knowledge and information, processing and communication, Castells refers to the three distinct stages as "the automation of tasks, an experimentation of uses, and a reconfiguration of applications" (Castells 2000, p.31).

Castells' explanation of the stages can be applied to the way radio and its listeners adjusted to each other's needs and assumptions as content provider and listener/consumer through eight decades of history (See Figure 1.3).

In the first two stages, technological innovation progressed through *learning by using*, in Rosenberg's terminology. In the third stage, the users

3

FIGURE 1.2 Simplified Broadcast Production/Transmission Model

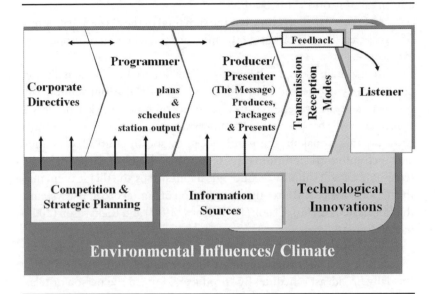

Rafael Oei 2002

FIGURE 1.3 Castells' Innovation Loop

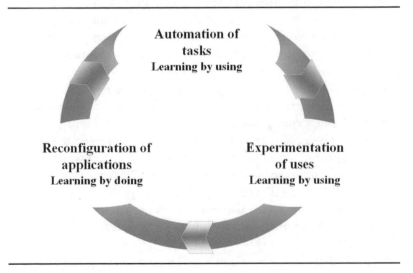

Rafael Oei 2002

learned technology *by doing*, and ended up reconfiguring the networks, and finding new applications (ibid.).

Superimposing this model onto radio history, as radio integrated into the fabric of homes through each stage of its development, radio provided services that defined its own place within society, reinventing itself at times, surviving for "new" audiences as new assumptions defined new services, demonstrating how evolution and adaptability are processes that follow consumers' familiarity with existing technology. This familiarity, as observed by Castells, will ultimately cause the consumer/user to experiment with and demand an improvement in the user/receiver interface. This is obvious within the digital environment, where listeners are given the opportunity to input personal listening and information preferences through a website or through digital receivers equipped with customisable options, "learning by doing" and "finding new applications" as institutional radio and its consumer/listeners function in a digital environment.

In Chapter Two, I will extend this focus to look at how the consumer/listener influenced institutional radio and radio production/presentation processes.

1.1 THE LITERATURE

In considering material from Singaporean publications, I chose to concentrate on output from government-based publications, academic textbooks, periodicals and brochures. I find these the most reliable though the referenced historical data on radio in Singapore (Oei 2002; Liu 1999; Chen 1997; Koh 1995; Tham & Tay 1995; Rediffusion Singapore 1995; Tay 1995; Tan & Soh 1994; Radio Singapore 1959) is not as extensively or comprehensively documented.

Gretchen Liu's (1999) lovely volume titled *Singapore: A Pictorial History 1819–2000*, provides information from the period covering World War II. Chen Ai Yen's (1997) chapter on "The Mass Media, 1819–1980" from the book *A History of Singapore* (Chen 1197, pp. 300–311), reinforces the accounts of the role and function of media from the 1950s onto the troubled period in Singapore's history in the late 1960s.

A significant contributor to the local media landscape is Rediffusion Singapore. Up to my account of this cable broadcasting service's establishment in Singapore in 1949 (Oei 2002)—its first in the Far East—there was limited awareness and information about Rediffusion in

Singapore's media literature. I was able to piece together the little known Rediffusion Singapore story from information published in Rediffusion brochures and original newspaper clippings from the late 1940s through to the 1950s graciously provided by Ms Juanita Melson, English Programme Director of Rediffusion Singapore at the time of my research. These articles reflect the impact Rediffusion had on Singapore media and its influence on media habits in Singapore. Many of the issues raised with the introduction of Rediffusion services in Singapore at the time reflect poignantly some of the issues that institutional radio faces today, with the introduction of digital media.

The real gem of a find was a 1959 Radio Singapore corporate information publication about radio in Singapore. The author is unknown, and there are no attributions or credits mentioned apart from the imprint of the Government Printing Office, Singapore. This little booklet is titled *Radio Singapore: How it all began*, and is a window to Radio Singapore as it was then, with some statistical information pertaining to listenership and programming. Although primitive by research standards today, the content of the booklet nevertheless provides an almost definitive account of Radio Singapore as it was then. Until the publication of *Borderless Bandwidth* (Oei 2002), it was difficult to find one document that traced the history of Singapore radio chronologically from its inception in 1936.

As part of marketing efforts that were in line with the restructuring and repositioning of the Singapore Broadcasting Corporation (SBC), there was a brief deluge of interviews, articles and features on radio in the press in 1995. As I was actively involved in that campaign as well, material from those sources provided much of the reinforcement that supports my account of more recent Singapore radio history. Amongst the articles and features, I have included material from Gemma Koh's article, "Radio: The Way We Were" from the October issue of *Female* magazine, Singapore (Koh 1995, p. 135) and Derek Tham and Dora Tay's interview of Mr Anthony Chia, Chief Executive Officer of Radio Corporation of Singapore and a feature on the restructured Radio Corporation of Singapore published in the December 1995 issue of *Accent* magazine.

Material for the popular history of radio comes from a variety of sources that include textbooks, academic papers and readers (Straubhaar & LaRose 2002; McLuhan 2001; Richardson 2001; Campbell 2000; Castells 2000; Keith 2000; Oravec 2000; Douglas 1999; Crook 1999;

Folkerts, Lacy & Davenport 1998; Hanson 1998; Fang 1997; Norberg 1996; Ang 1991).

Of the collection, Richardson's reader on *Internet Marketing* is unique in that it has within it papers that discuss the history of radio and provides a detailed overview of the impact and influence of media on the concept of "Internet marketing." In the volume, Richardson brings together a comprehensive study of Internet marketing theory and how these concepts are applied. Richardson's intention is to offer an integrated "nonperishable" approach to the discipline of Internet marketing (Richardson 2001, p. vii). The content suits my purpose, as it seems to me a holistic approach to a process that attempts to systematise and rationalise marketing in a virtual environment, similar to my efforts in proposing an approach to programming in the digital environment as presented in *Borderless Bandwidth: DNA of Digital Radio* (Oei 2002).

A History of Mass Communication: Six Information Revolutions by Irving Fang (1997) provided me with an approach to explore each segment in the history of communication within specific influential periods. While Fang describes the periods as "information revolutions," I consider these, like the emergence of digital broadcasting, evolutionary; although by comparison, digital radio today may be perceived as a vast transformation from the early wireless receivers. This is because I believe that by evolving processes into functions within a digital environment and setting up systems to deliver value on an enhanced broadcasting platform, the transition and progression becomes a consequence of operational practices if viewed in a progressive and linear fashion along a historical context.

Fang defines the use of "Information Revolution" in his text as "profound changes involving new means of communication that permanently affect entire societies, changes that have shaken political structures and influenced economic development, communal activity, and personal behavior" (Fang 1997, p. xvi). While we ostensibly differ in tone, we actually agree on the fact that when changes occur to adapt to new practices and expectations, these become permanent as the "new approach" in media communication. Fang goes on to explain the rationale behind his "Six Information Revolutions" in "Western history" from 8th century B.C. to the present time. From Fang's broad framework of the media-communication landscape, we will begin our journey through radio history eventually narrowing our focus to innovations pertinent to wireless transmissions. Without those preceding inventions and innovations, radio or digital technology, and all of their internal production processes, would not have been realised.

1.2 EVOLVING AND ADAPTING

Fang's first revolution is labelled the "Writing Revolution" which he says begins in the 8th century B.C. with the convergence of the phonetic alphabet from Phoenicia with papyrus from Egypt, enabling knowledge to be stored in tangible fashion (Fang 1997, p. xvii). Castells (2000) concurs and adds that the alphabet was significant in laying the foundation for "the development of Western philosophy and science as we know it today. It made it possible to bridge the gap from spoken tongue to language, thus separating the spoken from the speaker, and making possible conceptual discourse" (Castells 2000, p. 355). Progress in Chinese society, resulting from the standardised use of writing and language, brought with it a system of education, examination, philosophy and technological advances, even before occurring in Western civilisation.

The second revolution, according to Fang, is the "Printing Revolution" that began in the late 15th century—a convergence of paper developed by the Chinese and the German printing system developed by Johannes Gutenberg, although printing had already been in existence in China before the birth of Christ. Printing enabled the dissemination of information across many layers of society. Printing launched the Reformation and the Renaissance, and basically "marked the start of the modern world" (Fang 1997, p. xvii).

Fang describes the third revolution as the "Mass Media Revolution" and he dates that in the middle of the 19th century. Building on advances in printing and paper production, his rationale in placing the "Mass Media Revolution" in the 19th century is the change in the way information was conveyed with the invention of the telegraph. With the expanded reach of information, "literacy came within reach" for the masses (ibid.).

The fourth revolution occurred, according to Fang, with the influx of technologies that enabled sound to be stored, the production of affordable cameras for the masses, and motion photography. Mostly propagated in Europe and America, stories and entertainment could now be replicated and packaged, launching the world's obsession with entertainment and personalities. Fang attributes this "Entertainment Revolution" to the late 19th century (ibid.).

The mid-20th century brought with it the creation of what Fang calls the "Communication Toolshed Home" (ibid.). The term refers to the convergence of the telephone, broadcast receivers, recording facilities and print technologies that transformed the home into a central location for receiving information and entertainment. Fang observed that: "The media of communication have become inseparable from our lives" (ibid.). This is the fifth information revolution.

We are currently in the sixth information revolution which has the world engaged in the "Information Highway." Fang describes this as the "convergence of computer, broadcasting, satellite and visual technologies" (ibid.).

As we are still in its midst, the revolution is still being constructed where the "information elite can live anywhere" (Fang 1997, pp. xvii–xviii), opposing the demands of the Industrial Revolution where populations converged on cities and towns for specific economic and social interaction. What we find in this "revolution" is a decentralised fluid exchange of information that allows individuals to bypass communal interaction and transactions. This, in itself, will bring its own set of social and intra-personal problems.

Fang states that each information revolution interweaves and share overlapping characteristics. Each revolution entails converging technologies, anchored in economic and social causes that influence communication practices in those periods. As each "age" progresses, technological tools expand to allow producers to broaden content and communication processes. This inevitably signals the end of one period and heralds the emergence of another that produces technology that replaces the previous (ibid.). The same bodes for radio as digital technologies converge various communication delivery methods to create an enhanced communication platform.

Radio continually adapts itself, spawning variations in daily programme content and approaches to programming that content. This caters to the expectations of each period with new technologies being developed, replacing the old, reinforcing Castells' theory cited above. Each milestone in radio's history redefines radio broadcasting and its perceived value to society, the listener-testing, using and re-applying and adapting to an altered expectation. From a public service broadcaster, and a government-controlled entity, to commercial format radio, the listeners' perceptions and attention to radio's importance as a medium of communication and entertainment also affects the services and information they will seek to receive from radio.

Having said that, the constant review of radio's attributes is useful because the radio experience is different today from 30 or 40 years ago. Expectations evolve and change.

> But while radio listening has been a constant fact of twentieth-century life, the *way* people listened to radio was profoundly shaped by the era in which they began to listen. (Douglas 1999, p. 6)

And so, growing up during World War II, a grandfather's view of radio would differ from his son or daughter who lived through the 1950s, as it would be with the grandchild's perception, living through the 1980s. Tim Crook in his book *Radio Drama Theory and Practice* (1999) outlines his version of the communication evolution/revolution. He cites Hilda Matheson's book *Broadcasting* (1933) drawing from her hypothesis that uses H. G. Wells' five different stages in communication and technological development: Before speech, speech, writing, print, and mechanical transport and electrical communication (Crook 1999, p. 13).

On drawing on these stages, Crook builds on a framework that reflects the years when various media achieved mass consumption, useful in considering points of reference though somewhat limited compared to Fang's hypothesis above, and Castells' massive work (1997, 1998, 2000). Crook divides the ages as follows:

1890	Phonograph
1925	Radio
1955	Television
1960	(Transistor radio—portable)
1980	Video/satellite receiver
1994	Personal computer (PC)

(Crook 1999, p. 21)

With the advent of Digital Audio Broadcasting (DAB–Eureka 147), we are at another juncture in the evolution of communication media, along with the portable versions of the personal computer in the laptop and the palmtop or personal digital assistants (PDA). To Crook's timeline, I include 1991 for the emergence of the notebook personal computer (portable) and 1995 with the Palm Pilot that eventually led to the birth of PDAs. These innovations are key to current user expectations in what constitutes an information, entertainment and communication device.

In a study such as this, one may be tempted to focus on demarcating clear distinctions between each evolutionary period, such as the beginning of the information age. Exactly when the digital or information age began depends on whose hypothesis one supports. Crook's choice is 1994, with the proliferation of PCs and the Internet in the 1990s. Marshall McLuhan had already begun arguing for a new media theory back in the 1960s during the inception of the Internet with the ARPNET. McLuhan's pivotal volume, *Understanding Media: The Extensions of Man*, systematically explores each medium and its influences (McLuhan 1964/1994). Castells pays tribute to McLuhan with:

> Indeed, one of the major components of the new communication system, the mass media of communication, structured around television, have been studied in minute detail. Their evolution toward globalization and decentralization was foreseen in the early 1960s by McLuhan, the great visionary who revolutionized thinking in communications in spite of his unrestrained use of hyperbole (Castells 2000, p. 357).

Amongst other dates that may be considered as the "start of the information age" is the year 1982, with the release of Epson's HX-20, the first notebook-size portable computer, which made Internet-information access portable for the first time (Meister 2001: http://www.wagoneers.com/UNIX/computing-history.html) and paving the way for other mobile information devices.

The nature of recent technology has also been imbued with provisions for an interface with the consumer/user that allows for experimentation and innovation by the consumer/user. These allowances have resulted in hybrids and new applications. Castells perceives the situation as self-perpetuating.

> The feedback loop between introducing new technology, using it, and developing it into new realms becomes much faster under the new technological paradigm. As a result, diffusion of technology endlessly amplifies the power of technology, as it becomes appropriated and redefined by its users (Castells 2000, p. 31).

My stand is, as stated above, in agreement with Fang that even though his hypothesis states six distinct information revolutions, each period, along with its innovations and thinking, converges and influences the other. Establishing a fixed start-date does not alter the importance of the pervasiveness and influence of information and the sharing of knowledge on a global scale at the present moment. As we look at the consumer/user in the next chapter, I will include other views on the media landscape along with the emergence and impact of the "information age."

Crook also observes that the development and emergence of new media have accelerated in recent years (Crook 1999, p. 21). This may be attributed to what McLuhan referred to as the "global village" made manifest through the World Wide Web and electronic media, an idea that McLuhan alluded to in his writings (McLuhan 1988, 1994, 1995). It is precisely the borderless nature of communicating via the Internet, its innovations and its reach that contributes to the perception of acceleration in communication technological developments today.

Now, earth-shattering news can be broadcast instantaneously to every home as it happens, as was the case with the attacks on the World Trade Center in New York on Tuesday, 11 September 2001. Never in the history of television and radio broadcasting has it been possible for an historic event of such tragic proportions able to unfold for all existing electronic media simultaneously. The murder of Lee Harvey Oswald cannot rival the multimedia coverage of an event that had the world witness the instantaneous loss of thousands of lives as the two towers of the World Trade Center in New York collapsed. The same could be said for the Gulf War in 1991, when the Cable News Network (CNN) beamed, via sate lite, live coverage of the war as it unfolded in the Middle East.

The ability to execute such potent and timely media coverage in recent times is the consequence of years of media evolution. From whatever starting point, the consumption of media as a means of communication has within it various key influential milestones that invariably involve the development of technologies either directly or indirectly related to specific media, and the operational assumptions that go with it.

1.3 EARLY RADIO

In the 1800s, two scientists, Michael Faraday and Joseph Henry, developed the theory of induction that paved the way for wireless communication. Induction is the ability for the current flowing in one wire to induce a current in another without being physically connected to each other (Harper 2002, p. 8). Other seminal events include the invention of the telegraph by Samuel Morse in the 1840s, the idea of electricity and magnetism by Scottish physicist James Maxwell in the 1860s, Heinrich Hertz who proved Maxwell's theories, and Guglielmo Marconi in 1894 who made wireless transmission practical, the first to send Morse code in his garden and then over the Atlantic using a transmitting and receiving device that he had invented.

Ward Hanson, writing in 1998 on *The Original WWW: Web Lessons from the Early Days of Radio* opens by asking how does one evaluate technology that is perceived as rich in promise and innovation. This is technology, he states, that has led to the creation of companies, brands and industries that would revolutionise public culture, education and commerce (Hanson 1998, p. 3). His reference to the dilemma could well apply to the Internet or digital media services prevalent today, in reshaping communication assumptions, entertainment and the dissemination of information, data and knowledge. However, the above quoted sentiment, according to Hanson, actually confronted the radio broadcaster in 1922. In his words, this was the impact that "the original WWW, World Wide Wireless" had on the world (ibid.).

Much like the Internet today, the interest in radio technology caused many amateur radio enthusiasts to either acquire a receiver or construct their own sets. These were times long before regulation stepped in to curb the widespread and indiscriminate use of wireless radio technology. This phenomenon paralleled web surfers creating their own websites to put up their own content, as reflected in the early amateur radio operators. Evidence of the interest of early radio technology is through the appearance of popular American publications like the *Radio Broadcast* and *Radio News* magazines in the 1920s (Brown 1998, pp. 68–81). Articles in these magazines "provided technical information and training for all levels of skill and interest, promoted a common language for the standardization and exchange of technical information, and provided a site where the information could be shared" (Brown 1998, p. 79).

> Yet it is clear that with the introduction of the telephone, the phonograph, and then radio, there was a revolution in our aural environment that prompted a major perceptual and cognitive shift in the country, with a new emphasis on hearing (Douglas 1999, p. 7).

No doubt, there has always been a tradition of story-telling in many cultures. Families around campfires, and grandparents relating folk tales to enthrall their grandchildren. These are aural traditions that are still with us. Douglas' quote above underscores the cultural and perceptual shift that influenced the listening habits of individuals and families, reaching unprecedented audience numbers due to pervading technology in the case of the phonograph and the radio, and the ability to hold a private conversation with someone miles away through the telephone.

In fact, it is interesting to note that before radio began to broadcast entertainment and music, the telephone filled that role. The wealthy paid to listen to opera, theatrical performances and concerts fed through telephone wires to earphones. At various venues, like hotels, restaurants, hospitals, waiting rooms, pubs and taverns, patrons could even hire earphones to catch the latest programming. From 1893 in Budapest, Telefon Hirmondo transmitted scheduled programming over the telephone to thousands of subscribers (Fang 1997, p. 86). This was significant, observes Fang, as Telefon Hirmondo obviously fulfilled a latent public desire for regular information and entertainment through available technology. It is an early example of the use of transmission technology to provide regular entertainment for a fee.

Radio was known originally as "wireless telegraphy or wireless telephony" (Richardson 2001, p. 4; Douglas 1999, p. 9; Fang 1997, p. 89). Once considered a glorified wireless telegraph transmitter and receiver, it is interesting that radio's initial intended role as a point-to-point communication device bears some irony with the present as mobile telecommunication now provides some complex and sophisticated communication services that include radio reception as one of its many services. Douglas eloquently describes radio as revolutionary:

> Radio is arguably the most important electronic invention of the century. Cognitively, it revolutionized the perceptual habits of the nation. Technically, culturally, and economically, it set the stage for television. It forever blurred the boundaries between the private domestic sphere and public, commercial, and political life. It made listening to music a daily requirement for millions of Americans. For the entire span of the twentieth century, listening to radio— first introduced to America as "wireless telegraphy" in 1899—has been a major cultural pastime (Douglas 1999, p. 9).

Lee De Forest, who considered himself the "father of radio", understood the extent and inherent potential of Marconi's invention and sought to make his mark in history by going beyond the point-to-point services that Marconi's enterprises, Marconi in the United Kingdom and American Marconi in the United States of America, were offering. In 1899, De Forest wrote the first doctoral dissertation on wireless technology. Two years later, in 1901, he challenged Marconi to an information relay competition by signing up to report the New York International Yacht Races for a news service. The two transmitters jammed the other's signals, and race officials resorted to communicating the event's proceedings through hand and flag signals (Campbell 2000, p. 105). The following year, De Forest formed the Wireless Telephone Company to compete with American Marconi, set up by Guglielmo Marconi, the leader in wireless communication then (ibid.). While De Forest grappled with Marconi, another party, independent of the rivals, made a breakthrough in using the technology to transmit palatable content.

In 1906, Canadian engineer Reginald Fessenden was credited with the first voice wireless broadcast. It was Christmas Eve and Fessenden sent a voice transmission from his station at Brant Rock, Massachusetts along with a rendition of *O Holy Night* that he played on the violin and music played from some phonographic records (ibid.; Fang 1997, p. 93). A year later, De Forest transmitted voices and a performance by tenor Enrico Caruso. De Forest and his wife followed that feat the next year with transmitting music from phonographic records from the Eiffel Tower in Paris (Campbell 2000, p. 106). In 1914, De Forest continued his broadcasts of music and voice that included promotions of his "audion tube" (Douglas 1999, p. 51).

Amidst the excitement on the potential of this new wireless invention, future head of Radio Corporation of America (RCA), David Sarnoff, reportedly wrote a memo to his boss at American Marconi in 1916. He had proposed a plan for the development of radio to make it a "household utility," like the piano and phonograph, and to bring music into the house. The receiver would be designed as a "Radio Music Box" that would tune in to different wavelengths with a flip of a switch (McLuhan 1994, p. 304; Benjamin 2002, p. 97; Straubhaar & LaRose 2002, p. 152). As for revenue, he initially opposed commercial services and suggested for a listener tax instead (Straubhaar & LaRose, p. 152).

15

The accounts above reveal attempts by individuals to exploit the innovative wireless technology, to create a purpose for its existence in society. Apart from the delivery of entertainment over the telephone, the use of wireless technology was clearly in its infancy and not a medium for delivering extensive entertainment programming to the masses yet. While individuals grappled with its use, and society was yet to be totally enamoured with the potential of wireless technology, regulation and governance was the next inevitable step, spurred into action by a devastating event.

1.4 RADIO REGULATION AND THE SHIFT TO "BROADCASTING"

The Radio Act of 1912, a consequence of the *Titanic* tragedy, was the first evidence of radio stations requiring a transmission licence from the Commerce Department. A modification of the 1910 law to require tighter control of the use of radio aboard ships, it was instituted to prevent similar tragedies from recurring and addressed two issues: the question of competency in handling the radio equipment, and the need to have wireless equipment and at least two operators onboard all ships. This arose from the fact that ships near enough to the *Titanic* to rescue survivors either had their wireless turned off for the night, or did not have a wireless installed at all, missing the opportunity to assist the sinking ship (Fang 1997, p. 92; Douglas 1999, p. 60; Campbell 2000, p. 106; Straubhaar & LaRose 2002, pp. 149–150).

The implementation of the Act of 1912 was also to curb the misuse of the wireless transmitter. Through the chaos of inquiries and messages about the *Titanic*, a message that claimed that all survivors of the *Titanic* were safe, was received by and printed in all the major papers. That message was an unfortunate hoax, blamed on amateur radio operators. So the act required all amateurs to be licensed, that they were restricted to operate sets with up to 1,000 watts, and they were restricted "from transmitting on the main commercial and military wavelengths" (Douglas 1999, p. 60). Control of the medium had only just begun with that legislation. This law was in force until the boom of radio as a mass medium forced a review that resulted in the Radio Act of 1927 (Fang 1997, p. 92; Campbell 2000, p. 106; Straubhaar & LaRose 2002, pp. 149–150). With the Radio Act of 1927, the broadcast band was defined, frequencies were designated, and a limitation was set as to the number of stations operating at night. The act also stated that radio operations had to serve "public interest, convenience, or necessity" (Fang 1997, p. 116; Campbell 2000, p. 112; Straubhaar & LaRose 2002, p. 153).

1.5 RADIO AS A MASS MEDIUM

Using the technology for a different purpose, the US Navy were the first to use that "wireless telephone" as a wartime communication device in 1915 during World War I, after much testing (Fang 1997, p. 88; Campbell 2000, p. 106; Straubhaar & LaRose 2002, p. 150). Having acquired wireless operations, the US Navy were to be instrumental in what was to happen next. But what is interesting at this time is that wireless transmission was considered "narrowcasting" or point-to-point, as stated above. With Fessenden and De Forest, we see the beginnings of "broadcasting", an agricultural term that refers to the process of casting seeds over a large area (Fang 1997, p. 93; Campbell 2000, p. 105; Straubhaar & LaRose 2002, p. 151). By this time, the impact of the wireless transmission of voice and sound was tremendous. It would not be long until the term "radio" replaced the word "wireless."

With the US Navy using wireless technology, the potential of radio technology presented a need to control its access to the people and companies. In 1917, when the Navy entered the war, all amateur radio operations, telegraph, telephone and ocean cable systems were shut down to ensure military security (Fang 1997, p. 95; Campbell 2000, p. 106). After the war, the American president at the time, President Woodrow Wilson, along with corporate and government leaders, saw the necessity, as a world power, to use radio communication to serve American interests (Campbell 2000, pp. 106–107). It was a source of some discomfort at the time that the British-owned American Marconi Company was the dominant supplier of radio components (Folkerts, Lacy & Davenport 1998, p. 60). So as to promote the American plan to control wireless operations, British Marconi was forced to sell its American subsidiary, American Marconi, to General Electric (GE) in 1919. Then to ensure the successful development of radio, GE developed alliances with several stakeholders including American Telephone & Telegraph (AT&T) and Westinghouse, forming the Radio Corporation of America (RCA), the first radio institution. Through RCA, the United States had almost total control over radio as an emerging mass medium. Being a commercial entity, RCA led the way that enabled America to be the "world's largest exporter of information services and popular culture" (Campbell 2000, p. 107; Richardson 2001, pp. 4–5). Developing these alliances meant control of emerging and subsequent technological developments from these stakeholders as well.

In the process of developing operations to ensure the viability of the technology, several related innovations were key to ensuring the future of radio. While De Forest invented the "vacuum tube" in 1906 (Fang 1997, p. 93; Campbell 2000, p. 117; Castells 2000, p. 39; Straubhaar & LaRose 2002, p. 151), after modifying a tube developed by John Ambrose Fleming from Marconi (Douglas 1999, p. 51) and calling it the "audion tube," the collaboration between GE and AT&T Bell Labs resulted in many other innovations that we take for granted in the broadcast and recording industries today.

De Forest's "audion tube" detected radio waves, regulated the flow of electrons and amplified them (Fang 19997, p. 93). With the vacuum tubes that amplified voices in 1920, preamps and amplifiers were created. Other developments were the microphone, loudspeaker, and the recording and playback stylus (Fang 1997, p. 111). So when loudspeakers on radio receivers eventually replaced earphones, a new social dimension was created in radio listening as a shared activity in the home (Fang 1997, p. 115). As users of the microphone tested, used, explored and reapplied its technology, mirrored in what Castells later modelled as the innovation loop explained above, we see innovations in the microphone—the dynamic microphone, the condenser microphone, the "gun-microphone," the different pick-up patterns like the cardoid, bi-directional microphones, omni-directional microphones, uni-directional microphones and wireless microphones. Similarly, the loudspeaker technology introduced a series of speakers for different purposes and configurations that now bring us the surround digital experience through up to 10 well-placed speakers, and even through two speakers using "Q-sound" technology and surround headphones. These have all contributed to the science of audio production as we know it today.

Going back to the 1920s, and the early days of radio, initial radio receivers came with heavy 12-volt lead-acid batteries to pump in the power that it needed to receive and amplify the radio waves streaming through it. It was not until 1924 that radios were sold with wall plugs attached. Inconveniences aside, radio was a success, with RCA achieving radio sales of over US$10 million in 1922. By 1924, that figure reached US$50 million (Hanson 1998, pp. 6–7). Despite the high sales volume, radio receivers at the time still had difficulty locking onto a signal. And before regulation and control, the sharing of radio frequencies by different radio stations was a regular frustration which did not help matters. But like the present, sales of radio receivers and broadcasting stations were a combination of hype, media coverage, and public fascination (ibid., p. 7). Perhaps an approach to creating awareness of digital radio that would help in its acceptance in society today may be found in the early infiltration of radio to the masses. According to Hanson,

> The impact of three forces propelled the explosion of radio: Rapid radio set sales, mushrooming growth in signal sources, and intense public attention. ... Fascination leads to sales, sales lead to stations, new stations lead to more fascination. (ibid.)

For reference, this discussion is explored in my book *Borderless Bandwidth: DNA of Digital Radio* (Oei 2002).

In America, by 1923, two million people were served by more than 500 stations, with a count of a half-million sets in 1923 rising to two million in 1925 (Fang 1997, p. 115).

> In 1925, 10 per cent of American households had a radio. By 1933 the proportion had jumped to 62.5 per cent, double that at the beginning of the Depression. Already there were 599 stations broadcasting in the country, with three networks—CBS, NBC-Red, and NBC-Blue—offering national programs (Douglas 1999, p. 128).

> By 1927, 700 stations were operating, and $135 million worth of sets was sold in 1929 (Folkerts, Lacy & Davenport 1998, p. 61).

Radio technology developed rapidly, producing affordable sets that became more mobile. By 1947, and the invention of the "transistor" by Bell Laboratories, we see radio technology revolutionising "hearing aids" as the durable and less expensive "transistor" was smaller and required less power and generated less heat than the older vacuum tubes. The result was the release of the first transistor radios in 1953 by Texas Instruments that coincided with the re-emergence of radio in teenage popular culture as the "music box" that Sarnoff had envisioned (Campbell 2000, p. 117) accompanying the rise of rock-and-roll and the "Top 40" radio format.

From the initial point-to-point use of wireless technology, as a wireless telephone, the one-to-many broadcasting mode eventually took hold of the masses through the use of the technology to "exert government leadership, spread national culture, and share information" (Fang 1997, p. 89). And so for about six decades after Fessenden, the business of broadcasting entertainment and information to the masses grew into a very lucrative enterprise. Ironically, the reverse seems to be occurring today with digital technology, as we begin to redefine service distribution to specific audience profiles, and even individual preferences with the intention to "narrowcast." Is this "radio broadcasting"? It is this very debate that left the digital radio revolution in a stalemate for almost a decade. Only in recent years have there been some compromises to engage in digitising audio for digital data storage and retrieval broadcast systems, and in aggregating content for Internet radio. But as discussed in *Borderless Bandwidth* (Oei 2002), in most sectors, this move has been half-hearted, operating in a radio organisational system that is not structured to accommodate teams or divisions that are responsible for producing digital data and content in tandem with the audio services that are transmitted daily.

Perceptual acceptance of the new is the challenge. Today, it is the acceptance of digital radio being able to provide visual and textual data content along with normal audio programming. At the dawn of radio broadcasting, the important consequence of the "radio experience" is the altering of the perception of distance and time. Radio presenters reported on global events, making breaking news, information and the weather accessible in the living room as they happened. Mass markets emerged, shifting economic borders and revising the theory and approach to business and commerce. The concept of "scheduled mass culture" changed the daily life of millions (Hanson 1998, p. 3). Here was a chance to influence and direct audience listening habits. By June 1921, there were over 23,000 wireless stations in the world (ibid., p. 4).

1.6 BIRTH OF COMMERCIAL RADIO AND THE NETWORK

The business potential of radio "dramatically accelerated the economy's push to a mass market" (Hanson 1998, p. 3). With radio programmes expanding beyond "public service," radio began to wrestle with creating a revenue base to develop into a self-sustaining entity. Digital radio is undergoing a similar dilemma at the moment, going directly into addressing the revenue issue without going through the "public service" route. The issue in adopting this line of attack is in not generating public awareness of the technology first, which was the model taken by early analogue radio. Rather, the debates in digital radio committees and conferences I have attended focus on the need to create a rationale to launch digital broadcast technology without first providing sufficient public education of its presence and demonstrating its potential. If digital radio had followed a public service model in the early 1990s, people would have been allowed to experience the services first-hand and enjoy its benefits sooner. Radio institutions would also have been able to cater for and understand the processes needed to competently deliver digital services. Then like all new technology, the question of purpose and common social good would inevitably surface as a consequence; other services and business models could then be explored.

> This new technology raised a host of questions about what the act
> of listening to emanations from "the ether" was doing to the nation
> and the individual. In the early 1920s pundits predicted a massive
> cultural uplift through radio, with opera and lectures brought to the
> most isolated and uneducated in the country. (Douglas 1999, p. 129)

Purpose aside, viability is the main concern in business enterprises. The shift from using wireless technology for direct communication to broadcasting to a mass audience was a dilemma of indirect communication. Then—as now for digital radio—issues that emerged included revenue generation and the source of payment to generate that income to sustain radio services. The revenue model for RCA was simple from the beginning, to provide services for a fee (Hanson 1998, p. 5).

Research conducted in 1924 to ascertain the penetration depth of wireless services revealed that the role of radio manufacturing companies was also important in the equation. People would only be able to listen to radio if sets were available. With relatively few players on the market, key manufacturers and retailers engaged in category development (ibid., p. 8). The other factor was the idea of "goodwill" by key radio sponsors whose names would be mentioned in shows and content from the radio station. The hope was the generating of loyal retail customers from brand and name exposure "over-the-airwaves." What finally emerged from these approaches was, of course, the idea of on-air advertising, although the general public initially opposed the idea (ibid., p. 9).

In 1922, New York, AT&T set up WEAF, now known as WNBC, as the first radio station to sell commercial air time to advertisers calling it "toll broadcasting." By August that year, WEAF sold its first advertisement space to a New York real estate developer for US$50. This was a 10-minute broadcast about "the joys of living in the apartments they offered for sale in the Long Island countryside" (Fang 1997, p. 117; Campbell 2000, p. 108). With the growth of radio listening, the novelty of the approach and perceived potential in listening to an advertisement over the radio receiver, that initial US$50 investment brought in US$127,000 in subsequent airtime orders (ibid.).

In order to leverage on its lucrative potential, AT&T positioned WEAF as the flagship of its radio network in an effort to monopolise advertising on this new medium (Straubhaar et al. 2002, p. 152; Folkerts et al. 1998; p. 209). AT&T's first broadcast network linked several of its stations via telephone line to forge a way for radio advertising. You see, up to the birth of the "network", radio stations around the US transmitted their own programmes (Fang 1997, p. 118). By sharing and offering better programmes over a network, operating costs decreased and advertisers would be exposed to a larger listener base (ibid.). So according to Folkerts, Lacy & Davenport (1998), the consequence of having a player like AT&T involved in the development of radio resulted in AT&T inventing the "broadcast network." By 1925, AT&T had a network of 26 stations "from New York to Kansas City" (Folkerts et al., 1998 p. 209). AT&T's domination of broadcasting and telephony was not welcome by the emerging media industry stakeholders (Straubhaar & LaRose 2002, pp. 152–153), resulting in AT&T finally withdrawing from the radio industry to keep its telephone monopoly, selling its radio subsidiary to RCA in 1926 (Folkerts et al. 1998, p. 209).

This brings us to David Sarnoff, RCA's general manager from 1921. Sarnoff was among the first to envision the wireless innovation as a mass medium. In his youth, Sarnoff had his first taste of the effective use of wireless communication when he transmitted information about the *Titanic* survivors to newspapers in 1912 (Campbell 2000, p. 109; Hanson 1998, p. 5). With his acquisition from AT&T, and along with GE and Westinghouse, the National Broadcasting Corporation (NBC)—the first national network broadcaster—was created in September 1926 (Fang 1997, p. 118; Hanson 1998, p. 11; Folkerts et al. 1998, p. 209; Campbell 2000, p. 109; Straubhaar & LaRose 2002, p. 153). RCA soon acquired all stock in NBC and became the dominant network (Folkerts et al. 1998, p. 209). By January 1927, NBC launched two networks, NBC Red and NBC Blue. NBC Blue would later become the American Broadcast Company (ABC) in 1942 (Lewis and Booth 1990, p. 40).

The Columbia Broadcasting System (CBS) was founded in 1927 with 16 stations (Fang 1997, p. 118; Douglas 1999, p. 63; Keith 2000, p. 5). This network consisted of United Independent Broadcasters (UIB) and the Columbia Phonograph Company (CPC). However, after losing US$100,000 in the first month, CPC was jettisoned (Campbell 2000, p. 111). And so;

> By the 1930s radio was under oligopoly control, managed almost exclusively by two networks, CBS and NBC, who in turn had their content tightly regulated by advertising agencies and their corporate clients and, to a lesser extent, the FCC. (Douglas 1999, p. 6)

AT&T, on the other hand, continued to act as a transmission medium for all radio networks, reinforcing the policy of the "common carrier principle" that lasted until the US Telecommunications Act of 1996 (Straubhaar & LaRose 2002, p. 153). This model of operations between the broadcaster and the telecommunications transmission provider has been a point of contention in recent debates on providing content over digital radio services. While ownership of the process will not be addressed here, I will discuss how the issue of content services may be subsumed into the radio programming process.

The advantage of having big networks was the high quality of programmes, with money flowing in from commercials, paying for the many writers, actors, musicians, announcers, journalists, producers and engineers involved in the daily operations of the stations (Fang 1997, p. 118). The above "American model" was a calculated "result of diplomatic and commercial dealings," from the formation of RCA to the setting up of the major broadcast networks. It was part of the "cultural and economic domination of the US," a feature of post-war America (Lewis and Booth 1990, p. 50).

1.7 THE PUBLIC SERVICE MODEL

With the formation of networks, public service broadcasting was overshadowed by commercial enterprises in America, proving very lucrative for the corporations. And while broadcasting in America became competitive and very competent in cornering markets, the reverse was true in Britain (Fang 1997, p. 118). As a comparison to the commercial model that emerged in America, let us now explore the development of the "Public Service Model" adopted in Great Britain.

While the focus of the previous section was on radio's growth in America, the growth of radio beyond that continent provided alternate ways of providing radio services to listeners. The importance of being aware of the different philosophical approaches to providing broadcast services is in understanding that these dictated the way content was selected, produced and presented to the masses. These approaches eventually influenced the evolutionary process of production and presentation styles that define radio as it is now. Having seen the birth of the network and commercialisation of radio services, we now focus on the other spectrum—that of radio as a public service. While this was the state of early American radio, this was radio as perceived and experienced by the subjects of the British Empire.

Between 1922 and 1923, a commission from Britain was in the United States to study the potential of radio. This fact-finding mission was based on the need to properly utilise this technology for the common good of English society as the rush then was toward domination by musical entertainment that was paid for by advertising which the English commission saw "as a waste of the medium's cultural and educational potential" (Straubhaar & LaRose 2002, p. 155).

To capitalise on radio's "cultural and educational potential" (ibid.), in 1922 the Radio Society of Britain was formed. British Marconi and Metropolitan Vickers began broadcasts in England that same year (Shingler and Wieringa 1998, pp. 4–5).

The Metropolitan Vickers were the Metropolitan Vickers Electrical Company established on 8 September 1919. Operating mainly in Manchester, the Metropolitan Vickers was the result of the firm British Westinghouse, owned by American George Westinghouse, breaking away from American ownership of its operations using capital from the Metropolitan Carriage, Wagon and Finance Company, and the acquisition of British Westinghouse by Vickers Limited (http://www.marconi.com/html/about/metropolitanvickershistory.htm).

Meanwhile, with enthusiasm in wireless sets increasing, the Postmaster-General announced in April 1922 that measures had to be taken to control wireless broadcasting in contrast to the situation in America, and that the "question of broadcasting was to be referred to the Imperial Communications Committee (ICC) (Lewis and Booth

1990, p. 52). It was a question of the allocation of wavelengths between the amateur radio enthusiasts who were building their own transmission and receiver sets, commercial wireless telegraph companies, ships and the armed services (ibid.).

The ICC drew up guidelines that included the provision of one single wavelength (440 metres), a restriction of power to 1.5 kilowatts for radio stations, the prohibition of advertising and sponsorship, the use of news that had already been published in the newspapers, and broadcasts to be limited to music, education, religion and entertainment between the hours of 5 am to midnight (ibid.). These drastic recommendations obviously drew protests, mainly from radio companies. With the inclusion of Marconi and the Metropolitan Vickers, the next meeting by the ICC broadened the recommended spectrum to include the 350- to 400-metre band range.

By May of the same year, discussions with a number of companies began, under the constraints of two major concerns of the Post Office, "to avoid monopoly and to achieve efficiency" (Lewis et al., p. 53). Set manufacturers agreed for the need for protection from foreign competition and that there should be one broadcasting company. In October, the British Broadcasting Company was formed (Lewis et al., p. 54), and on December 15 that same year, the BBC was registered, receiving its licence on 18 January 1923 (Shingler and Wieringa 1998, p. 5).

The task to manage and operate radio services in Britain was given to John Reith, a son of a Presbyterian minister. Reith knew nothing about the new wireless technology that confronted him, or the fundamentals of broadcasting. Like any new technology, it was open to innovation and experimentation (Ang 1991, p. 108), so Reith began exploring possible uses to establish relevance for this new wireless technology in English society.

In conscious opposition to the "Americanisation" of popular culture, Reith's vision was to provide content that would "develop a sense of discrimination in the audience by giving it the opportunity to listen to 'better, healthier music'" (ibid.). Reith wanted to create an independent British broadcaster "to educate, inform and entertain the whole nation, free from political interference and commercial pressure" (BBC website, accessed 1 October 2002). With the help of newly-appointed chief engineer Peter Eckersley, Reith set about to achieve his vision.

The daily fare then was drama, variety, talk, children's programmes, and popular and classical music. The news was only broadcast after 7 pm "to avoid upsetting the newspapers" (ibid.). From the start, the decision was to maintain "good taste and decency" (ibid.), which is the hallmark of the BBC, along with credible coverage of the news.

Reith's approach articulated values and standards of the British upper middle-class, particularly those educated at Oxford and Cambridge (Ang 1991, p. 108). The thrust for this approach to broadcast music was "to 'raise' the musical taste of its listeners because Britain was considered a backward musical nation" (ibid.). While internally this may have alienated the local listening population who were not within the upper middle-class circles, it created a perception to the rest of the world that the English generally had upper middle-class values, tastes and behaviour. This impression of the English had a significant influence on the popular definition of being "English".

In England, early BBC listeners were within a 25-mile radius from the stations as that was the limited range of the radio signal. Because of this, much of the early content catered to locals performed by local talent (Straubhaar & LaRose 2002, p. 155) from the shires.

To extend services, signals were re-transmitted over a relay using telephone cables. By 1924, BBC chief engineer Eckersley laid the foundations of regional broadcasting (Lewis and Booth 1990, pp. 54–55). A series of relay stations were set up in Sheffield, Plymouth, Edinburgh, Liverpool, Leeds-Bradford, Hull, Nottingham, Dundee, Stoke-on-Trent and Swansea. These stations carried programmes from London and provided an alternative to local regional programming (Lewis et al., pp. 54–55; Shingler and Wieringa 1998, p. 5).

An integral part of providing wireless services was the question of funding. How were operations going to be financed? The British commission of 1922/23, after the study-trip to America mentioned above (Straubhaar & LaRose 2002, p. 155), recommended that radio services under the BBC were to be financed by licence fees, paid by listeners, and governed by a board to keep operations "independent of both government and private interests" (ibid.). However, as the BBC reach grew, the Crawford Committee, appointed in 1925, recommended that the monopoly over broadcasting should remain and that the company be "replaced by a public corporation, licensed for 10 years and 'acting as a trustee for the national interest in broadcasting'" (Lewis et al., p. 56). Consequently, Reith's vision of being independent of government control took a turn as the BBC was given a Royal Charter with the government retaining power to control the programme content of the BBC. For the next 50 years, the BBC operated along those lines.

As the number of licenses increased, income for the BBC increased (Lewis et al., pp. 56–57). In the end, Reith acknowledged BBC's advantageous position under this framework, enabling the BBC to develop broadcasting in a way no other country was able to make it (Lewis et al., p. 57). Lewis and Booth (1990) describes Reith's ideal of public service broadcasting in the following extract:

> They were, first, that the BBC did not aim for profit. Second, it strove to extend its service to the whole population. Third, "unified control" was the guiding principle, not sectional pressure or regional initiative. Fourth, "there is an emphasis on the 'public' or the series of 'publics' which together constitute 'the great audience'. The 'publics' are treated with respect, not as nameless aggregates with statistically measurable preferences, 'targets' for the programme sponsor, but as living audiences capable of growth and development". The National Programme and the alternative which the Regional Programme was at any time meant to offer were the means for this growth and development. (Lewis et al., p. 58)

Shingler and Wieringa (1998) add to the above sentiment and define eight key principles as Reith's Public Service Broadcasting model.

The first is geographic universality where broadcast programmes are made available to the whole population.

The second is to have one main instrument of broadcasting funded by its users, for example by a licence fee, as is the case of the BBC, like a contract between the citizen and the broadcaster.

The third refers to having a structure that competes in programming rather than numbers as the organisation does not compete for the same source of revenue.

The fourth principle describes the necessity to have universal appeal. In this, the Public Service Broadcaster is expected to provide a wide range of programmes "that will explore and extend the possibilities of the medium and stimulate new ideas and new talent" (Shingler et al., p. 17).

The fifth principle refers to Public Service Broadcasting having a "special regard for the needs and interests of minority groups" (ibid.).

The sixth addresses "national identity and community" and how Public Service Broadcasting can provide opportunities for citizens to indulge in discussions of national and communal concerns. This will help create "a shared sense of national identity" (Shingler et al., p. 18).

The seventh principle refers to the autonomy of Public Service Broadcasting. By its very inference, Public Service Broadcasting "should not be subservient either to governments or advertisers" (ibid.).

The final principle is "editorial freedom", according to Shingler et al. The spirit of this principle lies in the need for broadcasters to "create an arena" in which to "experiment and innovate" (ibid.) so as to attract people who will continue to develop the medium.

Reith's management style at the time was not unlike public servants of the time. Staff recruitment was generally from the same educational and social background as those who "served the Empire", which under Reith achieved a kind of domestic diplomatic service representing the British (Lewis et al., p. 69) creating a sense of elitism. With the control and expansiveness of the BBC, the image of the broadcaster as the best discerner of listeners' preferences emerged—an attitude adopted by the BBC that has remained an enduring legacy of Reith (ibid.). With the development of Public Service Broadcasting, the legacy of the system in short, as observed by Shingler and Wieringa (1998), is based on "ethical broadcasting" (Shingler et al., p. 14). As for the content, according to Hendy (2000), public service radio generally offers a broad range of programming that combines popular entertainment with "minority-taste cultural and news programmes, targeted through different services which collectively reach the *whole* population" in terms "of age, class and geographical spread" (Hendy 2000, p. 17).

With this approach to broadcasting, content, production and presentation styles that emerged along the vein of a BBC-esque style produced a particular approach and thinking that had to be employed in order to conform to the prescribed broadcast culture. After all, to subscribe to the idea that a broadcaster had to be "proper"; ethical; act as the guardian of cultural legacies and "good taste"; an educator while also an entertainer; and at the same time a custodian of diplomacy for the British Empire, it is no wonder that production values and nuances within a BBC production differ from the more ostensibly liberal and sensational American productions.

The different approaches notwithstanding, the crucial element in the broadcast equation remains the listener. Conveying the message to the listener remains the prime motivator for delivering content over the air. Being understood, influencing and creating an emotional bond with the listener are key to good broadcast communication as the ephemeral nature of conventional audio radio, as opposed to the potential present in digital radio, demands that the message be concise and comprehensible in the first instance. The ability to deliver this lies in the talent and creative dexterity of the radio presenter.

1.8 RADIO AS A PERSONAL MEDIUM— THE RADIO PRESENTER

The fascination with radio broadcasts lies in the vast array of content that can be received. The preceding sections outline the increasing demands for specific content by listeners, the influences behind presentation and production approaches, economic and political demands by the broadcasters to maintain programming quality, ensuring credible, entertaining and accurate content output, creating a revenue base, and balancing ethics and regulation. What slowly emerges from meeting these expectations in the early 1920s and 1930s are the attributes of radio that are now recognised as key to radio's accessibility and efficacy.

Consider the following. Radio is traditionally an audio medium that informs, educates and entertains. Radio comes across as a personal medium that is considered by many as a friendly companion. Radio as a personal medium got a boost in the 1930s through another innovation that helped to spread the use of radios in America.

Radio sets in the home were battery-powered until 1926. With the development of the battery eliminator, and thanks to the Galvin brothers operating under a business with a name that implied sound in motion, "Motorola" introduced William Lear's 1928 invention to the world. This was the car radio, which provided more mobility to radio listening (Fang 1997, p. 118) and which became instrumental in the re-emergence of radio listening in the 1950s during the rise of the music-format "Top-40 hit radio" stations.

The invention of the transistor by Bell Laboratories in 1947 (Campbell 2000, p. 117) also contributed to the mobility of radio listening by enabling the manufacture of smaller receivers. The timely fashion in receiving information and news makes transmission of content immediate. With that attribute, radio is often used as a conduit for political and social debate, review and commentary. Along these lines, radio as a medium provides opportunities to provoke thought and commentary; raises pertinent issues; and challenges and influences public and personal opinion. In many ways, it influences, serves and reflects the community.

While the first regular broadcasts may be attributed to Charles Herrold (Straubhaar & LaRose 2002, p. 151), the first inkling of any perceivable format coming onto radio was in 1919, when Westinghouse engineer, Frank Conrad, set up a radio studio above his garage in Pittsburgh. From his premises, with a microphone placed in front of his phonograph, Conrad transmitted information, news and music to his friends through receivers he provided, making him the first disc jockey for radio. He also invited listeners to send postcards, and these often arrived with requests for specific tunes. Due to the number of requests, Conrad eventually "tried to oblige by transmitting the broadcasts according to a schedule". A record storeowner even agreed to lend him records to enable him to meet these requests in exchange for mentioning the name of the store "on air" (Fang 1997, p. 114; Campbell 2000, p. 108), probably making that the first "on-air promo."

This method of presenting content over a wireless service was novel at the time. And so radio as merely a point-to-point direct communication device, as it was initially intended, came to an end and extended to a wider audience when an executive from Westinghouse adapted Conrad's idea and established KDKA in Pittsburgh Pennsylvania. With this concept of scheduled broadcasting to the masses, KDKA made the first professional broadcast on 2 November 1920, transmitting the "national returns from the Cox-Harding presidential election" (Fang 1997, p. 115; Campbell 2000, p. 108; Straubhaar & LaRose 2002, p. 151).

With the establishment of KDKA, the "radio experience" begins to take root in the listeners' psyche. McLuhan, writing about radio in *Understanding Media* (1994) had this to say:

> Radio affects most people intimately, person-to-person, offering a world of unspoken communication between writer-speaker and the listener. That is the immediate aspect of radio. A private experience. (McLuhan 1994, p. 299)

The main staple for radio at the time was drama, musical entertainment, comedy, information, mostly news and weather reports, and variety shows. And while the 1920s and 1930s is known as the "Jazz Age," as radio listening firmly established itself into the daily lives of individuals and households, the record business stalled and almost collapsed (Straubhaar & LaRose 2002, p. 154).

Talents that were broadcast frequently over the radio came from the stage (Campbell 2000, pp. 114–115). In fact, the term "DJ" or "Disc Jockey" was first used in "1941 to describe someone who played recorded music on radio programs" (Campbell 2000, p. 114).

In America, with an increasing number of voices being transmitted into homes, what became evident were the different accents and pronunciation styles that demanded translation in order for the speech to be comprehended (Douglas 1999, p. 102). With it came the assumptions about the presenter's intelligence and character through the vocal delivery and tone of voice. In Britain, this issue was addressed in 1929, when the "BBC imposed a single standard of pronunciation for all its announcers" who also had to be phonetically trained (ibid.).

In British colonies, the colonial legacy of traditional British-style radio presentation that provided information and entertainment to the masses generally employed the terms "radio producer" or "radio presenter". Back in the 1950s, it was the radio announcer.

As mentioned previously, this legacy of ensuring proper diction and pronunciation from British radio presenters, who had the responsibility to also be educators and custodians of information, was borne out of the need, with the proliferation of radio to the masses in the 1920s, to be understood. Shingler and Wieringa (1998) write that "Received Pronunciation was designed to set the standard of spoken English in Great Britain" as it was "part and parcel of Reith's ambition to establish through broadcasting a distinct national identity beyond class and regionality" (Shingler and Wieringa 1998, p. 45). Some of the justifications of implementing the above include technological grounds that

> … clear and precise speech (hence formal and standardised speech) was necessary to overcome the poor quality of microphones and receivers during the 1920s and 1930s. The same argument was also used to favour the male voice over the female voice. The deeper register of the male voice was judged to have better definition. (ibid.)

I will not include the arguments for and against the implementation of this "standard" in Britain as it is not the scope of this book. While this biased approach to presentation may have its disadvantages, it nonetheless provides a foundation, discipline and benchmark for presenters to latch onto and measure themselves against. Knowledge of and employing phonetic symbols to annotate one's presentation script provides a definitive guide to pronouncing the most challenging words. Knowledge and the ability to verbalise phonetically in no way encourages a presenter to sound more British, or American. Rather, it is a means to enable the presenter, or disc jockey, to minimise mispronunciations, especially during news presentations and important announcements. Being able to decipher, read and translate phonetically is a useful, fundamental skill to be acquired as a professional presenter. Ironically, especially when presenting a written script, it can sometimes enable the presenter to sound more natural—especially when the presenter annotates, phonetically, nuances of the spoken-language above perfectly spelled and printed words in that script. Once basics like this are internalised, the presenter will then be able to develop style and informality, having been familiar with the "rules of the game." What remains important is the ability to maintain an aural, visceral and emotional connection with the listener.

> Broadcasters on the air had to calibrate how they would speak so that they appealed to as wide a range of socio-economic classes and geographic regions as possible. They had to figure out how people would remember specific information and particular personalities. (Douglas 1999, p. 12)

Frances Dyson had this to say about the "radio voice." She believes that the radio voice has a heritage in public speaking and oration with a set of conventions (Shingler and Wieringa 1998, p. 42). However, she says that the "radio voice" is a technological construct as opposed to speech that is natural and not subject to amplification or editing (ibid.). Dyson also claims that the listener has a vested interest to believe in the credibility, spontaneity and currency of the radio voice because the "radio experience," being immediate, cannot afford to draw attention to the fact that its speech may be, in fact, a recorded reconstruction (Shingler et al., pp. 42–43).

While this may be true, I believe that even if the announcer is not being totally understood, just the sound of the human voice can be calming and reassuring. In this, radio is considered a companion to the listener who may be engaged in some other activity like reading a book or doing one's homework. And being an audio medium, placing the radio receiver in close proximity to the listener, the listening experience often becomes personal and solitary. McLuhan (1994) describes this process in his usual fashion:

> Radio is provided with its cloak of invisibility, like any other medium. It comes to us ostensibly with person-to-person directness that is private and intimate, while in more urgent fact, it is really a subliminal echo chamber of magical power to touch remote and forgotten chords. All technological extensions of ourselves must be numb and subliminal, else we could not endure the leverage exerted upon us by such extension. Even more than telephone or telegraph, radio is that extension of the central nervous system that is matched only by human speech itself. (McLuhan 1994, p. 302)

In 1931, Arthur Godfrey, a young radio announcer then, made this discovery, causing him to change his approach to radio presentation. After all, if the content of a radio show entertained the listener, it would help if the announcer were to be able to relate to that listener on a personal level as well (MacFarland 1997, p. 120). His personal revelation is useful in representing the evolving nature and method of radio presentation at the time.

Having been involved in an accident, Arthur Godfrey was hospitalised for several months. While convalescing, Godfrey had the opportunity to listen to a lot of radio. He observed that announcers mostly addressed groups of listeners in the course of their radio shows. This implied that the perception of the announcer was one of speaking to the entire population of the town, county, state or country. The announcer spoke to everyone "out there" except the person in front of the radio receiver (ibid.).

From this experience, Godfrey realised that radio listening was an individual and personal experience. Godfrey concluded that it would be more a powerful and effective approach for the radio presenter to speak to each listener personally, one to one. If radio is personal in nature, then references made by the presenter had to take on a more personal approach using a more intimate tone. Realising that the radio listening experience was personal and solitary, Godfrey altered his presentation style and was more intimate and personal thereafter (ibid.). While Godfrey's contribution may have been all but forgotten, it was not an entirely new approach to radio presenting. In the 1920s, personalities like Betty Crocker also had a "chatty" style to introduce advertising copy to the home while German radio had already developed a similar style to "reach a mass of listeners who were viewed in feminized terms" (Hayes 2000, pp. 80–81). Godfrey's reputation, however, certainly lives on. Casey Kasem paid Godfrey a tribute in an interview with Michael Keith (2002):

33

> There wasn't any single influence on my career, but I thought Arthur Godfrey was one who did it all. He not only did radio programs, but he did thousands of commercials, like me. … my grandmother told me, "You know when you're going to be a star when you're like Arthur Godfrey." … the enormous talent that he had in the area of comedy and in presiding over a semitalk show. (Keith 2002, p. 93)

Whilst Godfrey's realisation may not have been an earth-shattering milestone, being mindful of a more personal delivery was instrumental in making the presenter conscious of the way language was used on radio. Having a more intimate approach goes directly to the psyche of the listener, the effectiveness of which is often attributed to the famous "Fireside Chats" made by President Franklin D. Roosevelt during the American Depression and World War II. This series of broadcasts are recognised for their persuasive and immediate impact on listeners of the time (Hayes 2000, p. 76). It shifted political communication to a more conversational style of "mass intimacy" (ibid.).

In these broadcasts, President Roosevelt used an informal approach and addressed the American public with "my friends," "you," "I want to tell you," " I can assure you," "I know you will understand," and "let me make it clear to you" (Hayes 2000, p. 78).

By extension, the spoken word delivered through the radio by the presenter would generally originate in a written script in some form, even if it were put together in "bullet-point form." To be clinical about creating this intimate and personal approach, the implication for the presenter, then, is to have the ability to write a "conversational" script—at least until the presenter is proficient enough to converse freely "on-air" with a script of "bullet-points" and going as far as "ad-libbing".

Although this is not an argument for the use of colloquialism in radio speech, it is reinforcing the need to use "simple language" to reach the masses. This was the observation made after the fracas created by the broadcast of Orson Welles' production of *The War of the Worlds*. Douglas describes it saying "many in the industry took the panic as evidence of the intellectual simplicity of much of the audience, and the need therefore to speak to them in simple language" (Douglas 1999, p. 165). Other examples come from radio news reporters like William Shirer, who reported from Prague in the 1930s using language that "helped listeners see and even hear what it had been like", and Edward R. Murrow and Robert Trout, who "spoke to and for everyday Americans in a conversational, personal style, often using 'I', using 'the first and second person to address their listeners directly and involve them in what the war felt like'" (Douglas 1999, pp. 179–180).

This approach to radio presentation implied that radio writing then, by consequence, uses the active voice, short sentences, contractions, the present tense and simple language. After all, the experience of radio is transient, ephemeral, and the presenter has only "one chance" to be understood. That is the nature of the "spoken word" as opposed to the "printed word" that may be referred to at any time after publication. This has since been shared to all rookie radio presenters in radio script writing classes. Writing radio scripts would certainly not all be in the same rigid announcer-type form.

> Radio talk relied often heavily on repetition, on rhythmic cadences, on alliteration and mnemonic devices to facilitate ready recall and retention. People learned an "acoustic shorthand" that evolved from one era to the next. The constant reinvention of radio talk, and the way its signatures and cadences got grooved into our inner lives, also powerfully shaped generational identity. (Douglas 1999, p. 12)

It is this mannerism that presenters attempt to recreate in writing their presentation script in order to "sound natural." And so, as described by McLuhan (1994) and has been my experience, the spoken word written onto radio scripts take on a life of its own especially in the dark at night when the listener is left alone with the imagination.

> If we sit and talk in a dark room, words suddenly acquire new meanings and different textures. They become richer, even, than architecture, which Le Corbusier rightly says can best be felt at night. All those gestural qualities that the printed page strips from language come back in the dark, and on the radio. Given only the *sound* of a play, we have to fill in *all* of the senses, not just the sight of the action. (McLuhan 1994, p. 303)

Today, speech is still an integral part of radio. Shingler and Wieringa (1998) state that "speech is a crucial part of a radio station's branding, its construction of a particular image. Speech can be (and is) used to articulate a station's identity, helping it to attract specific types of audience" (Shingler et al. 1998, p. 31).

A last word on speech, or the "radio voice" is that for many years, according to Shingler and Wieringa, women were banned from reading the news on the BBC. This, they offer, was due to the close association the female voice had with gossip and rumour that was considered inappropriate in conveying information credibly and with "veracity as well as clarity" (Shingler et al., p. 46). The same bias seemed present in American radio stations in the 1930s as well because it was felt that "people did not like and would not trust the female voice over the air" (Douglas 1999, p. 164). Today, this has been proved otherwise.

Much like the vast amount of content that can be found on the Internet today, the thread that has been mentioned time and again throughout broadcast history consists of issues of authenticity, credibility and accuracy. And as radio began to increase its information content, credibility and accuracy were the main issues with radio news; the issues arising as a consequence of the misinformation received from wireless operators about the *Titanic* that included "news" at the time that all *Titanic* passengers had survived the *Titanic* disaster (see above).

1.9 RADIO NEWS

Early radio listeners had, by now, come to expect radio content to include music, entertainment, information and news. As patterns in programming demands emerge, we find the creation of necessary teams or sections to address various programming needs. One of these is radio news.

Shingler et al. (1998) considers the history of radio news as "synonymous with the development of the BBC." In the 1920s, it was "nothing more than a soap box for government"and a "propaganda machine during the Second World War" (Shingler et al., p. 19). Its importance and rise, however, was recognised by the newspapers, resulting in influential editors orchestrating the BBC prohibition against broadcasting any news before 7 pm and any commentary on public events (Shingler et al., pp. 19–20). In America, Douglas (1999) describes the problem:

> You could hear it in the very way that H. V. Kaltenborn, in 1939 and 1940, reported the news from Europe: he used words like *lugubrious*, *salient*, and *temporise*; he pronounced *at all* "at tall," and *chance* "chahnce." Yet in the next breath he would become much more colloquial, saying of the Germans, "All their stuff is censored," or that French lines were holding except for "a couple of unimportant spots." He frequently prefaced information from foreign communiqués with "what this means is" or "what this shows." Upper-class pedant or guy next door—what should the radio newscaster be? (Douglas 1999, p. 161)

The quote above reflects the sentiment that while there was a need to broadcast more than just entertainment and information, the early days of radio did not have a yardstick by which broadcasters could format news broadcasts over the radio. The radio newsroom was non-existent as were trained presenters or radio news editors. The situation in both America and Britain was the same; radio news then relied on and was essentially a repeat of what was reported in the newspapers (Shingler et al., p. 20; Harper 2002, p. 143). Carefully controlling the broadcast medium, radio was not able to initially compete with the newspaper. Newspapers restricted access to wire service reports (Harper 2002, p. 143) and did not welcome competition from this new wireless medium. So apart from the 1920 election returns from KDKA in Pittsburgh, there were virtually no news programmes on radio. In fact, news was an afterthought in daily programming that "was dominated by talks, music, and fledgling variety shows" (Douglas 1999, p. 166).

In Britain, World War II and the General Strike of 1926 were pivotal events that helped establish BBC news (Shingler and Wieringa 1998, p. 20). In America, the first regular news programme was reported to be in Nebraska, started by the *Norfolk Daily News* in July 1922 (Folkerts, Lacy & Davenport 1998, p. 214). This was a noon news programme that used the wire service material only available to newspaper sources. Events over the next decade galvanised efforts in developing radio broadcast news.

In 1931, Columbia Broadcasting System (CBS) produced a more popular quasi-news programme: *The March of Time*, with *TIME* magazine as its sponsor (Douglas 1999, p. 166; Harper 2002, p. 143). This Friday broadcast was fast-paced with news events recreated by news actors.

The kidnapping of Charles Lindbergh's baby in 1932 was also pivotal in the evolution of broadcast news. WOR in New York interrupted its programming to make the announcement, and forty minutes later CBS followed, interrupting a dance programme on its network. Both CBS and NBC subsequently established links to reporters in Hopewell, New Jersey and kept vigil until the body was found. What this dramatic event established were the technical and journalistic possibility of "on-the-spot radio reporting" (Douglas 1999, pp. 166–167). This event, because of newspaper and radio competition, caused the courts to ban radio and photographers from all proceedings after the Bruno Hauptmann trial (Harper 2002, p. 143), a rule that remained in force until recently.

Another key event that catalysed the establishment of radio news broadcasts occurred in 1932, when the Roosevelt–Hoover presidential race had radio networks beating the newspapers in broadcasting the election results, because the broadcasters had been receiving the information through the wire services. Events like these heated the competition between the newspapers and radio.

It was until 1932 sources for radio news bulletins were mainly from the newspapers with restricted access to wire services. Then, in April 1933, at the American Newspaper Publishers Association annual convention, there was a vote "to stop providing the networks with news bulletins and to discontinue publishing daily schedules of radio programs unless the stations paid for them, as if they were advertising" (Douglas 1999, p. 167). After this resolution, NBC and CBS began to build their news departments (ibid.). Newspapers boycotted CBS. The irony was that newspapers owned many radio stations, and it was really an issue about on-air advertising and how broadcasters were stealing clients from the newspapers (ibid.). The wire services only agreed to provide access to the information provided the broadcaster did not broadcast news "that was less than 24 hours old" (Douglas 1999, p. 167) and not more than 30 words, with fees charged for the use of additional material on radio (Folkerts, Lacy & Davenport 1998, p. 214). And so in December of 1933, broadcasters signed the "Biltmore agreement" that detailed the above and which also included an agreement to limit news items to two five-minute newscasts daily that ended with the line "For further details, consult your local newspaper" (Douglas 1999, p. 167).

The following year, a new service independent of the American newspaper industry emerged, the Transradio Press Service, providing domestic news and news from wire services like Havas from France and Reuters from England. In its first year of business, it acquired 150 clients. With this new competitor, local wire services in America realised that the development of radio as a legitimate information service could not be prevented, and so the wire services "declared independence from newspaper dominance and sold news to radio stations" (Folkerts et al., p. 214). Finally in 1934, United Press (UP), International News Services (INS) and Associated Press (AP) began to sell their news services to radio (Keith 2000, p. 153).

Beyond the battle for news sources, we turn to the impact and development of the news presenter and of radio news reporting.

1.10 RADIO NEWS PRESENTATION

The power of radio was reinforced with a radio news report on 6 May 1937. Chicago reporter Herb Morrison was describing the arrival of the first trans-Atlantic commercial airliner, *Hindenburg*, in Lakehurst, New Jersey when suddenly it burst into flames. The emotionally distraught Morrison, accompanied by the sound of chaos in the background, produced a most powerful aural report and record of a major historical event (ibid.).

A year later, on Halloween, Mercury Theatre's production of *The War of the Worlds* provided further evidence of the peoples' growing dependence on radio news reports. The simulated news reports in the radio drama caused panic and people began to flee their homes. That episode in broadcast history has been used to reinforce the growing influence of radio in the home and the "people's newfound dependence on radio news, which, in the fall of 1938, had been bringing Americans increasingly urgent and disturbing bulletins about Hitler's conquests in Europe and particularly about the Munich crisis and Neville Chamberlain's capitulation" (Douglas 1999, p. 165).

By 1938, radio rendered the newspaper almost obsolete. Rather than buying newspapers to follow the developing crisis in Europe, people stayed home to tune in to reports of what was happening in Munich. A year later, over nine million new radio receivers were sold (Douglas 1999, p. 162). By the time of the Munich Accord, a *Fortune* poll reported that radio listening in America became "the nation's favorite recreational activity" (Douglas 1999, p. 174). People who preferred radio news, according to the poll, shared that they received the news more quickly, "it took less time to find out what was going on, and they found it more interesting and entertaining" (ibid.).

As demands for credible reporting and presentation of news increased, so too did demand for creating tools for the craft. With the audiotape, the radio journalist was able to expand and record news reports. Actual sounds from location reports, the ambience, the reactions and political speeches could now be recorded for listeners to hear. More importantly, these could be archived (Fang 1997, p. 113).

In the early days, only CBS had a system to preserve its war coverage (Douglas 1999, p. 161). This was because during World War II, firsthand reports by CBS journalist Edward R. Murrow from battle-scarred London established CBS as the premier radio-news network, a reputation that was carried onto CBS television (Campbell 2000, p. 111). Today, production and journalistic tools include the mini-disc, the compact disc and digital audio editing software operating in mobile laptops, and static computer workstations. We will review these technologies and innovations in later chapters.

As a consequence of all the early radio reports, standards of objectivity became concerns for broadcast news. This was because the nature of radio had reports delivered through the human voice. With slight inflections of timbre and tone, opinion and bias may be unduly projected to listeners (Douglas 1999, p. 164). At about this time, the "male archetype—the newsman"—was "being designed as well" (ibid.). Ed Klauber, CBS-owner William Paley's personal assistant, concerned about objective broadcasts, imposed certain guidelines for CBS news (Douglas 1999, p. 181). CBS was not to have an editorial position about the war, reporters should not express their feelings and commentators should not judge for the listener. Presenters had to have an "unexcited demeanor" at the microphone and should only convey the facts (ibid.).

> Commentators were now called analysts, and they were not to indulge in editorialising on the air. Nor were CBS reporters to reveal any emotion or bias. They were not supposed to say "I believe" or "I think" but instead to use phrases like "it is said" or "there are those who believe" or "some experts have come to the conclusion".
> (Douglas 1999, p. 182)

Given the ephemeral nature of sound received over the radio, and the style of news presentation, information and news material had to be carefully selected and edited for the most effective impact on radio. Shingler and Wieringa (1998) suggest, however, that while radio's immediacy provided "up-to-the-minute" news and information, "it can be seen as being less comprehensive" (Shingler et al., p. 99). They then go on to compare the number of words an average newsreader utters, "160–180 words per minute" (ibid.), with the number of columns print news copy carries. While I agree with being highly selective of information and news material, I disagree with the comparison on the basis that it is like comparing chickens to horses. They are fundamentally different in substance and nature.

At this point, let us consolidate all the innovations and demands upon radio as an information and entertainment service.

FIGURE 1.4   Radio Broadcast Production Output

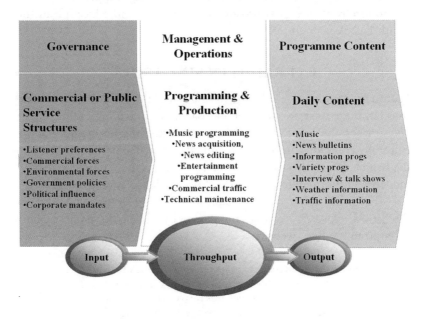

Rafael Oei 2002

Looking just at the three areas of "programming," "production" and "presentation," I have attempted to outline the key events that have influenced and shaped each process in the radio broadcasting production chain that contributes to the "radio experience." The indirect effect is the formation of certain traits that determined the processes and structure that make up "institutionalised radio." A visual representation as a signpost in our discussion may take the above form as shown in Figure 1.4.

Having established the fundamental components that make up much of how radio content is produced and delivered, we continue our radio journey in Singapore where radio begins to take root in the 1930s. Formerly a British colony, Singapore is a good example of having been influenced by the BBC and then having to adapt to and evolve in order to operate within a more commercial oriented environment to survive in the 1990s. The journey of Singapore is significant as its transformation within the broadcast industry from a rigid bureaucratic organisation to one of the most commercially-savvy broadcasters in the region, paved the way for it to be the first South East Asian country to launch Digital Radio services, using DAB-Eureka 147 technology. Singapore remains in the forefront of digital broadcasting research and education in the South East Asian region.

1.11 RADIO IN SINGAPORE

From a programmer's standpoint, having traced the development of radio thus far, there were two distinct approaches to providing radio content and services: the music and entertainment fare of the US model, and the culturally conscious, information and educational approach to radio by the British. We could also simply refer to them as the "commercial radio model" and the "public service broadcast model."

To further underscore how radio was used in Britain, embodied in the "British approach" to programming, here are some anecdotal accounts taken from the BBC website:

> The monarch could speak to his people as never before. King George V was first heard on radio during a broadcast from the British Empire Exhibition of 1924. The speech was relayed on loudspeakers outside major department stores and the crowds were so large they stopped the traffic in the road. (BBC website 2002, http://www.bbc.co.uk/thenandnow/history/, accessed 1 October 2002)

> The first running commentary for a sporting event was England vs. Wales Rugby at Twickenham in 1927. Other early outside broadcasts of major national events included the FA Cup Final, Wimbledon, The Boat Race and Trooping the Colour. (ibid.)

> "It is said that there are only six jokes in the world, and I can assure you that we can only broadcast three of them ..." John Watt, the BBC's Head of Variety in the 1930s. (ibid.)

> Good taste and decency had become a BBC issue very early on. Comedians overstepped the mark at their peril. (ibid.)

As was Reith's intentions when deciding on the policies that governed his approach to using the wireless radio, BBC output certainly reflected "everything British" to reinforce and reflect the values of that society. Under this influence, radio services in Singapore began on 1 June 1936 under the British Malaya Broadcasting Corporation formed in 1935. By this time, the functions and listener expectations of the radio station included music scheduling, news acquisition and reporting, variety entertainment and public service announcements that contributed to community building. Services were broadcast from Caldecott Hill while operations were housed in a government building at Empress Place.

The daily fare was news and information with music largely being "Hawaiian and light classical music" (Siow 1995, p. 135). News was gathered in a newsroom that, in 1959, claimed to be the provider of "one of the biggest domestic news services in the world" (Radio Singapore 1959, p. 9) broadcasting "11,680 bulletins in seven languages and dialects, 1,150 news talks, 10,500,000 words and 1,560 hours of news" (ibid.). There were also direct relays of programmes from the BBC (Chen 1997, p. 300).

Operational processes in programme scheduling were still under the "Reithen Model" of the broadcaster being the best authority of "listener tastes." The consequence of a rigid approach to administrative and operational processes in local institutional radio kept the radio services in Singapore unchanged until the late 1980s (Oei 2002).

In 1940, the British Colonial Government took over control and transferred the station to the quasi-government Malayan Broadcasting Corporation in April 1941 (Siow 1995, p. 135). The corporation consisted of governments from the Straits Settlements and the United Kingdom (Koh 1995, p. 135).

Of historical significance to Singaporeans is the completion of an apartment project at that time, in an area called "Dhoby Ghaut." The Cathay Building was the tallest building in Singapore then, and the apartment block came equipped with a 1,300-seat cinema and 32 luxurious apartments that boasted "hot and cold water, refrigerators and the use of a squash court" (Liu 1999, p. 181).

The project was opened on 3 October 1939. The cinema was plush, with an air-conditioned auditorium fitted with armchairs, "black marble pillars, green tiled floors and gold ceilings" (ibid.). Standing 16 storeys, it was twice as tall as the tallest building of the time, the Union Building. After its launch, the apartments were not to fulfil their intended purpose. The Department of Broadcasting leased the entire apartment block for its offices (ibid.).

With the invasion of Singapore by the Japanese in 1942, the broadcast station at the Cathay Building went under the name of "Syonan Hoso Kyoku," transmitting propaganda. Programme content included reminders to respect the Japanese flag, playing of the Japanese national anthem, drilling to Japanese music and providing Japanese language instruction (Chen 1997, p. 300; Siow 1995, p. 135).

After the war, broadcasting came under the service of the Publicity and Printing Unit of the British Military Administration, still based at the Cathay Building. This was soon to be reorganised by the British civil government into *Radio Malaya*.

Programming at this time included educational school programmes, news, entertainment and discussion services that encouraged and stirred public interest on matters of the government and Malaya. At the time, "Malaya" included both Malaysia and Singapore. The languages used in broadcasts were in English, Malay, Tamil and seven Chinese dialects, appropriate to the racial mix (ibid.).

Essentially, radio in Singapore was a vehicle for the dissemination of information, and the bulk of programming consisted of "spoken-word" programming. Music, while still remaining the staple popular entertainment, generally filled the space between the information, packaged radio shows and news segments. This legacy is still reflected in the way cue-sheets and scripts are generally written in Singapore today. Non spoken-word segments are separated by a "Cons" or "Con", abbreviations of "continuity" or "continues with" that indicates an audio insertion within the script.

While radio took a hold on Singapore listeners in the 1930s and early 1940s, other developments were taking root in America and England that would be pivotal in radio's developmental history, influencing the history of music as well.

1.12 THE TELEVISION INVASION

In America, Vladimir Kosma Zworykin and Philo T. Farnsworth are considered the fathers of television, developing a system that converted images into electrical signals in the 1920s (Harper 2002, p. 9). In England, credit was with John Logie Baird, who pioneered television at around the same time. In fact, viewers in London were able to receive regular BBC television transmissions by 1935/36. These experiments were interrupted with the outbreak of World War II, resuming after the war in 1946 (Ang 1991, p. 114; Shingler & Wieringa 1998, p. 21).

It was in 1939 that David Sarnoff demonstrated the television system at the World's Fair in New York. Sarnoff had invested $50 million in Vladimir Kosma Zworykin's invention (Harper 2002, p. 146). During the fair, President Roosevelt, who had used radio to reach the living room of his electorate through his "Fireside Chats" became the first president on television (ibid.). With the launch of television to the world in 1948, radio's place as a primary broadcast service in society was in jeopardy.

Without the benefit of visuals, radio listenership fell drastically. In England, the key events that redistributed media consumers were the coronation of Queen Elizabeth II in 1953 and the introduction of a commercial television network aptly called Independent Television (ITV) in 1955 (Ang 1991, p. 114; Shingler et al., pp. 21–22). In America, radio personalities left radio for lucrative offers in television. As listenership declined, so did advertising revenue (Harper 2002, p. 146).

> By 1954 that futuristic novelty television, which David Sarnoff had showcased as if it were his firstborn son at the 1939 World's Fair, was in over 26 million, or 56 per cent, of America's households. The number of television stations had soared, from six in 1946 to 354 in 1954. (Douglas 1999, p. 219)

As McLuhan observed, new media uses the content of the medium it displaces; television adopted a radio variety programming approach to its daily content, pre-dating the programming approach of MTV in recent times. Campbell describes this in the following extract:

> Remarkably, the arrival of television in the 1950s marked the only time in media history in which a new medium virtually stole every national programming and advertising strategy from the older medium. Television snatched radio's advertisers, its program genres, its major celebrities, and its large evening audiences. In the process, the TV set physically displaced the radio as the living-room center-piece across America. (Campbell 2000, pp. 116–117)

For the first time, listeners were able to see radio personalities on television monitors. For some this was a boost to their careers. However, there was still something to be said about the power of the imagination.

Radio had to do something to recover listenership. The world was on the verge of the birth of rock-and-roll, and the advent of the "Top 40" music format. There had to be mass appeal to create a need for radio once again. That was over the horizon. First, back to Singapore.

1.13 THE FIRST COMMERCIAL SERVICE IN SINGAPORE

The March 1949 issue of *Far East Trade and Engineering* announced the following:

> A new era in the history of broadcasting in the Far East opens with the introduction of Rediffusion into Hong Kong, Singapore, Kuala Lumpur and Penang. ... There is no aerial or receiving set to worry about, no need for electric current or batteries. The loudspeakers, volume control and selector switch, which are supplied by Rediffusion, are all that is required. (p. 180)

Having an independent radio station in Singapore being granted a licence to broadcast made the headlines the year before. "New Radio Station for Singapore" declared *The Free Press* on Tuesday, 20 January 1948.

> It will broadcast sponsored (advertising) programmes and will also relay items from the BBC and Radio Malaya. ... The station will be a powerful receiver which will be able to pick up broadcasts from all over the world. ... Subscribers will be supplied sets connected directly to the station on the same lines as a telephone system. (*Free Press*, 20 January 1948)

This made Rediffusion the first private radio operator in Singapore in 1949. Essentially, Rediffusion broadcasted content from the United Kingdom. Eventually, programming included Chinese-dialect variety content to meet local demands, transmitting mainly through a cable network.

Rediffusion started in the early 1920s from the small town of Clacton in South England. A pioneer in relay broadcasting, the idea here was to boost radio reception via cable to loudspeakers installed in subscribers' homes. This form of transmitting is known as radio diffusion, hence the name "Rediffusion" (re-diffusion). This was especially useful for areas with poor radio reception.

Using telegraph or telecommunication lines, however, required some regulation review. This gave rise to a submission to amend the Telegraphs Bill. A *Straits Times* report stated that while under "the Telegraphs Ordinance authority is given to the Telegraph authority to place and maintain a telegraph line under, over, along or across, and posts in or upon any immovable property" (*Straits Times*, 5 April 1949) amendments were proposed because "... the Bill is intended to provide facilities specially for Rediffusion (Singapore) Ltd" (ibid.). This extended "that authority and the protection of the existing ordinance to any person to whom a licence has been granted by the Governor-in-Council to establish and maintain a telegraph line" (ibid.).

Digital radio, datacasting and the carrying of other forms of communications besides the audio stream, have caused similar concerns to regulators. Data and Internet services traditionally fall under the umbrella of telecommunication services, while audio radio content falls under the regulatory framework of the broadcast regulator.

With the presence of a commercial broadcast enterprise, public debate arose on whether the "pan-Malayan Department of Broadcasting, popularly known as Radio Malaya" should be handed over to Rediffusion, already a self-sustaining commercial enterprise (*Straits Times*, 4 August 1949).

> Sponsored broadcasts, recommended for immediate Government consideration by the Committee appointed by the Federal Council to investigate the workings of the Department of Broadcasting, might cut Radio Malaya's deficit of $1,500,00 a year by at least one-third ($500,000) (*Straits Times*, 4 August 1949).

> If Government departments are going to be judged by their ability to support themselves out of their own revenue—which was the only test applied to the Broadcasting Department by the Federation committee—then perhaps this is merely the first of a series of novel recommendations (*Straits Times*, 17 August 1949).

While the Federal committee felt that "... the Rediffusion company would be the best repository of broadcasting responsibility ..." (ibid.) the issue of control was of utmost concern. A *Free Press* staff reporter expressed these in this extract:

> Broadcasting is, under modern conditions, a powerful instrument of policy; and any civilised government which had not under its control, whether directly of indirectly, a broadcasting organisation would find itself at a serious disadvantage in times of national emergency or even of political tension. (*Free Press*, 3 August 1949)

In contrast, the same article goes on to say, "broadcasting is not an activity which lends itself very readily to direct Governmental operation" (ibid.) because both organisations have different ends and different cultures.

The emergence of Rediffusion services was opportune because the reality was radio sets were priced beyond the means of many households. Rediffusion services provided an opportunity for many Singaporeans to gain access to the rest of the world.

> They regarded radio diffusion as a valuable means of extending the benefits of radio to people who were unable to afford radio sets. (*Free Press*, 20 January 1948)

For five dollars a month, subscribers in Singapore were able to listen to long-distance stations clearer than many receivers could receive at the time. Many households benefited from the gift of music and drama that it brought, with dialect opera being the most popular offering. After more than 50 years, subscription prices in Singapore still remain low, rising only to 10 dollars a month today!

The conditions for granting the licence included relaying a certain amount of Radio Malaya and the BBC along with in-house Rediffusion content. For many local subscribers, this was a small detail compared to the opportunity to tap into a world beyond their living room. It was an indication of better things to come, having just survived Japanese occupation during World War II.

An advertisement in the *Sunday Tribune* (12 March 1950) announced that Rediffusion had 9,600 subscribers since its launch in 1949, rising to 11,700 two months later, according to another advertisement on 28 May 1950.

By the late 1950s Rediffusion was a part of Singaporean life, even making the news when Radio Malaya's Mike Ellery left Radio Malaya to join Rediffusion as English Programme Manager on 1 March (*Straits Times*, 1 February 1957). He was replacing Vernon Martinus who was leaving to pursue a career in entertainment.

Programming differences between Radio Malaya and Rediffusion's commercial programming included ticket give-aways to events like "live" recordings of a popular programme *The Teenage Special* (*Standard*, 25 July 1958) and having contests like *Top Tunes of the Week* where listeners submitted their predictions of songs that would hit the charts (*Free Press, Hi Fi and Radio Supplement*, 25 July 1958). It was the "popular radio" format of its time, providing popular entertainment to the masses.

Currently, Rediffusion offers two channels, the Gold Channel and the Silver Channel. The Gold Channel transmits programmes in Chinese 18 hours a day while the Silver Channel, 24 hours of entertainment in both English and Chinese. Rediffusion also runs a Commercial Production Unit called Studio9 and a Central Antennae Television System, providing excellent reception of PayTV, Teleview and Satellite Television to subscribers. According to Rediffusion Singapore, 30 per cent of the government-built Housing and Development Board apartments (HDB flats), privately-owned apartments, condominiums and commercial buildings are fitted with Rediffusion systems.

Rediffusion also projects "lifestyle" and tries to reinforce this through offering the leasing and sales of a range of specialised audio-visual systems and services. Rediffusion also has a line of household products under the name "Redimart." Many Singaporeans would recall leasing the Sierra, EMI-Thomson and Rediffusion television sets from Rediffusion, especially during its heyday based at Clemenceau Avenue, Singapore. Rediffusion's offices are presently at Harper Road in Singapore.

Rediffusion Singapore's legacy was in providing the first challenge to the local public-service radio broadcast model. It was the first commercial popular radio service in Singapore, and the first cable transmission service in Singapore. Here, for the first time in Singapore, was a radio service that was more entertainment-based and for all intents and purposes, was the first format service. Compared to the government-run service that was Radio Malaya, it was a breath of fresh air. Affordable for lower income households, listenership shifted to this cabled box that used no electricity. Radio Malaya, however, was unmoved and programming remained pretty much the same through the 1950s and 1960s.

1.14 THE BIRTH OF FORMAT RADIO

While Singapore radio came to grips with Rediffusion in the early 1950s, radio in America was undergoing change.

By the early 1950s radio *was* thought to be dead, a victim, like the movies, of television. The famous "talent raids" of 1948–49 lured stars like Jack Benny, Bing Crosby, and Ozzie and Harriet away from radio to television, inaugurating the death knell. "Within three years," proclaimed NBC's president, Niles Trammell, in 1949, "the broadcast of sound or ear radio over giant networks will be wiped out." Trammell was right: by 1954 network radio, with its primetime programming that brought national stars to a huge national audience, *was* all but gone (Douglas 1999, p. 220).

Although the "power" of the networks may have diminished, it was actually evolving and re-emerging with an influence generated from a different source. This was the force of popular culture, and of music.

> Competition over markets *within* markets led to the staking out of the youth market, which was, of course, growing exponentially in the 1950s and 1960s. DJs, in an effort to earn listener loyalty, cultivated a distinct generational identity among teenagers, addressing them as cool, different, in opposition to those who would blanket the airwaves with Mantovani and his orchestra (Douglas 1999, p. 222).

This next wave was to be known as "format radio," specifically the rise of the "Top 40" radio music format. Though there may be different versions of how the radio format was born, the popular story involves a station owner from Nebraska, Todd Storz and programmer Bill Stewart.

> As with all inventions, there are disputes about who thought of Top 40 first; the two most frequently cited inventors are Todd Storz, who owned a string of stations by the mid-1950s, and Gordon McLendon, the former sportscaster and founder of the Liberty Broadcasting Network, which eventually consisted of over 400 stations (Douglas 1999, p. 247).

Storz and Stewart observed the behaviour of staff and patrons at a particular bar in Omaha as they went about choosing music selections on a jukebox. They noticed that favourite tunes were chosen and played frequently over a span of time, with selections recurring after being chosen by different patrons and staff. Storz and Stewart surmised that limiting their station's output to a music playlist that included popular tunes would increase listenership on their station when played repeatedly through the day. After working out a formula to rotate specific categories of songs based on their popularity, they reprogrammed their radio station to implement this idea. Their audience share rose by 50 per cent (Norberg 1996, p. 1; MacFarland 1997, p. 64).

Apparently, Todd Storz had been experimenting with a formula-driven or format-approach to programming for radio as early as 1949, as a response to the advent of television. This management-controlled approach to programming combined with the rock-and-roll explosion in the mid-1950s, giving birth to the "Top 40" format (Campbell 2000, p. 119) based on the charts from record sales.

What began to emerge in the early 1950s and led to the invention of the Top 40 format was "programming by the charts"—selecting music for broadcast based on record sales and jukebox plays (Douglas 1999, p. 246).

So, according to record sales, the programmer or music director would select the top 40 selections on the sales charts and schedule those songs based on rotation policies and rules. Along with other programmed events like the regular news bulletins, weather report, commercials and information segments, a scheduled playlist may look like the following.

FIGURE 1.5 The Playlist Sequence

Air Time		Cart	Intro	Length	Status	
12:00:00		News in brief		5:00.00	✓	
12:05:00	⬚	Station ID		0:10.00	✓	Information and audio programming that are scheduled for broadcast per broadcast hour to be executed in sequence.
12:05:10		Weather/Traffic		1:00.00	✓	
12:06:10	$	Johnson's		0:30.00	✓	
12:06:40	$	Visa Promo		0:30.00	✓	
12:07:10	⬚	Station Stinger		0:05.00	✓	
12:07:15	♫	Living Years	0:15	5:37.00	✓	
12:12:52	♫	Nothing's Gonna Stop	0:22	4:35.00	✓	

Rafael Oei 2000

McLuhan had an interesting comment, comparing the "jukebox" approach to radio with the largely information-based approach prior to "format radio."

> The uniting of radio with phonograph that constitutes the average radio program yields a very special pattern quite superior in power to the combination of radio and telegraph press that yields our news and weather programs. It is curious how much more arresting are the weather reports than the news, on both radio and TV (McLuhan 1994, p. 306).

By 1954/55, this approach to radio programming latched on to the minds and hearts of the teenager, catalysed by the introduction of rock-and-roll to American radio listeners by Alan Freed. The business of radio experienced a shift in dynamic, as the music content was now inter-dependent on record sales and the popularity of singers and songs.

> As the record and radio industries became more mutually dependent in the early 1950s, and as DJs like Alan Freed gained the power to make or break a song, record company reps offered a variety of incentives to play their records on the air (Douglas 1999, p. 250).

This eventually gave rise to more legislation and programming control as what emerged were unethical transactions between record companies and radio personalities. This was to be known as "payola," a term that was a contraction of two words—"pay" and "Victrola"—referring to the long-playing record player.

> The Special Committee on Legislative Oversight took testimony on payola, and Alan Freed and Dick Clark were singled out as exemplars of the problem. ... and legislation prohibiting payola followed. But the real impact of the hearings was the further erosion—some might even say elimination—of DJ autonomy in favor of programming by committee, meaning increasingly by management, who followed the lists of best-selling records (Douglas 1999, p. 251).

What had happened was at the urging of the American Society of Composers, Authors and Publishers, (ASCAP), the House Oversight Subcommittee Chairman Oren Harris looked into the recording industry's practice of payola, which was not illegal before 1959. However, commercial bribery was. Alan Freed was indicted for accepting an amount of $2,500 and Dick Clark was found to have had partial copyrights to 150 songs. There were also "ties to 33 music-related businesses, including publishers, recording companies, and pressing plants, most being located in Philadelphia" (ibid., pp. 251–252; http://www.history-of-rock.com/, accessed 11 March 2004). One of these, Jamie Records, was found to have paid out $15,000 in payola to Clark, which he denied having received.

Of the two, Clark had the most to lose, having invested in concerns in the recording industry. Under orders from ABC-TV, Clark gave up his outside interests and was let off with a warning. Freed, on the other hand, refused to deny involvement and was promptly fired by WABC-New York. Freed was later tried in December 1962 and pleaded guilty to 29 counts of commercial bribery. He was fined and received a six-month suspended sentence. Later, on 15 March 1964, the federal grand jury indicted Freed on tax evasion. His career ruined, the "father" of rock-and-roll was admitted into hospital that same year, suffering from uraemia. He died early the following year, 1965, on January 20. Dick Clark went on to create the American Music Awards and to host America's longest running variety show, *American Bandstand*, which he retired from hosting in 1989 (ibid.).

The distinctive nature of rock-and-roll music lay in the sound that it created in radio output and the way DJs presented their shows. Douglas describes it as a tussle between cultures in the following extract:

> Radio—more than films, television, advertising, or magazines in the 1950s—was *the* media outlet where cultural and industrial battles over how much influence black culture was going to have on white culture were staged and fought. Increasingly, teenager's music was written or performed by African–Americans, and many of the announcers they loved, who were white, tried to sound black (Douglas 1999, p. 222).

And it was the case as the emergent musical genre of the time, jazz included, had its roots in African–American culture that presented some problems for the image of radio in America.

> There were, in fact, many advertisers who refused to advertise on Top 40 stations because they didn't want their products associated with *that* kind of music. *That* kind of music, just like the jazz of the 1920s, had started out as race music. Once again, this time in the form of rhythm and blues and then rock 'n' roll, it was African American music that spoke to the cultural alienation, rebellion, and sexual energy of the younger generation (Douglas 1999, p. 228).

However, history has shown that this was indeed the transition that led to the "second wind" for radio, further supported by the development of the transistor radio that became the icon of the time, enabling radio listening to reach beyond the living room, into the car and onto the beaches.

> With rock 'n' roll broadcast over car radios and transistors, it was the mobility of the music, not its fidelity, that mattered (Douglas 1999, p. 252).

With the choice of music, mobility of radio and the rebellious streak of youth, radio listening became the biggest trend to follow and escape into.

> The mystic screen of sound with which they are invested by their radios provides the privacy for their homework, and immunity from parental behest (McLuhan 1994, p. 303).

> Since TV, radio has turned to the individual needs of people at different times of the day, a fact that goes with the multiplicity of receiving sets in bedrooms, bathrooms, kitchens, cars, and now in pockets. Different programs are provided for those engaged in diverse activities. Radio, once a form of group listening that emptied churches, has reverted to private and individual uses since TV. The teenager withdraws from the TV group to his private radio (ibid., p. 306).

1.15 SINGAPORE RADIO MOVES ON

Back in Singapore, Radio Malaya moved its station and offices to its present location at Caldecott Hill, on Andrew Road, in 1952. By 1954, the station was broadcasting free-to-air a total of 230 hours a week.

In an interview with Gemma Koh of *Female Magazine* (October 1995), Tan Siew Loon, a librarian, radio orchestra member and later classical music producer recalled:

> Everything was on one channel, programmes were very fragmented. Hours of transmission were short, closing in between programmes for schools broadcasts. But we had a lot of material from two main sources: BBC (parlour games and quiz games) and Voice of America programmes including orchestral concerts and recordings of opera.

There was light music in the morning (programmes like Waltzing and March) and pop tunes (like soppy love songs and songs of the 20s) in the evenings. Once a week at lunchtime, the radio orchestra played live. And on weekends, we'd go out to various hotels. On Sundays were live church programmes.

Interview programmes with VIPs and live commentaries of boxing were very popular. Later came badminton and horse racing commentaries. Outstanding were announcers like Kingsley Morrando (Koh 1995, p. 135).

By 1958, household radio licences had risen to 91,259 from 11,818 in 1947. In 1959, Radio Singapore was established, after having been part of Radio Malaya until the end of 1958.

Multicultural Singapore at the time received broadcasts in the four languages with a breakdown of 84.5 hours for Chinese programming, 78.25 hours for English, 63.75 hours for Malay, and 40.5 hours for Tamil services (Radio Singapore 1959, p. 3). This included extra transmission hours during school terms that carried "Schools Service Programmes" in all languages.

Listenership for Radio Malaya had been steadily rising from 11,818 household licences in 1947 to 91,259 by the middle of 1958 (Radio Singapore 1959, p. 2). This figure includes Rediffusion subscribers. There was a total of 267 hours of programming in 1958/59 with the following breakdown.

TABLE 1.1 Table of Programming (Radio Singapore publication 1959, p. 4)

Items	Hours	Items	Hours
News bulletins and news talks	24.5	Talks including adult education	35
Music	140	Schools broadcasts	20
Drama and documentaries	25	Variety	8
Sports	4	Religion	5
Announcements	1.5	Programmes for special groups	4

Programming content, evident from the table, was community-focused, with the inclusion of adult educational programmes, programmes for special groups and schools broadcasts. In 1958 alone, there were 2,507 registered "listening" schools (Radio Singapore 1959, p. 10). Radio in Singapore clearly served the community to reinforce the message of social and cultural integration. The programming was fixed with specific content and radio was used to cater to the needs of the "general public." It was after all a public service radio station. It educated, informed and was all things to its listeners.

In 1959, Radio Singapore broadcast approximately 27,000 programmes, totalling about 13,500 hours on air. Programmes produced from in-house studios made up 46 per cent of total output. 52 per cent were locally produced commercial productions and 2 per cent were relays and overseas transcriptions. Looking at the staff numbers, the 403 staff then is a far cry from what MediaCorp Radio of Singapore has today (ibid., p. 5). Transmission coverage in 1959 was from three medium wave transmitters for Singapore and three short wave transmitters for the Federation. These were operated from the Jurong station of Radio Singapore (ibid., p. 7).

Generally, the entertainment content on radio and its personalities came from the stage. Bands played and were transmitted "live," or they were pre-recorded in the studio. In Singapore, presenters were still dressed for their shift as though they were going for some grand function. The legacy was the "Reithen formality" and "properness," a culture that transferred itself into the delivery and programming of Singapore radio (Koh 1995, pp. 133–134). Another radio personality, Steven Lee recalled in an interview with Ms Koh from an article in *Female Magazine* (October 1995):

> ... Before radio turned commercial, broadcasting styles were very stiff—prim and proper, almost like BBC ... (Koh 1995, p. 136)

Radio Singapore merged with the Federation of Malaya once again in 1963, forming Radio Malaysia. The daily fare then was from four channels in English, Tamil, Chinese and Malay. An external service called *Suara Singapura* incorporated educational programmes in these four languages (Koh 1995, p. 136). This merger was short-lived as soon after, Singapore gained independence in 1965, and with that, Radio-Television Singapore (RTS) emerged.

Up to this point, the above examples of rock-and-roll, "format radio" and the change to a more personal presentation illustrate some evolutionary stages that radio had to undergo to adapt to each time and circumstance. The emergence of the commercial entertainment approach to radio, presented by Rediffusion in Singapore and format radio in America, contrasted the then "mainstream approach" to informational programming, presenting the listener with radio-listening options. This suggests a need for some constant level of reflection and review in programming culture, philosophies and styles in order to remain relevant, especially against increasing technological innovations.

Radio in Singapore remains an information channel for the government today, playing a crucial role in nation building, and transmitting social and cultural heritage. In the words of the Singapore Broadcasting Authority's mission statement:

> To develop quality broadcasting and make Singapore a dynamic broadcasting hub, so as to help build a well-informed, culturally rich, socially cohesive and economically vibrant society (SBA website, accessed 3 June 2002).

The above mission reinforces the SBA Act that replaced the Broadcasting Act in October 1994 when the Singapore Broadcasting Authority was instituted. Part of its functions includes:

(2)   The Authority shall have the following duties:
    (a)   to regulate the broadcasting industry so as to achieve an adequate and comprehensive range of broadcasting services which serve the interests of the general public;
    (b)   to ensure that the broadcasting services provided by licensees are maintained at a high general standard in all respects and, in particular, in respect of their content, with quality, proper balance and wide range in their subject-matter, having regard both to the broadcasting services as a whole and also to the days of the week on which, and the times of the day at which, such broadcasting services are broadcast; and
    (c)   to ensure that nothing is included in the content of any broadcasting service which is against public interest or order, national harmony or which offends against good taste or decency (SBA Website, accessed 3 June 2002).

This function was critical for the politically volatile years between 1959 and 1969 when radio was used to rally diverse ethnic and cultural groups together (Chen 1997, pp. 300 & 303). The influence of radio in Singapore is described by the managing editor of *Accent*:

> ... The up-side is that our lives have been made easier and more comfortable than ever before. For those people living in the wayward regions of the world, technology is a godsend that puts them in touch with the world outside. For them, radio, particularly, is a medium of communication that surpasses geographical boundaries and frontiers. ... For many Singaporeans, radio is a lifeline, a voice in the night, the friend who understands. ... You can tune out the vision, but the sounds of silence can be deafening (Tay 1995, p. 14).

The Singapore Broadcasting Authority has since expanded its mandate to address the issues of the media in the present digital age. Now known as the Media Development Authority, the MDA has issued a "Code of Practice for Market Conduct in the Provision of Mass Media Services" for both broadcasting and print: setting the guidelines for content management and industry practices in Singapore (http://www.mda.gov.sg/content/index.html).

1.16 FM STEREO SERVICE

In 1960, Radio Singapore recorded and broadcasted its first commercial advertisements from Coke and Ovaltine. In that same year, more FM (Frequency Modulation) spectrum space was released, increasing format stations and services in America and around the world.

> FM radio, and the new stereo systems that showcased it, represented at that time the ultimate use of technology to magnify, extend, and deepen the capabilities of the human ear. The new technology separated sounds, highlighted how they were layered, made the components of music more distinct and pure (Douglas 1999, p. 258).

The beauty of FM technology lay in the lack of electrical and static interference. FM transmission accentuated the distance and pitch between radio waves, giving greater clarity and fidelity to the transmitted audio. AM, or amplitude modulation on the other hand, relied on the volume or height of the radio waves (Campbell 2000, p. 117; Straubhaar & LaRose 2002, pp. 170–171). With the crisp fidelity and superior sound of FM services, it became the preferred mode of transmission for music as opposed to AM (Amplitude Modulation) services.

FM transmission had been developed in the 1920s and 1930s by RCA engineer Edwin Armstrong. It had begun with Armstrong's appreciation of the potential in De Forest's "vacuum tubes" resulting in his *superheterodyne circuit* that was developed in 1918. This circuit laid the foundation for FM transmission and reception because it enabled a radio receiver to remain on one specific frequency after being selected by the listener (Harper 2002, p. 136). Although described by Sarnoff as a revolutionary breakthrough in broadcast sound, Sarnoff and his executives at RCA consciously delayed FM's launch to concentrate on developing and promoting the television (Campbell 2000, p. 117; Straubhaar & LaRose 2002, p. 171). While protecting their AM stations, RCA had wanted to ensure that channels were allocated to television before they were released to FM transmission (Campbell 2000, p. 118).

Armstrong's belief in FM led him to found more than 20 experimental FM radio stations between 1935 to the 1940s after leaving RCA. In 1941, the FCC allocated space for commercial FM licences and by 1949 there were up to 700 FM stations in America. But the journey and legal battles for FM and for numerous patents were arduous and took their toll. Armstrong did not live to see his dream fulfilled. After prolonged efforts to promote FM and bitter from Sarnoff's betrayal, Armstrong jumped from his 13th-storey New York apartment on 31 January 1954, just before radio experienced its "second wind" with its music format programming and the popularity of the transistor radio (Campbell 2000, p. 170).

With the ability to transmit stereo sound, and with its fidelity, music was the staple for FM services, transmitting classical music, easy listening music, and popular tunes. With more music and less talk, listeners began to tune in more frequently to FM radio stations, shifting from AM-services because of all the talk programming that increased on those stations. By the end of the 1960s, FM listenership grew 120 per cent.

A few figures only begin to convey the magnitude of the FM revolution. In 1964 total net FM revenues were $19.7 million. Ten years later that figure had increased 13 times to $248.2 million. In 1962, according to the FCC, there were 983 commercial FM stations on the air; in 1972 their number stood at 2,328. Four years later there were nearly 3,700 FM stations on the air. By 1972, in cities such as Chicago and Boston, it was estimated that 95 percent of households had FM sets (Douglas 1999, p. 259).

The first FM transmission in Singapore was on 17 July 1967, with the official stereo service launching two years later on 18 July 1969. Subsequently, AM-band listenership in Singapore fell drastically, resulting in AM services being discontinued in 1993 without any incident or fanfare.

The journey and development of radio as a medium of communication, then entertainment, and the journey of FM radio, are accounts of long and difficult odysseys. In Singapore, radio was about to undergo a significant shift within a compressed span of five years. This was the preamble to the implementation of digital radio services in Singapore on 19 November 1999. For an explanation and description of the potential of digital radio, see my book *Borderless Bandwidth* (Oei 2002) where I discuss the need for structural changes in the radio organisation in order to function systemically to deliver digital audio and data content from a programming perspective. In this volume, I discuss radio content, and I have been exploring the evolution of aural

FIGURE 1.6 Listener-Oriented Value Chain

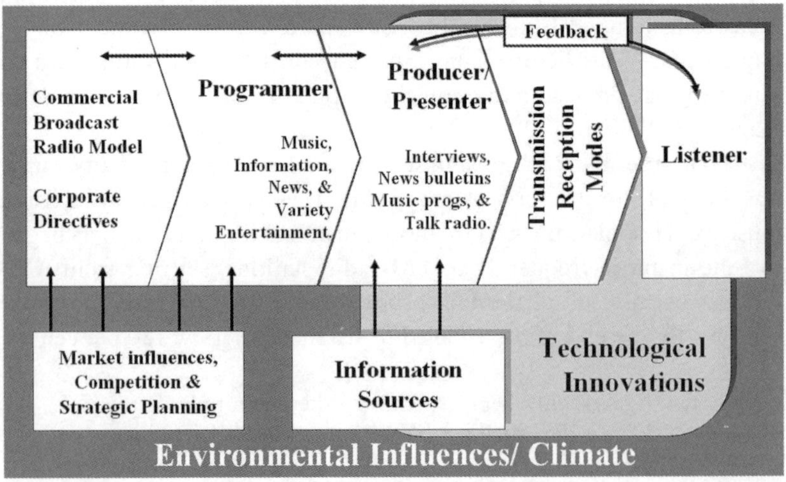

Rafael Oei 2002

content in radio services through its history before discussing content generation for a digital radio platform.

Up to this point, I have attempted to trace the influences that have made radio listening the experience it is today. Compare the illustration, Figure 1.6, with a similar depiction in Figure 1.2 above. This illustration represents a listener-oriented value chain that has since influenced programming approaches in radio. It is a model that takes into account the preferences of listeners, market influences, competition, the environment, corporate directives, and technological innovations that allows for interaction and feedback from various quarters in order to provide the best radio service for the intended listener base with the most lucrative revenue generating model possible.

My intention in laying this foundation is to bring you one step further into exploring radio-listening that now transcends mere aural listening experiences through recent technological innovations, going beyond Marconi's or Sarnoff's dreams. We are now living in an age where listener expectations are different, given the presence of the global communication network that enables communication between individuals across continents and oceans in an instant. Radio technology has advanced onto a digital domain that has within its system the potential for multi-dimensional programming possibilities. In the next chapter, we look at the listener as a consumer of digital products in an attempt to discern possible patterns that may be used to formulate and design relevant and compelling content that may be broadcast through digital radio technology.

CHAPTER 2

Listener to
Co-Producer/Consumer

In the previous chapter, we looked at the evolution of radio as a medium of communication. We saw how services evolved and adapted to the needs and assumptions of the time. It may be simplistic to sort the movements into two camps, nonetheless for convenience, it is generally accepted that there have been two overall approaches to radio broadcasting that have emerged from the US and the UK. Lewis and Booth attempts to summarise the dichotomy in the following:

> It is noticeable that the pressure for new radio forms comes from two different directions—those seeking to set up commercial stations and those who wish to use radio for community development. In many places the 'new' form of radio has been locally based, but that is not the ground on which either side has most to gain (Lewis and Booth 1990, p. 188).

While I may have alluded to the necessity for the Singapore Broadcasting Corporation to institute organisation-wide change and the benefits of adopting the American commercial-entertainment radio model, I am by no means implying that the commercial model is better than the public service model. Given the scenario SBC was in, and the market share it was losing, it could not function in a prescriptive mode and programme for a faceless and blanket "general public." Numerous studies reveal diversity in audience makeup and that the "general public" is a myth. And to say one model is above another would be naïve.

In this chapter, I will address this diversity and look at the listener regardless of broadcasting model. I will explore how the consumer/listener has evolved, and how institutional radio and radio production/presentation processes are influenced to provide necessary content and services.

Ang (1990,1996), Castells (1997, 1998, 2000), Douglas (1999), Hendy (2000), Lury (1996), Rifkin (2000) and Zyman (2000) have commented on the changes to the understanding of the term "audience," within the new digital and interactive communications technologies. In proposing a framework to modify existing institutional paradigms and processes, this chapter will examine the concept of "the listener" as opposed to the emergent "consumer/user," and proposes that current radio listeners are "co-producer-consumers," participating more actively within daily radio programming beyond the figurative inference made by Hendy, into the possibility of personally altering programmed content.

As listeners, then, we are the co-producers of radio. We all create our own images in listening to radio, and we each inhabit domestic worlds which mould our listening in different ways (Hendy 2000, p. 145).

As I explore the influences that have produced the "co-producer-consumer," I will inevitably include the proliferation of Internet-based services that have shaped the formulation of digital-centric assumptions that govern behaviours and perceptions of what constitutes digital media and services. With the improvement of cable transmission through broadband, fibre-optics, fire-wire and wireless broadband carriers, mobile telephony communication services have gone deep into the realms that once were dominated by broadcast media by providing similar services on the cellular telephone. Once the basis of these assumptions and consumer/user expectations are identified, the nature of digital services that may be offered on a medium like digital radio may be juxtaposed against the architecture that is Eureka 147-DAB, which will be explained in the next chapter. Only then will a modified institutional structure emerge to reveal the processes needed to be implemented to support these services.

To be sure, radio production processes have moved far beyond the simple voice over music to be transmitted over the airwaves. In the first chapter, we saw the first "programmer" and provider of information and entertainment through an electronic medium was the telephony service provider via institutions like Telefon Hirmondo, fulfilling the public's desire for regular information and entertainment through available technology, which was at the time telephones. Today, once again, mobile telephones surge ahead of broadcast media in providing more than just verbal communication services. We fax, email, surf the Internet, receive information and data, listen to MP3 audio files and listen to the radio using the cellular phone.

2.1 THE LITERATURE

The groundwork for this chapter centres on the nature and extent of cabled and wireless-broadband Internet access. I will use data relevant to broadband Internet access, the use of personal computers, and consumer behaviour with regard to online access to music, information, video services and online radio and television. The behaviour and attitude toward these digital services would influence the consumer/user's assumptions when faced with the prospect of now having to slowly consume digital radio and television services.

Data will be compared across the Asia-Pacific, the United Kingdom and the United States. This extended triangulation is important in gathering information that would help us understand the consumer/user's acceptance and perception of digital-reality.

Studies I have read and will refer to include fact sheets from the Radio Advertising Bureau of the United Kingdom (http:// www.rab.co.uk/, accessed 24 January 2003); the *Radio Ad Effectiveness Lab Research Compendium* (Peacock 2002); the *Survey on Infocomm Usage in Households 2000* by the Infocomm Development Authority of Singapore or "IDA" (IDA 2001); the *Survey on Broadband Usage in Singapore 2001* (IDA 2002); data from the *Connected Homes Programme* (IDA 2002); the report on *Singapore Youth in the Information Age* which was a focus group discussion organised by the Asian Media Information and Communication Centre (AMIC) for the National Youth Council (NYC), Singapore (AMIC 1998); and *A Study of Youth in the Asia Pacific* (ACNielsen and Optimum Media Direction 1998). There was one study that compared educational institutions and their existing media curricula against the observations and expectations of the media industry from the ASEAN member states. Edited by Drs Ang Peng Hwa and Sankaran Ramanathan (2000) this collection of studies, *Communication Education in ASEAN*, was particularly useful in identifying the gaps that may exist between media educational outcomes and expectations from the media industry.

From the US, interesting studies that reveal the next generation of digital media users include: *Radio Today 2001: How America Listens to Radio* (Arbitron 2002); *Internet and Multimedia 10: The Emerging Digital Consumer* (Arbitron and Edison Media Research 2003); *Internet 9: The Media and Entertainment World of Online Consumers* (Arbitron et al. 2002); *How Kids and Tweens Use and Respond to Radio* (Arbitron 2001); and *Radio*

Station Web Site Content: An In-depth Look (Arbitron and Edison Media Research 2000).

The above quoted studies are particularly interesting in revealing how consumers have received the onslaught of the Internet and digital wireless telephony through their purchase behaviour, online access and reasons for surfing the Internet.

Other books that discussed consumer behaviour in Singapore and the region include: Dr Rappa's (2002) *Modernity and Consumption: Theory, Politics, and the Public in Singapore and Malaysia*; Dr Madanmohan's (2002) *The Asia-Pacific Internet Handbook, Internet in Asia*, edited by Drs Sankaran and Becker (2001); *7 Faces of Singaporeans: Their Values, Aspirations and Lifestyles* (Kau, Tan and Wirtz 1998); *IT2010: Beyond the Web Lifestyle* (Chan 1999); and *Global Culture: Media Arts, Policy and Globalization* (Crane, Kawashima and Kawasaki 2002).

Readings that have also influenced my study include: Ien Ang's (1991) *Desperately Seeking the Audience* and (1996) *Living Room Wars: Rethinking Media Audiences For a Postmodern World*; Brown and Duguid's (2002) *The Social Life of Information*; Castells' (1997, 1998, 2000) trilogy; Crisell's (1994) *Understanding Radio*; Fairclough's (1995) *Media Discourse*; Hendy's (2000) *Radio in the Global Age*; Brian D. Loader's (1998) *Cyberspace Divide: Equality, Agency and Policy in the Information Society*; Lury's (1996) *Consumer Culture*; Jeremy Rifkin's (2000) *The Age of Access: How the Shift from Ownership to Access is Transforming Modern Life*; Shingler and Wieringa's (1998) *On Air: Methods and Meanings of Radio*; Negroponte's now classic *Being Digital* (1995); and Thomas A. Stewart's (1998) *Intellectual Capital: The New Wealth of Organizations*.

2.2 INTERACTIVITY ON TRADITIONAL RADIO SERVICES

The media have tried to bridge the gap between the public conditions of media production and the private conditions of consumption by evolving a "communicative ethos" and a "communicative style" which adjust towards the priorities, values and practices of private life. This includes the development of a "public colloquial" language, a public language for use in the media which is modelled to varying degrees and in varying ways upon the practices of informal, colloquial, conversational speech (Fairclough 1995, pp. 37–38).

The existence and social relevance of broadcast media depend on the people it programmes for. The appeal of media content goes only as far as it is useful, relevant and valuable to the audience for which it is intended. Broadcast professionals have attempted to define the role of the radio through the years so that it would become accepted as part of the listener's lifestyle, as related in the previous chapter. David Hendy breaks down the influence of radio into three main areas:

> The first is in the area of democratic life, and specifically the way in which radio lives up to its reputation as a medium of information and discussion. The second is in the more diffuse area of identity—how radio might nurture, or destroy, people's sense of "belonging"; "belonging" to communities that can be defined, for example by ethnicity, language, place or even by patterns of consumption. The third area has a more specific focus: the way in which radio might shape trends in popular music (Hendy 2000, p. 194).

Hendy's reference to radio's influence on music trends seems a narrow one. I would extend that phrase to include the influence of radio on the listeners' preferences and perspectives in daily life. And so as I discuss radio's role as "a medium of information and discussion," as an integral element of communities, it would also include radio as a commercial vehicle, leading into my arguments for the latest incarnation of the radio listener—the "co-producer-consumer."

Looking at Hendy's reference to radio programming as being "democratic," responding and "living up to its reputation as a medium of information and discussion," let us once again look at the process of radio production and programming to explore how "democratic" this process is.

Communication models have the message as the originating input, going through processes and filters before emerging as an output that is received by the receiver (Ang 1991, McLuhan 1994, Crisell 1994, Fairclough 1995, Hendy 2000). This message, although having been subjected to various levels of scrutiny from concept through to production and market research to transmission, is also subjected to the listeners' perception of the output that may not be aligned with the initial intended message of the broadcaster. Whether these messages find their mark, or are perceived to be relevant to the listener is a tenuous assumption if not subjected to rigorous research.

FIGURE 2.1 The Production Workflow

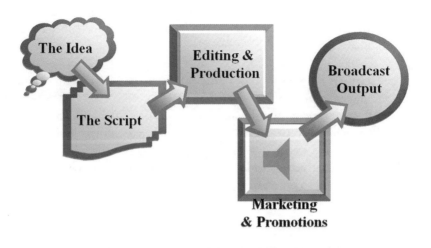

Rafael Oei 2002

In order to find a rationale for determining the nature and type of content suitable for broadcast we may consider gratification theories applied to radio listening. Based on McQuail, Blumler and Brown (1972), Crisell lists four main kinds of gratification that will, if aligned with the listener's needs and behaviour at that moment, make for appealing listening, which would then be perceived as being successful programming.

1. Diversion – the need for escape from life's routine and problems, for emotional release.
2. Social integration – the need for companionship, to form relationships with others.
3. Self-awareness – the need to compare personalities to oneself, programme content to one's own situation.
4. Surveillance – the need for information about the world (Crisell 1994, p. 209; Bucy 2002, pp. 37–38)

The discriminating consumer-user will select her preferred medium and forms of "content according to her psychological and social needs and her physical circumstances, all of which vary in time" (ibid.).

In Bucy's (2002) excellent new media reader *Living in the Information Age*, the chapter on "New Media Theory" includes a reference to the study by Katz, Gurevitch, and Haas (1973) who view mass media "as a means used by individuals to connect themselves with others" (Bucy 2002, p. 38). Bucy's edition lists five categories:

1. Cognitive needs – acquiring information, knowledge, and understanding.
2. Affective needs – emotional, pleasurable, or aesthetic experience.
3. Personal integrative needs – strengthening credibility, confidence, stability, and status.
4. Social integrative needs – strengthening contacts with family, friends, and so on.
5. Tension release needs – escape and diversion.
   (ibid.)

Both references cited in Crisell and Bucy describe the media user as one who is seeking to gratify personal needs to belong, to escape, to be entertained and to be part of a larger community at the same time. This only reinforces the individuality of the listener or media user, and the conditional nature in one's behaviour for accessing entertainment or information from the media.

> Radio provides a speed-up of information that also causes acceleration in other media. It certainly contracts the world to village size, and creates insatiable village tastes for gossip, rumor, and personal malice. But while radio contracts the world to village dimensions, it hasn't the effect of homogenizing the village quarters. Quite the contrary. In India, where radio is the supreme form of communication, there are more than a dozen official languages and the same number of official radio networks (McLuhan 1994, p. 306).

The varied roles of radio and the attempt to meet these demands have been described in the previous chapter, reflecting the evolution of radio programming content from a combination of spoken word services, news and commentary along with musical interludes to a more populist scheduled music programming approach. With World War II, community reports and news coverage became more extensive as listeners craved to know more about the world around them.

And there are few devices with which people from different generations and backgrounds have had such an intimate relationship. Ask anyone born before World War II about the role of radio in his or her life, and in the life of the country, and you will see that person begin to time-travel, with an almost euphoric pleasure, to other eras and places, when words and music filled their heads and their hearts (Douglas 1999, p. 3).

As technologies and creativity over the radio matured, productions became more elaborate resulting in examples like the infamous Mercury Theatre production of H. G. Wells' classic *War of the Worlds* and various complex documentaries, features and commentaries, many of which are dominated by the BBC due to its long standing tradition.

One constant in the use of radio was that it entered and remained a part of the home. Radio listening became a habit, an integral part of life and a means to maintain contact with a wider world.

Since the 1930s, many millions of people all over the world made the radio an integral part of their daily lives, turning to it the moment they awake and, from that point on, relying on it to accompany them through the day, providing not just company in periods of solitude but also an organising structure and timetable (Shingler and Wieringa 1998, p. 110).

Douglas has a similar observation:

Radio structured people's days, waking them up in the morning, punctuating their routines, separating the afternoon from the evening, and putting them to sleep at night. It provided audio markings of time and space, an aural signifier of people's schedules. It was still, in the 1950s and early 1960s, the major source of news for most people (Douglas 1999, p. 220).

The creation of various genres to satisfy audience expectations and needs seem endless as what may seem popular today may be passé tomorrow. Crisell observes:

Consequently we adapt radio to our *physical* circumstances and requirements in the way uses and gratifications theory argues that we adapt all the media to suit our *psychological* circumstances and requirements (Crisell 1994, p. 211).

This brings us to the question of access. To find a service, entertainment or information relevant and valuable there needs to be the ability to access it, whether it is through a radio receiver or calling into the station for a song, some information, to join in an interview talk show, or just to chat with the presenter over the airwaves. When the interaction is made, the content becomes accessible in both comprehension and for gratification.

> All forms of mass communication give rise to questions about access. In mediated quasi-interaction, the issue of which categories of social agent get to write, speak and be seen—and which do not—assumes considerable importance (Fairclough 1995, p. 40).

When listeners are tuned to a radio programme, focussed and interested, they tend to be immersed totally. The power of the spoken word, sounds and emotion create a picture in the listener's mind as was in the case of Orson Welles' *War of the Worlds*. Apart from the enactment being complete with actuality and sound effects, the impact of that radio drama was due to the accepted role of radio as a source of credible news, which was the manner in which the story was adapted for radio by Welles. The story of the landing of Martian aliens on earth was related through the mock commentary of a journalist interrupting a mock daily broadcast of programmes and music. Even though the radio programming in the drama was fiction, being a replica of an actual broadcast format, listeners were convinced the alien landing was real Given how new the medium was, the limited number of sets available nd the inexperience of a war and depression-weary listening audience, t.e listeners reacted in dramatic fashion and evacuated themselves.

A similar occurrence may be unlikely to happen today, as the media consumer has access to multiple media to verify broadcast information and breaking news. The most significant example in recent years was the terrorist attack on the World Trade Center in New York, broadcast live as it happened, transmitted through various broadcast networks and over the Internet. By all counts, it was an unbelievable event. Like me, many viewers watched in disbelief as the second airliner crashed into the remaining tower, the first having been hit slightly earlier. My first response was, is this a Hollywood stunt? On the spot accounts by eyewitnesses were powerful and dramatic over the radio, more so because the radio journalist was more mobile without having a camera crew on tow. The aural descriptions were vivid because of the listeners' imagination, combined with the sound of actualities recorded at the scene.

> Because sound is dynamic and fleeting, radio conveyed a powerful sense of "liveness"— it was, from the beginning, "an account of what *is* happening, rather than a record of what *has* happened." Radio was a perceptual technology that extended, deepened, and magnified hearing to completely unprecedented levels. (Douglas 1999, p. 7)

In the case of *War of the Worlds*, the incident illustrated how the listener was an unwitting active participant in the drama because the action that occurred in the mind was perceived to be real. Interaction with the radio station increased with the emergence of personality-driven radio as well.

> This natural bias of radio to a close tie-in with diversified community groups is best manifested in the disk-jockey cults, and in radio's use of the telephone in a glorified form of the old trunk-line wire-tapping (McLuhan 1994, p. 306.)

With that the flamboyant rapid-speaking creature, the disc jockey, became more prominent.

> Radio created the disk jockey, and elevated the gag writer into a major national role. Since the advent of radio, the gag has supplanted the joke, not because of gag writers, but because radio is a fast hot medium that has also rationed the reporter's space for stories (McLuhan 1994, p. 303).

It was this new approach in radio programming that met and dealt with the threat of the television. With listener and market segmentation in the Top 40 radio station format, FM stations begin their climb as the broadcast transmission standard.

Access to the radio was also increased with the emergence of the transistor radio. This enabled the listener to bring the radio receiver anywhere, and so radio became even more mobile and a part of youth lifestyle in the 1950s and 1960s, contributing to the beach and surf culture.

> Transistorized sets did not come onto the market until 1954, and at first they were relatively expensive, costing from 50 to 90 dollars. But competition from the Japanese drove both the size of the sets

and their price down, so that by 1961 one could get a transistor set for under 10 dollars. That meant that young people—even as young as eight or nine—could have their own radio sets (Douglas 1999, p. 226).

Interacting with the medium is key. When familiarity and credibility are established, listeners tend to want to participate and be associated with the station. And traditional radio is really a linguistic medium, relying on narratives and the spoken word to lead the listener into the imagination or into action.

> The importance of speech in determining audience preferences has been recognised throughout the radio industry. Most station controllers today are acutely aware of the need to closely monitor the uses of broadcast speech and to make careful decisions about its content, style and delivery (Shingler and Wieringa 1998, p. 31).

Negroponte, discussing speech recognition and synthesis, acknowledges the complexity of speech, language and nuance.

> Spoken words carry a vast amount of information beyond the words themselves. While talking, one can convey passion, sarcasm, exasperation, equivocation, subservience, and exhaustion—all with the exact same words (Negroponte 1995, p. 139).

In such a complex process of communication exchange, there are several levels on which the listener may respond and interact: cerebrally, emotionally, physically—by going down to the station, phoning the station and now, through the digital network.

The most widely used methods to interact with the radio station are the phone-in (during music request programmes, contests and quizzes, on-air promotional campaigns) and the interview-talk show. These provide avenues for on-air participation, dialogue and discussion between the station and the listener. It is no wonder that in recent years, the talk show has gained popularity, with callers phoning in for consolation, to seek advice, or just to indulge in mindless chatter to participate and own a brief moment "on-air." Hendy views this transaction positively:

> My essential point is this, though: that such a model of cultural mediation—one which is capable of breaching radio's habitual desire to segregate us—could, theoretically at least, hold true for similar

processes of 'intercultural trafficking' between local and distant cultures, between various ethnic identities, and—recalling our earlier discussion of talk-radio's role in democratic life—between various political beliefs and ideas (Hendy 2000, p. 238).

The talk show and the phone-in radio programmes have been quite the staple for radio stations around the globe because of all the above stated points. It seemed to bring the radio to the people and vice versa.

> Whilst the station gains and retains an audience, listeners get to have their say; they literally become the voice of the station and everything on that station (jingles, music, presenter personalities, advertisements, etc.) becomes geared towards establishing a suitable context within which the voice of the listeners (callers) can best be accommodated. In this process, the listeners themselves are the driving force behind both the content and style of the radio station: they are, ultimately, the power behind the broadcaster's throne (Shingler et al. 1998, p. 118).

Ironically, this view that radio is democratic is contradictory considering the fact that most radio programming is pre-scheduled and is not determined or altered "live", similar to the illusion "reality television" would have us believe that events unfold on the spur of the moment dependent on decisions made by the participants. There is still a programmed timeframe, a certain target audience to pitch at, and a particular production approach. Similarly, radio output is tailored to produce a desired effect on certain segments of the listening audience for the purposes already described above, and for purposes of fulfilling marketing strategies.

Radio programmes are pre-packaged as well. In all radio productions the same combination of elements is used in various configurations. Assuming that research into the project has already been done, the elements in the production process may be broadly simplified and represented using the following diagram labelled Figure 2.2.

Packaging is only necessary if the production has to be pre-recorded and produced prior to broadcast. The presenter, or disc jockey, of course, may present "live" broadcasts, in real time, in the broadcast studio using a combination of pre-edited, pre-produced and "live" elements to enhance the content being broadcast. To the listener, this is invisible and of no concern. As long as what is anticipated is produced and presented well, and at the published broadcast-time, the listener does not care how the programme was "brought to air."

FIGURE 2.2 Production Elements

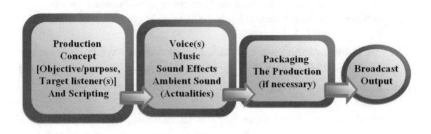

Rafael Oei 2003

Turning to the process of delivering a "live" on-air programme, what seems to be prevalent now is that listeners consider music to be synonymous with radio.

> Music on the radio, as on television, seems to perform two main functions. It is an object of aesthetic pleasure in its own right, in record shows, concerts, recitals, and so on; and either by itself or in combination with words and/or sounds it performs an ancillary function in signifying something outside itself (Crisell 1994, p. 48).

Of course music is only one component in the structure of a broadcast hour.

> Even music radio stations are liberally interspersed with DJ chat, news bulletins, time checks, weather forecasts and traffic news. Speech lends structure to the daily schedule and provides the context in which music operates as meaningful entertainment (Shingler et al. 1998, p. 30).

For an on-air presentation situation in a format radio station, the elements that fit into the "live" broadcast content would generally be a variation of the following elements (see Figure 2.3).

These elements, similarly invisible to the listener, are taken for granted in daily radio listening. The process that produces this broadcast output is elaborate and is the product of a combination of various roles and systems that keep the radio station functioning. The output model presented in Figure 2.3 satisfies the needs of a format radio listening

FIGURE 2.3   On-Air Output Model

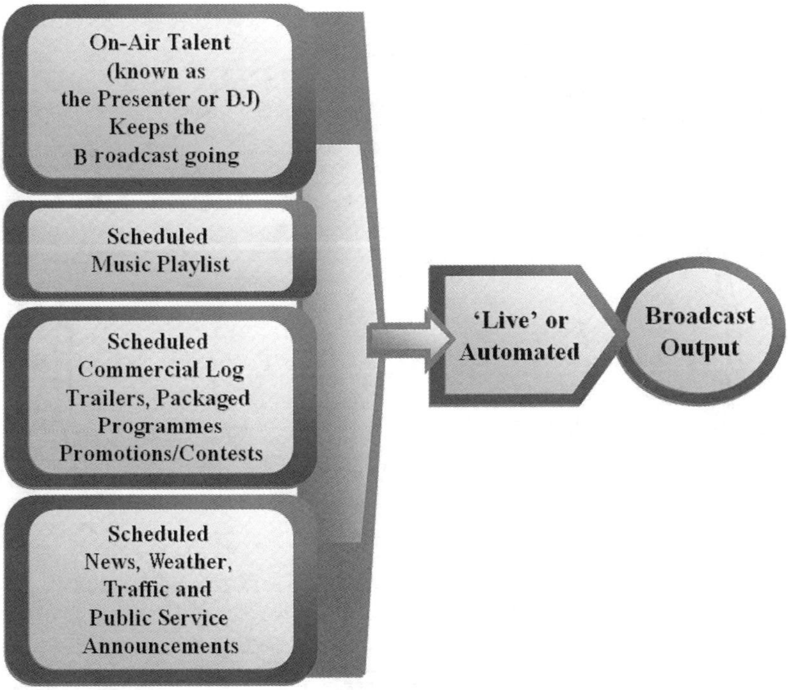

Rafael Oei 2003

audience, currently widely accepted as "mainstream radio." This model of radio listening is prevalent around the world and is largely a personality driven, music-based programming structure as opposed to the news and information radio station.

Central to this output model is a framework that is based on the "format clock" that provides the backbone and skeletal structure on which all schedules rest.

Putting together the blueprint and a discussion of the programming process has been briefly described in my book *Borderless Bandwidth: DNA of Digital Radio* (Oei 2002) and will not be repeated here. The entire process of scheduling and "clock design" itself warrants a separate workbook if this were an instructional manual. "Format clock" designing

FIGURE 2.4 Format Clock

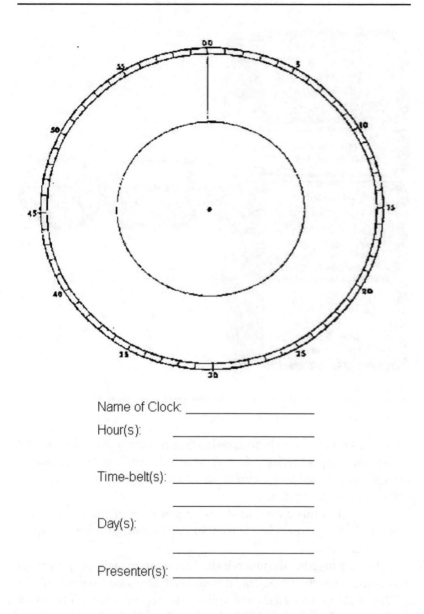

Name of Clock: _____

Hour(s): _____

_____

Time-belt(s): _____

_____

Day(s): _____

_____

Presenter(s): _____

Rafael Oei 2003

is a contextual process that must be practised and tested against actual output, not merely discussed. This extensive process is built into an assignment that third-year radio students have to go through and submit in the Mass Communications programme of the School of Film and Media Studies, Ngee Ann Polytechnic.

Having said that, we return to the point of radio's "democracy." While interaction, participation and communication with the radio station and its programmes are considered "democratic" (Hendy 2000, pp. 195–196), taking the systemic view on the delivery of radio programming I maintain that the process is hardly democratic. Programmes are structured and formulated to solicit listener responses. The radio station itself is positioned to cater to the profile of the market segments it means to transact with. Both the institution and its output are designed and fashioned for a specific transactional purpose.

> Listeners are therefore caught in the proverbial "catch-22" situation. Drawn to their radios to stave off depression and alienation, and yet excluded from any genuine act of communication, listeners run the risk of being confronted by further evidence of their alienation (Shingler and Wieringa 1998, p. 122).

Hendy is more accurate suggesting that radio has "an aura of democracy" (Hendy 2000, p. 195) the key word being "aura."

In considering and reflecting upon the elements that go into such a multilayered and multifaceted production for broadcast, you will appreciate the process that goes into the daily preparation and execution of a broadcast day. It is the integration of diverse elements into a discernible and comprehensible form within a context, whether it is information in the news to be taken seriously, a music talk show to be taken as entertainment, an issues-based talk show, a music phone-in request programme, or the documentary or feature where the information and experience is digested cerebrally. The listener will decode these accordingly.

Whilst we accept that radio disseminates information and entertainment, textured and designed to appeal to the needs described above, various marketing devices also determine the extent, reach and nature of the content and services a broadcast medium should provide. These then translate into revenue that keeps the station functioning. Ien Ang describes it in this way:

The institutional point of view is pre-eminently embodied within the institutions that are directly responsible for planning, producing and transmitting television programming (television industry, broadcasting organizations, but also, in a more indirect way, the state institutions that shape and regulate national media policies.) These institutions depend on the actual existence of the audience in very material terms (Ang 1991, p. 3).

This elusive creature that broadcast programmers strive to satisfy is crucial in the economic equation of a broadcast institution. Catering to the tastes of specific market segments requires a leap of faith on audience feedback and the numbers generated through rating sweeps. Each body of responses transmogrifies into an image that is assumed to be some semblance of the listener/viewer/consumer. One can only attempt to understand and formulate a recognisable entity on which to base one's programming assumptions.

This paradox is evident in the attempt to produce and programme broadcast content that will generally be accepted by specific segments of the public while knowing that attitudes, preferences and behaviour are highly personal and individual.

People create communities, construct elaborate codes of social conduct, reproduce shared meaning and values, and build social trust in the form of social capital. Only when social trust and social exchange are well developed do communities engage in commerce and trade. The point is, the commercial sphere always has been derivative of and dependent on the cultural sphere. That's because culture is the wellspring from which agreed-upon behavioural norms are generated. It is those behavioural norms, in turn, that create a trusting environment within which commerce and trade can take place (Rifkin 2000, pp. 11–12).

The convenience in sorting the market into some semblance of order is an illusory construct that has created the market culture that we have today (Douglas 1999, p. 131). It is the analysis of these numbers that influences the direction and approach to programming strategies.

Indirectly, however, it shapes the entire media environment in which we live. It determines who will anchor the nightly news or host a talk show, what our children will get to watch on Saturday mornings, and which political opinions we will and will not hear on our radio or television. Today this system integrates a range of technologies—telephones, computers, Nielsen boxes, audience measurement devices like the program analyzer—with other inventions—like the focus group, the questionnaire, or the survey —and a host of technically sophisticated mathematical approaches to assessing media appeal and effects. Back in the 1930s all this had to be invented (ibid., pp. 124–125).

In this, the media has the record companies and businesses to thank as these commercial entities tried to understand the effects radio had on the listener's psyche in order to develop more effective marketing and sales strategies to persuade the consumer to purchase their products (ibid., p. 129).

The consumer's interaction with the product is crucial in determining the nature of that relationship and the extent of its perceived value by the consumer. Celia Lury describes the relationship lucidly in her book *Consumer Culture*:

> One of the most important ways in which people relate to each other socially is through the mediation of things. *Material culture* is the name given to the study of these person-thing relationships; it is the study of things- or objects-in-use. [...] The term "material culture" is useful, then, because it implies that the material and the cultural are always combined in specific relationships and that these relationships can be subjected to study (Lury 1996, p. 1).

Being an aural/audio medium, radio's content and services are the "objects" of exchange with the consumer. The transactions occur daily over the airwaves and between the radio receiver and the listener. As illusory a construct as it is, without measurement and analysis, producers of products and services can only speculate about the effectiveness of one's output and its effect on the consumer.

For the media, audience surveillance and measurement began in the 1920s with broadcast institutions trying to second-guess the broadcast audience's "tastes and preferences." It was through the work of Austrian immigrant Paul Lazarsfeld, the father of market and communications research in America, who developed tools that enabled the beginnings of these studies (Douglas 1999, p. 125).

> Ratings are so important for the industry because they articulate the economic and the symbolic, the institutional and the discursive, power and knowledge.

> It is through ratings discourse that the social world of actual audiences is incorporated in the complex system of production and exchange that keeps the industry going (Ang 1991, p. 57).

The consequence of the activities described above result in an accepted perceived role of radio within popular culture.

The exchange of data and responses to gauge market sentiment provides one level of interactivity between the medium and the consumer in the way the output is consumed, perceived, and affects the life of the recipient. The influence of radio on its consumer and vice versa betrays the reliance each has on the other. Douglas describes this tension:

> There is a rift between the inherent technical properties of radio and the economic system in which it was—and is—embedded. The deeply personal nature of radio communication—the way its sole reliance on sound produces individualized images and reactions; its extension of a precommercial, oral tradition; its cultivation of the imagination—all work in stark contrast to the needs of its managers, who seek homogenized responses, and need a like-minded audience instead of idiosyncratic individuals (Douglas 1999, p. 17).

Other than the market surveys and amidst the battle for ratings, there is a simple and more direct means of communication for the listener and the radio station, interacting over traditional terrestrial radio:

> We can see already the extent to which increasing levels of competition in radio broadcasting in Britain resulted in the rise of the radio phone-in once radio stations recognised not only that these were one of the cheapest forms of programming but also, and more importantly, that they enabled stations to build up a large and loyal listenership (Shingler and Wieringa 1998, p. 118).

It was this "large and loyal listenership" that radio stations sought. After the telephone, marketing efforts extended beyond just relying on the telephone for listener participation and feedback, creating a culture for the radio listener as they began communicating with the station by writing and corresponding through the mail, and delivering fax messages as well.

> The phone-in was regarded as such a major development in broadcasting because for the first time it gave the viewer or listener a presence on the medium which was *audible*—not as the result of

her having a letter read out on the air or going into a studio or attending an outside broadcast in her neighbourhood, but spontaneously and away from broadcasting equipment, in her own home or local telephone box or at her place or work (Crisell 1994, pp. 190–191).

Today, these have also included listeners who communicate with the broadcast studio and presenter directly by sending electronic mail over the Internet, chatting in electronic-chat rooms and sending text messages through the *Short Messaging System* (SMS) via the cellular telephone.

The appeal of the phone-in is in an interesting occurrence that takes place during the on-air call. When a caller is given access to speak and converse with the DJ "on-air," this is an opportunity for the listener to actively participate in a broadcast scenario other than just writing in or calling in to make a song dedication or request. In talk show or phone-in programmes, the listener ostensibly has "a say" in the programme. Not quite playing the role of a producer yet—although requesting for particular topics for discussion, pre-packaged programmes, or songs does infer some form of influence on the scheduling of radio programme content. In this scenario, the caller symbolically represents the "general listener" communicating with the broadcast medium.

Even if the listener does not call into the studio, passive participants listeners do inadvertently express their opinions and views to the inanimate radio receiver, often quite graphically, if the response or reaction is adverse.

> The statement is something of a challenge for the rest of us to come out of this particular closet and admit that talking back to our radio sets is anything but a minority activity. Just how many of us do in fact regularly find ourselves talking back? It might be worth keeping an eye out in future for other drivers to see just how many people appear to be talking to themselves (Shingler and Wieringa 1998, p. 111).

However, when the listeners do call back what occurs with this semiotic relationship between broadcaster and recipient, for a brief moment, is that it reverses.

> Thus in a curious way the medium is inverted—turned inside out. The audience members become the broadcasters: they are, as it were,

enabled to reflect themselves. For the individual who is merely listening to the phone-in there is not only the likely and conventional pleasure of hearing a discussion—what Higgins and Moss describe as "argument as theatre"—but an impression, however misleading, created by those phoning in of innumerable *other* listeners who approximate to the community at large (Crisell 1994, p. 195).

In my view, this transient experience does not demonstrate the democratic influence a listening audience has on radio as suggested by Shingler et al., Hendy and Crisell as while the listener may seem to have some influence over the output of the station, it does not affect programming in such a way that warrants a change in the overall programming strategy of the station, nor does it shift the organisational foundation of institutional radio that requires a restructuring. It is only a device employed within traditionally structured radio programmes to solicit audience participation. Crisell cynically calls this device an illusion that presents radio as a communication medium.

> It creates the illusion of radio as a two-way medium and is concerned to verify that the station or channel has an audience and that this audience is capable of understanding and responding to the message which the station transmits (ibid., p. 189).

Briefly having gone through the components of traditionally structured radio broadcasts and programming, I will now explore the digital environment and its nature. It is the construct of digital technology that has modified the way information, entertainment, and services are accessed and retrieved by the consumer. This has in turn modified the behaviour and expectations of the radio listener.

2.3 THE NATURE OF THE DIGITAL MEDIA CONSUMER

> Much of what is now taken for granted has, in fact, only recently emerged. Just one human generation ago, at the beginning of the 1970s, electronic pocket calculators were just starting to compete with slide rules and mechanical adding machines; computers were big and impersonal; and AT&T was still a monopoly that leased nearly all private telephones in the United States. Portable communicators and voice interaction with computers only existed

in the imaginary 23rd century universe of the original *Star Trek* television series (Bucy 2002, p. 22).

It begins with the nature of accessing information in this digital age. The versatility to configure and customise personal preferences in software and hardware is now a widely accepted assumption of digital media.

> This model of the future is distinctly different from a human-factors approach to interface design. The look and feel of the interface certainly count, but they play a minor role in comparison to intelligence (Negroponte 1995, p. 159).

With the various ways of interacting with digital media, scholars have suggested that this has caused a shift in understanding the term "audience." Digital information-age radio listeners have acquired a set of information technology (IT) related skills and assumptions different from the radio listener of the 1960s, 1970s or even 1980s. George Gerbner, founder of the "Cultural Environment Movement," in discussing the power of storytelling expresses the magnitude of media influence in recent times:

> For the first time in human history, children are born into homes where mass-mediated storytellers reach them on the average more than seven hours a day. Most waking hours, and often dreams, are filled with their stories. Giant industries discharge their messages into the mainstream of common consciousness. The historic nexus of church and state is replaced by television and state (Bucy 2002, p. 146).

This generation is growing up in an instant on-demand oriented environment, in "an age of access" as Jeremy Rifkin calls it, with information, entertainment and communication just a touch of a button away.

> The Age of Access, then, is governed by a whole new set of business assumptions that are very different from those used to manage a market era. In the new world, markets give way to networks, sellers and buyers are replaced by suppliers and users, and virtually everything is accessed (Rifkin 2000, p. 6)

This is the generation that are growing up in an expansive and expanding environment. They predominantly perceive digital media and technology as standard appliances, similar to the way the more matured generation have perceived the telephone, the vacuum cleaner, the ironing board, the radio and the television. This is the generation who are also able to design and build their own Web pages, market their goods online and stream their own music. And so, they are familiar with dictating and customising what it is they want to see, play and hear.

> This strikingly widespread phenomenon is not going to abate or go away, but it is only one kind of behavior, one more like direct manipulation than delegation.

> Our interfaces will vary. Yours will be different from mine, based on our respective information predilections, entertainment habits, and social behavior—all drawn from the very large palette of digital life (Negroponte 1995, p. 159).

The digital environment and receiver interfaces have brought with it such a level of interactivity that the consumer-user has control over gaining access to the type of information and entertainment that is important to them.

> In the post-information age, we often have an audience the size of one. Everything is made to order, and information is extremely personalized. A widely held assumption is that individualization is the extrapolation of narrowcasting—you go from a large to a small to a smaller group, ultimately to the individual (Ibid., p 164).

The nature of accessing digital media is that it is customisable and can be subjected to individual preferences.

> The idea that the individualized technology of the information revolution will undo the massification produced by the technology of the industrial revolution underlies most such scenarios of disaggregation (Brown and Duguid 2002, p. 65).

Moreover, the nature of the medium allows its content to go beyond boundaries. Accessing information and services, and commercial transactions on the Internet are virtual and intangible.

> A further oddity—compared to transactions involving tangible items—is this: The fact that you have sold information to me does

not prevent you from selling the same item to someone else (Stewart 1999, p. 171).

And so the consumer-user is able to access information and products from Brazil in Singapore, as long as it is published over the Internet on a website. If the consumer so desires, a purchase can be made without having to meet anyone face-to-face.

> In the new cyberspace economy, money is becoming even less physical. Every day, more than $1.9 trillion passes through electronic networks in New York City (Rifkin 2000, p. 36).

This is further compounded and supported by banking institutions that have restructured to enable transactions over the Internet to have a convenience that traditional banking does not have.

> ATM machines, smart cards, and digital cash are remaking the rules of the money game. Businesses and consumers are increasingly exchanging goods and services and conducting a full range of business transactions electronically (ibid.).

On the other hand, Rappa (2002), writing about "consumption and its discontents" in his book *Modernity and Consumption: Theory, Politics, and the Public in Singapore and Malaysia,* has a rather cynical view on this "access culture." I include it here to acknowledge that while I am expounding the wonders of digital technology, I accept that it will not be effectively utilised all the time.

> Yet the new found information distributed to consumers worldwide is not any more substantive or anymore analytical. There's merely a larger distribution network. This has three main political impacts on the consumer: (1) more information in less time with less accuracy; (2) costs incurred on new technology are passed directly to consumers; and, (3) the rise of agency-generators that churn out repetitive and dull news-bites of similar views of one issue (Rappa 2002, pp. 231–232).

Negroponte (1995), Stewart (1998), Rifkin (2001), and Brown and Duguid (2002) have similarly described the misuse and abuse of the Internet and digital media services. Thomas K. Landauer, in his article "The Productivity Puzzle" (1995), suggested that the increase in productivity promised by the emergence of the computer is a similar disenchantment.

> There is some sign that some corporations, usually very large ones, have had major successes with computers in the last few years, but it is not clear yet whether these successes were due to the computers themselves or to dramatic business revamping bred of recession pressures. We expected computers to bring across-the-board productivity help, work efficiency improvements for small and large alike. This they have not delivered (Bucy 2002, p. 195).

Be that as it may, not all agencies are guilty of hosting trivial resources and boring content, nor have computers consistently been efficiently utilised to improve productivity. As with most consumer products and services, there will be the benign and the most inspired creations. The validity and usefulness of the means, that is the digital radio or the computer hardware/software, does not rely solely on the content it transports.

Already mentioned are recent advances in broadcast technologies that have provided various means to transmit traditional radio services. As outlined in *Borderless Bandwidth: DNA of Digital Radio* (Oei 2002), interactivity in digital radio services is evident in web streaming, telecommunication services that offer radio transmissions and Internet surfing, and the ubiquity that is currently mobile telecommunications. As described in the Introduction to this volume, the next generation cellular phones will be structured on Wide Orthogonal Frequency Division Multiplex (WOFDM), which is basically the DAB architecture developed initially for digital radio services.

With the proliferation of advanced communications technology, radio listeners are also web-surfers who communicate daily over the Internet and who are more than familiar with researching and information gathering through the "Web". This is the era of information users and contributors where radio listeners interact and are connected with information and entertainment on demand. Evidenced by the popularity of more music-based and game-based programming, we see the media consumer as a more leisure-oriented entity as digital technology has made living more comfortable and information/entertainment more accessible.

> While the industrial era was charactierized by the commodification of work, the Age of Access is about, above all else, the

commodification of play—namely the marketing of cultural resources including rituals, the arts, festivals, social movements, spiritual and fraternal activity, and civic engagement in the form of paid-for personal entertainment. The struggle between the cultural sphere and the commercial sphere to control both access to and the content of play is one of the defining elements of the coming era (Rifkin 2000, p. 7)

The "modern" radio listener is the consumer-user that will expect information and entertainment when it is needed. We are in an era that actualises what German playwright Bertolt Brecht argued against: that of "radio being a channel through which homes passively received information and entertainment." Brecht envisaged radio listeners being active, to also "become producers of radio as well as consumers" (Hendy 2000, p. 195).

Brecht's conception of radio as a public service was one which involved listeners not just as consumers but also as producers (suppliers) of its material. This, he argued, would make radio a truly social or public medium (Shingler and Wieringa 1998, p. 113).

Key to these services is the flow of information and the medium in which the consumer-user receives it. Castells (2000) in describing the "information technology paradigm" presents five characteristics. The first is that "information is its raw material," the second refers to the "pervasiveness of effects of new technologies" where information "directly shapes" society through new technological media. The third refers to the increasing complexity of the network in supporting "the creative power of such interaction" with the information. The fourth characteristic of the "IT paradigm" lies in its flexibility where "processes are reversible" and "organizations and institutions can be modified." The fifth characteristic is the "convergence of specific technologies into a highly integrated system" where "separate technological trajectories become literally indistinguishable" (Castells 2000, pp. 70–72).

In his chapter on "The New Economics of Information," Stewart observed that "the tangible and intangible economic realms coexist, connect, overlap, interweave, interact" in a way that "it is no longer accurate to say that the intangible economy is 'based' on the tangible one" (Stewart 1998, pp. 169–170). The digital realm is intangible. Output created and released onto networks like the Internet does not necessarily bring equal measurable economic returns. While the media has research that measures audience responses, these does not always translate into currency. The knowledge or information economy also brings other idiosyncrasies to the workplace and the organisational structure that produces these services.

Castells succinctly adds that radio services will evolve beyond audio programming and that institutional radio will reorganise to support this. He said: "Data transmission becomes the predominant, universal form of communication. And data transmission is based on software instructions of coding and decoding" (Castells 2000, p. 72). Unfortunately, it seems that institutional radio has been slow in meeting the challenge, evidenced by the development of mobile telecommunication services that have overtaken the broadcast media in launching enhanced multimedia capabilities. Castells observed that "business control over the first stages of development of multimedia systems" is imperative (ibid., p. 397). This is the point of this dissertation, and will be discussed in a later chapter.

If we look at the media models that have emerged historically, the "American model," as opposed to the "BBC model" of radio, seems ostensibly to be the easier of the two to adapt to the changing broadcast landscape, the US model having had its inception and nurturing in a commercial incubator. The intention of the "BBC model," where Reith tried to create "a common national culture" that "aimed to develop a sense of discrimination in the audience by giving it the opportunity to listen to 'better, healthier music' than pop music" (Ang 1991, pp. 108–109) seems to run contrary to a consumer-oriented broadcast service. What is interesting to note, however, is that Reith had intended a more "dutiful style of radio listening" through a varied approach to radio programming to create an active radio listening audience that listened "seriously and constructively" (ibid., p. 109) rather than passively as "background noise" which standardised regular format radio seemed to encourage (ibid.). Reith, then, had intended radio to be a primary medium with the listener being actively engaged while being informed, entertained and educated.

Ang (1991) argues that the "Reithean aspiration to create a disciplined audience has disappeared" to be replaced by "high-quality production standards" that offers "diversity to stretch interests and horizons" that does not impose but caters to "popular tastes" (ibid., p. 119). This suggests that programming and productions from the BBC developed along a different route from American radio that in many ways influenced the production culture, resulting in a reputation for creative and credible output that is the "BBC standard" which has the ability to engage the listener. My thoughts on this is that the present standards that have come to be synonymous with the BBC were a consequence of Reith's efforts, and that rather than disappearing, the disciplined audience has evolved and matured.

Having said that, the reality expressed above concerning the "American model" is seen in the speed in which American corporations have rallied to control media companies to control global communication networks, channels and cultural resources.

> Disney, Time Warner, Bertelsmann, Viacom, Sony, News Corporation, TCI, General Electric, PolyGram, and Seagram who will dominate the global media market and determine the conditions by which the public gains access to cultural resources and commodified experiences. The 10 companies alone enjoyed annual sales ranging from $10 billion to $25 billion in 1997.

> US-based media companies are the world leaders and have set the ground rules for the global contest to control communications and commodified cultural resources (Rifkin 2000, p. 219).

The digital environment is a place where the consumer is in control of his or her own experience. It is a reality where access is immediate and on-demand. Along with the launch of broadband connectivity, the speed of accessing online services have increased and extended to include higher quality resolution videos and audio output. The consumer also has the option of viewing or listening to the product online through streaming media, or downloading it onto the hard disk for repeated consumption at the consumer's leisure as in the case of archived products.

Digital consumers are also more than familiar with online communication tools like electronic mail (e-mail), cyber-chat rooms where communication is in real time, and video-conferencing. Distance learning takes a whole new meaning through the digital domain. This is where study is literally at one's own pace, accessible 24 hours a day, anytime, anywhere. Coursework, course notes and lectures can be digitised and packaged with all the multimedia interactivity and animation available to enhance the learning experience. All the above have moulded and influenced assumptions and behaviour in the consumer as to the fundamental protocol and nature of interaction in cyberspace.

Extending the argument, if we agree from all that has been said about the behaviour of the "digital media consumer", with technological advances comes the emergence of a "new society." It also follows that despite historical influences, structural transformation is inevitable, given the consumer-users' modified behaviour in adapting and assimilating new technologies into daily life. Castells (1998) in *End of Millennium* notes:

> A new society emerges when and if a structural transformation can be observed in the relationships of production, in the relationships of power, and in the relationships of experience. These transformations lead to an equally substantial modification of social forms of space and time, and to the emergence of a new culture (Castells 1998, p 340).

The framework of digital production processes for digital radio, Eureka 147-DAB, will be discussed in Chapter Five. Discussions on the restructuring of institutional radio can be found in my book *Borderless Bandwidth: DNA of Digital Radio* (Oei 2002).

Following along my discussion of the nature of the digital media consumer, and laying the groundwork for the "relationships of experience" identified by Castells above, I will now look at how the consumer has been able to immerse into digital culture, thereby acquiring the skills, knowledge, habits and behaviour that make up the digital experience.

2.4 THE USERS' EXPOSURE TO DIGITAL SERVICES

In search of influences that create the foundation of this new culture, and in exploring the extent of the influence of media in this respect, we begin in Singapore.

Singapore consists of "a highly literate and relatively wealthy resident population" that have been "raised on a generous diet of commercialism, consumerism, and capitalist choices" within a relatively stable political environment (Rappa 2002, p. 238). Given its size and global perspectives, Singaporeans are regularly reminded to "continue to serve the nation and to produce for the nation" (ibid.). Rappa acknowledges that with exposure to the inflow of information from the rest of the world, "it will become increasingly difficult to control the minds and decisions of future Singaporean consumers in the Age of the Internet" (ibid., p. 239).

In order to understand the mind of Singaporean youth and their media consumption, the National Youth Council of Singapore commissioned the Asian Media Information and Communication Centre (AMIC) to conduct focus group discussions in 1998. A sample survey of 150 Singapore youth aged between 15–24 years revealed that the mass media, particularly television and radio, are very much a part of the life of Singapore youth who generally rely on the media to keep them informed of the world around them (Goonasekera 1998, p. 4).

Media related leisure activities included listening to music, with a response of 37 per cent, followed by watching the TV. The AMIC study also showed that media was instrumental in the creation of values, attitudes and practices. 57 per cent of the respondents said they listened to the radio daily. Of these, 19 per cent listened to over five hours of radio a day, 11 per cent three to five hours a day and 9 per cent said they did not listen to the radio at all. 72 per cent of those who were spoken to preferred radio programmes that were music-based. News, current affairs and educational programmes came second at 4.7 per cent of the total respondents each. The most preferred music was western/pop (38 per cent), followed by Chinese pop at 26 per cent (Goonasekera 1998).

As for new technologies, to ensure that Singapore would have its share of savvy producers and consumers of information technology, over the past decade the Singapore government encouraged IT instruction in education and the use of IT in the neighbourhood to create an "Intelligent Island" for the 21st century.

Three documents were published describing the blueprints to exploit this technology: *Civil Service Computerization Programme* published in 1981, the *National IT Plan*, in 1986 and *A Vision of an Intelligent Island: IT2000 Report*, in 1992. Public access to the Internet for Singaporeans occurred in 1994. The following year, Singapore launched the world's first national homepage: *http://www.sg* (Ang 1998). Part of the S$5-billion *IT Master Plan for Education* was to ensure that all schools in Singapore were connected. And so schools, since then, aimed for a ratio of one computer per two students, with at least one computer per faculty (Rao 2002, p. 326).

Among the initiatives to develop Singapore into a networked nation were plans to cable all households, first with connectivity through telephone cables then with broadband services through operators like the Singapore CableVision, the provider of cable television in Singapore, SingNet under the Singapore Telecoms and Pacific Internet, an Internet service provider.

To facilitate the development of e-commerce, the Singapore government established the "Electronic Commerce Hotbed" programme in August 1996 (ibid., pp. 328–330).

There were 1.9 million computer users or 47 per cent of the total Singapore population accounted for in the Infocomm Development Authority of Singapore survey of 2000. Looking at the effect of these initiatives on Singapore at-large, a 1999 survey by the Infocomm Development Authority of Singapore (IDA) revealed that home computer ownership increased from 35.8 per cent in 1996 to about 59 per cent in 1999. This rose to 61 per cent in the year 2000, from a base total of one million homes. This meant that three out of five homes owned a computer by the year 2000.

Of these, the general trend in Singapore was to own more than one computer at home. There was a 10 per cent increase from the figures in 1990, with users spending an average of 6.3 hours on their computer per week. By the year 2000, the number of people owning two or more computers increased to about 23.5 per cent.

FIGURE 2.5   Number of PC Owners in Singapore

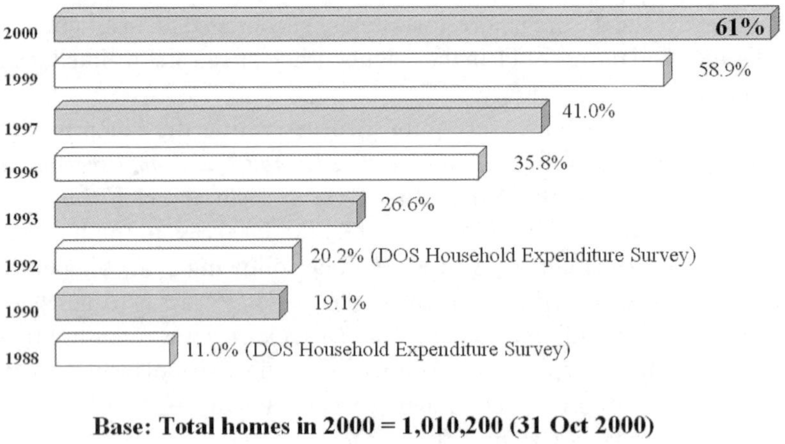

Year	Percentage
2000	**61%**
1999	58.9%
1997	41.0%
1996	35.8%
1993	26.6%
1992	20.2% (DOS Household Expenditure Survey)
1990	19.1%
1988	11.0% (DOS Household Expenditure Survey)

Base: Total homes in 2000 = 1,010,200 (31 Oct 2000)

SOURCE: IDA 2001, *Survey on Infocomm Usage in Households 2000*

Also in the year 2000, about half of Singapore homes had Internet access, six times more than the figure from 1996.

FIGURE 2.6   Households with Two or More Computers

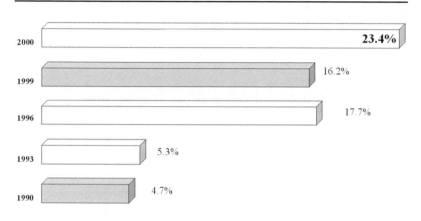

Base: Households with computers = 616,222 (2000)

SOURCE: IDA 2001, *Survey on Infocomm Usage in Households 2000*

FIGURE 2.7   Singapore Broadband Users

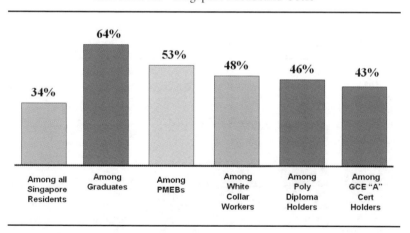

SOURCE: IDA Broadband Usage in Singapore 2001

With the introduction of broadband services, computer use and Internet penetration increased. Broadband users number among the students and professionals as Figure 2.7 shows.

The *Broadband Usage 2001* survey by IDA revealed that one in three, or 34 per cent of Singaporeans aged 10 years and above, were broadband users. Access was generally at home and at work. For the moment, broadband users rely on cabled connections, with ADSL leading the pack at 40 per cent from a sample of 3,000 respondents.

While the respondents were aware of the variety of services available to broadband users, the two main activities remained information retrieval (74.6 per cent) and email or chat (91.6 per cent).

Fairly popular on-demand activities include gaming, government transactions (Singapore having a very e-oriented government), online music listening, and financial services.

Despite the hype about the mobility that the Internet would bring us, in increasing productivity and the possibility of working from home for instance, the figures below show that this has not been the case, with video conferencing, teleworking, distance learning, online shopping and watching movies rating lowly.

What is interesting from the figures is what it reveals about users' awareness about online services and their willingness to engage in these services. For instance, while users are aware that online shopping is

FIGURE 2.8 Singapore Broadband Connection Modes

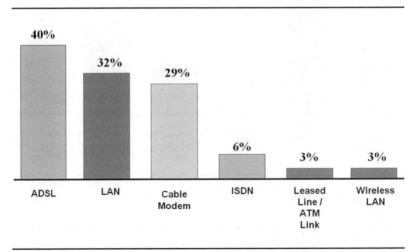

SOURCE: IDA Broadband Usage in Singapore 2001

FIGURE 2.9   Singapore: Popular Broadband Uses

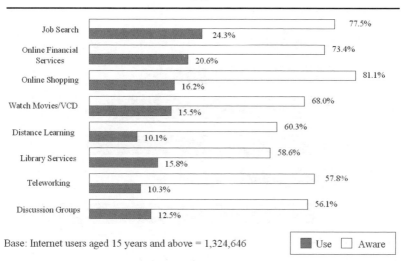

Email/Chat	98.2% / 91.6%
Information Retrieval	89.2% / 74.6%
Web Applications	73.5% / 40.3%
News/ Webcast	80.1% / 39.8%
Download Online Music	78.6% / 37.4%
Online Government Transactions	78.9% / 31.9%
Online Games	77.0% / 29.2%

Base: Internet users aged 15 years and above = 1,324,646   ■ Use   ☐ Aware

SOURCE: IDA 2002, *Broadband Usage in Singapore 2001*

FIGURE 2.10   Singapore: Broadband Uses

Job Search	77.5% / 24.3%
Online Financial Services	73.4% / 20.6%
Online Shopping	81.1% / 16.2%
Watch Movies/VCD	68.0% / 15.5%
Distance Learning	60.3% / 10.1%
Library Services	58.6% / 15.8%
Teleworking	57.8% / 10.3%
Discussion Groups	56.1% / 12.5%

Base: Internet users aged 15 years and above = 1,324,646   ■ Use   ☐ Aware

SOURCE: IDA 2002, *Broadband Usage in Singapore 2001*

available and convenient, only 16.2 per cent of those interviewed actually engaged in the activity. Similarly, the disparity between the knowledge that distance learning, teleworking and discussion groups were available, and the numbers who actually used the facilities is wide. Since these figures, there have been concerted attempts by various institutions to increase the credibility and security of these services. I will mention how these initiatives have been used in the context of our radio students, and how Ngee Ann Polytechnic on the whole has increased opportunities for students to use the Internet for study and assignments.

Singapore has relatively high computer ownership compared to Japan at 42 per cent, Australia at 47 per cent and in the US at 54 per cent. This is supported by the findings by World Times/IDC Information Society Index in 1999 where Singapore was ranked top in computer and Internet infrastructure (IDA 2000).

The following graphs are based on charts from the survey conducted by the Infocomm Authority of Singapore in the year 2000. If we look at the ages of home PC users we find that most users are under the age of 15, and the range of active users lies below the age of 39 years,

FIGURE 2.11 Home PC User Ages

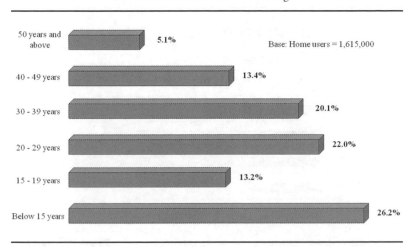

SOURCE: IDA 2001, *Survey on Infocomm Usage in Households 2000*

What is interesting, also, are the figures for children at age 12 and below–12 as that is the maximum primary school-going age. This is because

96

currently preschoolers and primary school children are already exposed to the computer with various subjects being taught through CD-ROM programmes as well. In fact, one of the initiatives by primary schools is an introduction to webpage designing, which is meant to help students hone their multimedia Internet skills and language ability through writing content for websites (for more information, access the Ministry of Education website at http://www.moe.gov.sg/).

FIGURE 2.12   The Educational Level of Singapore PC Users

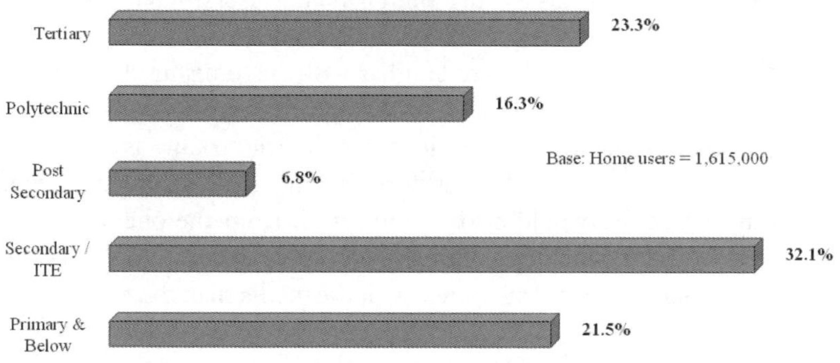

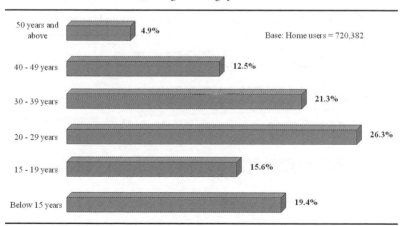

SOURCE: IDA 2001, *Survey on Infocomm Usage in Households 2000*

FIGURE 2.13   Age of Singapore Internet Users

SOURCE: IDA 2001, *Survey on Infocomm Usage in Households 2000*

Home Internet users in Singapore reveal almost the same responses, with a dip for those under 15 years, and an increase for those between the age of 20 and 39.

Their educational background can be seen from Figure 2.14.: Of these, we see quite a fair number of home PC users that surf the Internet are well-educated, and who would probably use the home PC for work and information retrieval, apart from communicating with their friends through online chat rooms and the email.

These charts suggest that the next generation of PC users would be more aligned with the digital media culture and would possess the skills and knowledge to be discerning digital media users, having had the foundation from as early as preschool. This would provide co-producer-consumers in the future who are familiar with customising their online information retrieval preferences and would, by extension, be able to configure their digital media experiences with little trouble as compared to the consumers of today. The workforce to build and operate the digital media infrastructure would also be improved, from the operators and producers of today, when this digital media savvy generation enters the industry having had more experience with the media than those currently in the industry.

The push for Singapore to be an information hub, and for the entire island to be networked, has been a matter of national policy. The reason why this has been relatively easy to achieve is given the size of the island,

FIGURE 2.14 The Educational Level of Singapore Internet Users

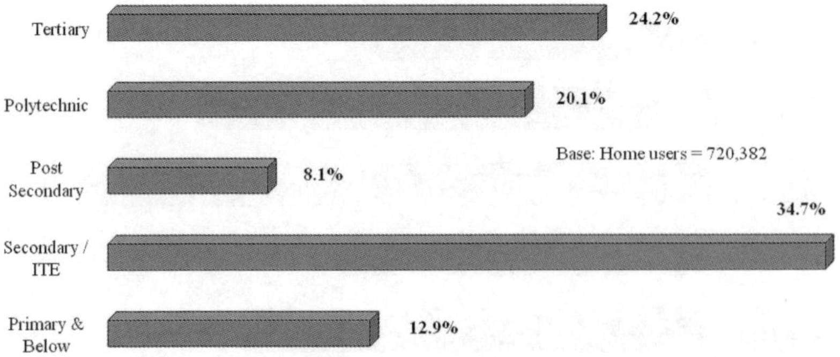

Education Level	Percentage
Tertiary	24.2%
Polytechnic	20.1%
Post Secondary	8.1%
Secondary / ITE	34.7%
Primary & Below	12.9%

Base: Home users = 720,382

Source: IDA 2001, *Survey on Infocomm Usage in Households 2000*

the skills present in its human capital, and the government infrastructure that has been in place since 1965. Clearly, the Singapore government sees digital technology and media as being advantageous to society. The survey ends with:

> Overall, the survey findings show that the foundation for an Information Society is in place. We are approaching the point where not having access to technology tools is likely to put an individual or home at a social disadvantage for being unable to participate fully in the digital economy. Hence for those who are yet to be digitally connected, there will be continued efforts to encourage adoption of Infocomm technology to improve their quality of life and enhance employability. For those who are digitally connected, the challenge is to raise the level of sophistication in using Infocomm technology, to include other useful and interesting applications and services available on the Internet (IDA 2001, p. 21).

In order to see how widespread this "new society/culture" is, let's take a quick glance around the world. The following chart shows that Internet broadband access in the US steadily increased over a three-year period.

When we look at how the media user behaves in the US, we find that conventional TV and radio use prevails, with time spent on broadband Internet access increasing to 13 per cent, as you would know if you checked the Arbitron reports.

FIGURE 2.15   US Internet Broadband Access

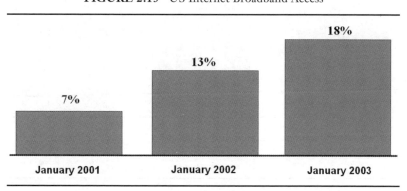

SOURCE: Arbitron Inc/Edison Media Research Fall 2002/Jan 2003.

FIGURE 2.16 US Time Spent on Media

Television 44%	Radio 35%	Internet 13%	Newspaper 8%

SOURCE: Arbitron Inc./Edison Media Research Fall 2002/Jan 2003

American broadband users see broadband Internet access as a means of communication, a source of information and entertainment, all the things radio is also attributed with as well.

What about the next generation and how are they perceiving traditional media like TV and radio? In the winter of 2000, Arbitron conducted a survey titled "How kids and tweens use and respond to radio." Arbitron defined children between the ages of 6 and 8 as "kids", and "tweens," between the ages of nine and 11.

The survey found that American children are very involved with radio, participating in games and phone-ins. The children were also found to be online, downloading, searching for and listening to music as well as actively buying products.

FIGURE 2.17   US Broadband Use

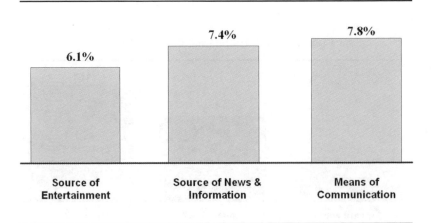

Source of Entertainment	Source of News & Information	Means of Communication
6.1%	7.4%	7.8%

Source: Arbitron Inc/Edison Media Research: Fall 2002/Jan 2003

FIGURE 2.18   Where US Children Listen to the Radio

Child's Bedroom 76%	Family Room 38%	Kitchen 11%	Other 10%	Play Room 2%

SOURCE: Arbitron Inc., Winter 2000.

FIGURE 2.19   UK: Where Radio is Accessed

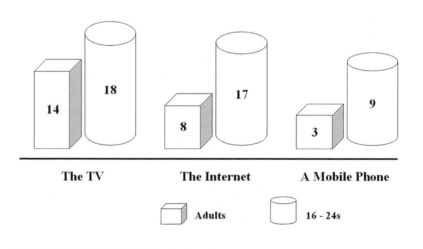

The TV   The Internet   A Mobile Phone

☐ Adults   ▯ 16 - 24s

SOURCE: Radio Days 3, UK.

Where do these children listen to radio most? In the privacy of their bedrooms, with girls listening to radio more than boys.

The trend is similar in the United Kingdom with a fall in the use of traditional broadcast media. In the UK, broadband Internet users use digital media to listen to radio programming, including the mobile phone and even the TV.

When we make a comparison, we see a 10 per cent difference between Singapore and the US and Hong Kong in terms of the percentage of home computers owned. As for home Internet access, Singapore also ranks on top, leading about 13 to 14 per cent from Australia, Hong Kong and the UK (see Table 2.1 and Table 2.2 on the next page).

TABLE 2.1 Home Computer Ownership 2000

Country	Access (%)	Survey by (Month)
Singapore	61	IDA's Survey (Dec)
Australia	56	Australia Bureau of Statistics (Nov)
US	51	US Department of Commerce (Aug)
Ireland	32	Central Statistics Office (Nov)
Hong Kong	50	Census & Statistics Department (Mar)

SOURCE: IDA 2001, *Survey on Infocomm Usage in Households 2000*

TABLE 2.2 Home Internet Access 2000

Country	Access (%)	Survey by (Month)
Singapore	50	IDA's Survey (Dec)
Australia	37	Australia Bureau of Statistics (Nov)
US	42	US Department of Commerce (Aug)
UK	35	National Statistics (Dec)
Ireland	20	Central Statistics Office (Nov)
Hong Kong	36	Census & Statistics Department (Mar)

SOURCE: IDA 2001, *Survey on Infocomm Usage in Households 2000*

The Asia-Pacific Internet Handbook (Rao 2002) provides some interesting insights to the projected economic influences instrumental to wireless mobile Internet access and the state of Internet and broadband use in Asia. Rao, quoting the *eMarketer: eAsia Report 2001*, states that in 2000, active adult Internet usage was 38 million users in Asia. This will grow in 2003 to 95.83 million online users (Rao 2002, p. 6). This figure is 25.7 per cent of the total worldwide community of Internet users. By 2005, out of an estimated 765 million users around the world, 228 million will be Internet users from the Asia-Pacific region. The same report predicted that e-commerce in Asia will grow from US$6.6 billion to US$88 billion in 2003 (ibid., p. 18).

With the popularity of cellular phones and wireless telephony services increasing, mobile telephony-services in the region looks impressive compared to cabled Internet access. The Singapore telecommunications market was liberalised on 1 April 2000. Since then, more than 6,000 multinationals and local wireless players have established research and development centres and test-bed activities in Singapore. As of August 2002, Singapore has one of the highest penetrations for wireless-telephony services at 75.1 per cent. The local mobile phone subscribers number 3,102,200 people. Asia alone has an estimated 250 million cell phone users. This is expected to increase to 600 million users by 2005. In fact, mobile phone-users are double that of Internet users. The positive outlook for wireless telephony services has caused ITU to predict that by 2010, 50 per cent of mobile phone users will be in the Asia Pacific region (ibid., pp. 18–19).

The preceding figures, discussions and details on broadband Internet access, home personal computer ownership and wireless telephony use and development around the Asia-Pacific region, the United States and the United Kingdom served to illustrate the exposure the media consumer has to digital media. This generation of consumer-users is conversant with a host of digital media knowledge and skills that were unfamiliar to the radio listener that institutional radio has modelled its operations upon. Institutional radio is, for the most part, still operating on a programming model that is over 70 years old.

Current media consumer-users have the ability to customise and personalise access to entertainment and information over the Internet. This expectation has extended onto wireless telephony services that have included Internet services traditionally accessed through the home personal computer, such as email, facsimile, e-commerce, Internet surfing and digital chat rooms. The figures above show the ubiquity of mobile telephones today. Digital radio has the potential to similarly allow the listener to customise and influence programming output according to personal preferences, transforming the listener into a consumer-user, or even a "co-producer-user".

The inherent potential of digital media to allow consumers to programme and customise digital broadcast output implies a medium that is more versatile than its predecessor. It will impact the organisational structure of institutional radio, including human resource issues, given that digital technology enables multi-functional operations to provide a varied listener experience and opportunities to access data and archived artefacts. These issues are discussed at length in *Borderless Bandwidth: DNA of Digital Radio* (Oei 2002). At that moment of customising access and output preferences for the medium, the notion of the "co-producer-consumer" crystallises beyond those suggested by Hendy (2000), Shingler and Wieringa (1998) and Crisell (1994).

CHAPTER 3

Putting It on Paper

In the creation of the radio experience lie a host of skills that would have to be employed in order to deliver a seamless and fluid presentation either live or pre-packaged. I have always held the belief that if one were familiar with the skills in conceptualising, writing and producing for radio, one would be able to be more succinct and effective in one's communication skills, both written and verbal.

The reason for this is in presenting for radio, there is only ONE attempt at communicating anything to the listener. It is a transient medium, unlike print. And if you can effectively communicate messages over the radio time and again, you will find that it will permeate into the way you think, use the language and structure your sentences. So writing and producing for radio, if internalised, can actually help you to be more focused. You will cut to the chase, you will get to the point, and you will be able to do it with an economy of words. Writing will be a different experience for you.

3.1 THINKING "AUDIO"

As a presenter, one of the things that has stuck with me is that I should always remember that I might be speaking to a blind man on the other end of the receiver. On more than one occasion, while performing an "air-shift," I've had calls from listeners who were visually challenged. In each case, they would convey how radio has been a window to the world for them, a source for information, a friend to them, and a companion in their most quiet and lonely times.

To people who have not had the faculty of sight from birth, there is no visual experience of colour, nature, physical structures, or you and I, i.e., the sight of another human being. They have not experienced the contrasting impact of light and dark. There are no visual references nor any concept of height, width, depth, or how vast the sky may be. They have no visual reference of where a corner departmental store may be or how it looks. They would have no idea about the impact colours may have from your business logo or a popular product.

If the above were taken into account every time a radio script is written, or a production is done, the result would be highly focused scripts that are succinct, filled with vivid word images, and excellently crafted audio productions. These would be audio productions that "come alive" in the imagination—in the mind's eye. In our business, the often-used phrase that describes this process is to create a "theatre of the mind". Sadly, the phrase has become a cliché and, in many instances, brushed aside with a "oh, that phrase again, yeah, yeah ..."; and then ignored.

Other excuses for not spending time on crafting radio scripts include not having enough time, or having to churn out a multitude of scripts daily and meeting impossible deadlines. Some radio students that I have encountered have said that they do not spend time on their scripts or are not bothered with it because their favourite presenters (or deejays) ad-lib and do not write "that way" anyway. Field trips or guest lectures correct this notion when I invite their idols. These students then hear it firsthand when their favourite presenters reveal that even ad-libbing begins with preparation, putting down on paper a basic structure and having a script written almost word-for-word until the words flowed freely. Without prompting from me, these lecture presentations then include production examples that demonstrate scripting for aural transmission using words and phrases that paint pictures for the "theatre of the mind." It is the nature of the medium.

3.2 RADIO IS THE "THEATRE OF THE MIND"

It is not easy to craft that "perfect" radio script, and I believe that it really takes some practice. But once the habit is formed, the approach to writing "radio-friendly" scripts will become second nature without too much of an effort.

> Since the medium is blind the words cannot be *seen* by the receiver but only *heard* by him: hence the linguistic code of radio approximates much more closely to that of *speech* than writing. But there is an important measure of difference. Much radio talk is first written down—scripted (Crisell 1994, p. 55).

It begins with realising that as in normal everyday conversations; each sentence would have to be short and precise. While being short and precise, sentences delivered in the course of a normal conversation are not often complete or well-crafted. Natural-sounding scripts would have to be written in a similar fashion if they were to be delivered "naturally" when it is finally read/presented. Each sentence and word carefully chosen to say what has to be said in the shortest possible structure. After all, when we are amongst friends and busily chatting away, very often we, ourselves, speak in short bursts, repeating phrases and using habitual pet-phrases or pet-words. It's almost like writing a personal "dramatic monologue."

Two things happen when you write a "radio friendly" script:

1. When you read it, you will sound as though you were speaking "off-the-cuff."
2. You will also sound as though you were "naturally" conversing with your listener one-to-one.

From experience I know the above to be true. It is true also for my friends in broadcasting and production as well. But as is the nature of books such as this, quotes and references are used to support ideas and statements. For the above, read McLeish, Wieringa & Shingler, Hendy, Reese and Mencher, to name a few. Crisell has this to say about radio-friendly scripts:

> Why should reading disguise itself as spontaneous talk? The act of reading implies *absence*—the separation of addresser and addressee. The addresser has been replaced by a text, so that if a radio listener is aware that a broadcaster is reading he will assume that she is either relaying the words of somebody else or erecting a barrier between herself and her audience. Hence to avoid creating this impression of absence and impersonality much radio talk which is actually scripted—programme presentation, weather forecasts, continuity, cues, trailers and so forth—is delivered as if it were unscripted and impromptu (ibid., p. 56).

The next challenge is to write in such a way as to bring the subject alive. To write so vividly as to paint and colour visual word-pictures.

Here are some exercises that are often used. I have been through these exercises myself and have used them with my students as well. While I am aware that we now live in a multimedia environment and digital radio now offers text and graphics, I reiterate that radio is still very much an aural medium. From that basis, I have insisted that radio students be consciously aware of the limitations of radio, being primarily an audio medium first, and to script and produce from that perspective.

3.3 TEXTURES, SHAPES AND SHADES

When going through this exercise, I remind my students to think about the blind, or to be politically correct—the visually challenged listener. Imagine what it is like not to have a reference point nor a prior experience of what you will be talking about or describing. Invariably, this limits the metaphors or analogies that they would be able to use in their scripts or descriptions. What this exercise does is cause the student to stop and ponder on what the visually capable have taken for granted when looking at colours, shapes, textures and sizes. The challenge is in translating what is normally taken for granted into something visceral so that what is described or said is communicated aurally as effectively as possible.

3.3.1 Shades and colours

1. How would you describe the colour RED?
2. What about describing the colour GREEN?
3. How will you do it, especially for someone who has never had a visual experience of it?
4. Take a moment now and attempt to describe any ONE of those colours to someone who has never seen their tints and shades before. Write it down.
5. After your first draft attempt, read it loudly.
6. Now take away words that seem redundant and shorten the sentences.
7. Now read it out loudly again.
8. Now read it to a friend.
9. What did they think of your description?
10. How would you improve on it?

Remember that when presenting over the radio, the listener has no idea what is being described if time is not taken to share as much detail as possible with the listener. Use emotion, the senses, the feel and the texture if that would help.

At this point, I have not discussed the nature of radio presentation scripts, so you may find that your script would sound somewhat rigid and stilted. You may feel like you sound as though you were reading.

If you were emoting while reading your text, you may feel unnatural and as though you were exaggerating or delivering your description in a "sing-song" fashion. Gone are the days when radio presentations sound like oratory. The radio experience of today is more personal and listeners are more familiar with a presenter who sounds as though they were conversing with you.

Here is an example of a possible description of the colour "red":

> The colour red is like anger; the warm feeling of rage building in me. It's like a hot summer day. The heat on my skin, so unbearable it may blister. Red is as fiery as the hot stove that burns my hand. It's the passion I feel when I'm with the one I love.

Some of my students would initially churn out something like the following, until I remind them that if a person were born blind, they would not have seen a red rose, nor seen blood or the blue sky.

> Red is the colour of a rose. It is the colour of blood, when a finger pricks on its thorns. The glow of a ruby, as luscious as lips ripe for kissing.

> Blue is the ocean on a clear day. The colour of the sky as the wind blows through your hair.

After the first round when the pieces are read to the class, each student comments on their friend's work. As feedback and comments are made, lights come on in their eyes as they realise that the metaphors and analogies they have used are familiar only to those who have seen and experienced what they have described.

3.3.2 Shapes

In the next exercise, describe a shape. Begin by looking at any one of these shapes, and then describe it. You may include a colour if you like. Your goal is to convey the chosen shape, through words, to your listener without their benefit of having seen it before.

FIGURE 3.1 Shape Exercise

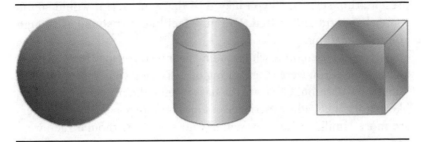

As with the "colour exercise" above, go through the steps of writing it down, reading it out loud, editing your text, then reading it out loud again to test it. Then read it to a friend to see if they know what in the world you're trying to describe.

For shapes, references may be made to everyday objects like the shape of a can of drink for the cylinder, or the edges and shape of a box for the square, and so on. Size and height may be included if you would like to orientate your listener to those attributes.

3.3.3 More exercises

The point of this section is to programme your mind to "see" suitable words in your head, to choose and use the best words to draw, colour, paint, and craft vivid images for the mind. Look at these pictures. How would you describe any one of these to someone who can't see it? Use colours, size and height comparisons, spatial adjectives, emotion, texture etc.

FIGURE 3.2 Picture Exercise 1

FIGURE 3.3   Picture Exercise 2

Now try these. Write a story on any one of these pictures.

As before, when you have finished your story, read it out loud and make the necessary changes until you sound fluid and the text describes the scene vividly. Ask your friend to close their eyes before you read your "script" to them.

What did they think of your story?

3.3.4 On location

Another exercise you may try is to go down to the corner of a street or sit down in a playground or at a park bench. Basically, find a location somewhere in your neighbourhood. Bring along pen and paper.

Begin by setting the scene. From where you are, place each object and item in our imagination. Create that space for us.

Now, describe what you see from where you are.

How would you describe that scene in front of you?

After completing your first draft, read it out loudly to yourself.

How did you do? Did you use reference points?

Did you use sizes?

Did you use comparisons?

In relation to where you were sitting, where was everything?

What was the weather like?

Use words to describe temperature, sound, touch, taste, smell, light, mood and feeling. Bring that scene alive for your listener. Did you sound as though you were describing it off the cuff or did you sound like you were reading?

3.3.5 Some examples:

- Just, I think it is ... four to five metres to my right ... about the length of a pickup truck, I see a man selling balloons. The sunlight's shining through the branches. His skin ... sweaty ... glistening in the sun.
- The garbage can in front of me is overflowing. Look at all those beer cans ...! The smell, bitter ... Stale! ... Someone had a party last night. Oh, the stench ...! Reminds me of dead, rotting fish.
- The sweet smell of early morning ... ah ... I love it! You can feel the dew, light on skin. It's in the air. On my left's the pond. At the edge ... there're some old folks ... moving slowly ... looks like Tai Chi.
- Two cold grey buildings, like ash, dwarf the entrance. I'm on the pavement. The towering monument's behind me. It's casting a shadow over the road. The rain's stopped. I can smell tarmac and rain-fresh air. The reporters are lining the streets, like a street parade. I'm told the delegation will arrive from my left. They'll turn 'round the corner about ten metres from where I am.
- It's drizzling tonight, the drops floating down ... against the floodlights. The pitch is wet. On the far end of the field, he's near the penalty box ... number-26's on the ground, beside the goal post ... rolling in pain. The players are now running to him. What's he doing? The manager's screaming instructions from the bench ... In front of me, at the Grand Stands, the crowd's on their feet.

Try to create width, height and depth in your descriptions. Everything written for radio has to be explicit. Stating the obvious helps to propel the listener along with the action. Words are important in creating context and in painting the image in the imagination of the listener.

> In other words, sounds require textual pointing—support from the dialogue or narrative. The ear will believe what it is led to believe. This pointing might be termed "anchorage," which is how Roland Barthes describes the function of words used as captions for photographs. Visual images, he argues, are polysemous. But so are sounds. Hence words help to *fix* the floating chain of signifieds in such a way as to counter the terror of uncertain signs" (Crisell 1994, p. 48).

And so since we are speaking to one person, remember to:

- Appeal to the human emotion. Deal with the human condition. Appeal to the heart and the mind.
- Deal with the familiar. Inform, educate and entertain. Be able to generate a response.
- Script for the ear not for the eye.

Production scripts are the blueprints that a sound engineer or producer uses to put the programme together. It would include directions for cross-fades, cold ends, voice over music beds and so on. Notice that the script example below (Figure 3.4) begins with a clear reference to the title of the programme, the station it will be transmitted on, the time and day it will be transmitted, and the name(s) of the producer(s). Unlike an "On-air" script prepared and used by the "duty-presenter," these production scripts are used in packaging programmes or information capsules. "On-air" scripts may begin fully written out. As the presenter gets more used to his or her own personal style, the "script" may end up reduced to just bullet-points. By this time, the presenter may be able to ad-lib as will.

3.4 FINE-TUNE THE WRITING

Radio is an aural experience limited to a time frame. One does not have the luxury of talking endlessly during an air-shift. There are commercials to be played, programmes to broadcast, music to play, letters to read, sponsors to appease, information to disseminate and news to present. If you are producing and scripting a programme, that would also be within a time frame of anything from three minutes to a one-hour segment. Within that broadcast window, as a presenter you would have to make sense, be focused, be interesting, in some cases to be interactive, and say all you have to say despite all that your research into the topic has yielded. Further to that, depending on the nature of the programme, you would also have to package it all with music, interviews and effects.

When scripting for the ear, the first premise is to be personal. Be mindful that the listener is listening to you alone—one to one—even if the listener is part of a group. The listening experience is a personal one. And so, write as though you are having a conversation with one person.

As there is only a limited time to speak with the listener, be highly critical about what is to be included in the script. Give it the relevance test by asking "So what?" to the information you want to convey. Will it benefit the listener? Is it relevant to the topic and focus of the programme? If the information or what you want to say is not relevant then why is it in the script? Exclude it.

Be succinct and handle ONE IDEA at a time. This also applies to talk breaks as well. The listener's attention span is limited. If a laundry list of information is being rattled off, the focus becomes dissipated and the listener's attention will be lost. By the third point, the first would have been forgotten. So keep it short, and keep it simple.

Using simple and easy to comprehend words would allow the listener to understand you immediately. If there's a shorter, more common word, use it. For example, words like precipitation, terminate, residence, purchase, countenance, and endeavour may not be part of your daily vocabulary.

Similarly, in conversation, the "active voice" rather than the "passive voice" is used. Writing in the "active voice" enables a presentation to be more dynamic when delivered. This includes writing in the *present tense* or the *present perfect tense*. Place the time element , if you need one, after the verb; and put words that you want to be *emphasised* at the end of the sentence, as in the following example:

"The chairman and board members reached agreement *this evening* on a *balanced budget.*"

Use shorter sentences to get to the point faster, keeping the subject and verb close together, and avoiding parenthetical phrases and clauses because these are invisible to the listener. This implies almost framing your sentences using a "subject-verb-object" approach. For instance, "police arrest the masked bandit" or "Elton John singing Crocodile Rock".

Writing in a conversational manner includes using "contractions". "Do not" becomes "don't", "I am" becomes "I'm" and "he is" becomes "he's". To reiterate, we are writing for the ear so the radio script would have to sound familiar, not stilted and staged.

While writing conversationally is essential, this does not mean being extremely colloquial or using sloppy language. Be mindful of writing sentences that may confuse the listener by inadvertently including the following:

- *Homophones*: Words that sound the same but have different spellings and meanings (e.g., "He was given *two* severe warnings" / "He was given *too* severe warnings").

114

- *Homonyms* or *homographs*: Words that are spelled the same way and that sound the same, but have different meanings (e.g., "*Close* your eyes and count to 10" / "Stay *close* to the path").
- *Redundancies* are unnecessary words that take up unnecessary time. Examples are "at this point in time" and "the end result." Why not use "now" and "the result is"?
- *Hollow* words are similar. Some examples are "45-degree *mark*," "falling to zero *degrees*," "one month *long*," "the test will run for a three-month *period*" and "storm *condition*." The same may be said for *pre-fabricated phrases* that are often used. Almost clichés themselves, and although there really is nothing wrong with writing them in, I am sure you are able to come up with better openings and endings:

TABLE 3.1 Prefabricated Phrases

In a surprise move …	Police are investigating …
This is the story of …	What happens next remains to be seen …
It's official …	Only time will tell …
Now it can be told …	Now the ball is in the opposition's court …
It shouldn't come as any surprise …	Don't count him out yet …
When was the last time you …	It'll probably get worse before it gets better …
Believe it or not!	No one knows what the outcome will be …
It was business as usual today at …	In the final analysis …
What we know now is …	There's no end in sight …
It's that time of year again …	

Being precise and accurate in your content are also necessary. Using clichés and beginning with phrases like "there is," "there are," "once again" add to a script's ambiguity. It is much better to state a fact and get to the point. For instance "there was a power failure that disrupted the game last night" would come across much better written as "a power failure disrupted the game last night."

Beginning with a quote may also lead to misunderstandings. For instance, the following may seem to be your opinion if the listener misses the attribution that follows the statement: "The economy is a joke!" says a city hall official. Begin with "A city hall official called the economy a joke …".

115

Reading your script aloud will often draw these elements to your attention. Upon listening to the script, if you find there is ambiguity and the listener might be confused, then opt to use another word. Having said that, do check your script for grammar and spelling. You would not want to confuse the person who will be reading your script, causing them to stumble over the words you have written.

When writing for the ear, or the mind, make what you are saying as tangible as possible. Use words that would paint an almost three-dimensional image in the listener's mind:

TABLE 3.2 Aspects of Writing for the Ear

• Length	• Texture	• Speed	• Orientation/reference points
• Breadth	• Tone	• Distance	• Touch
• Depth	• Colour	• Duration	• Smells
• Height	• Emotions	• Shapes	• Responses/reactions

Setting the "stage" is important as listeners are unable to see you, unless a web-camera has been installed in the studio. Scene setting is also essential when presenting on-location, doing live commentary at a live event, or in a packaged programme like a documentary or a feature. A mental landscape, environment and space is created in the listener's mind where action or events can occur. It orientates and brings the listener into the action, and to where you are. Scene-setting provides mental reference points that the radio presenter would be able to draw upon during his/her presentation.

If you need to attribute things, events, quotes and so on, put the attribution first as that is most natural. Some examples:

"Jeffery told me today that he loves to swim."

rather than:

"I love to swim." Jeffery told me today.

Another one:

"The minister says employment is in good shape."

rather than:

"Our employment situation is in good shape, according to the minister."

Radio listening is effective because its content communicates one-to-one, plays on the listener's emotions and the imagination. To have to pare information and scripts down-to-size is no mean feat. And writing the way you speak is not easy. We are often not detached enough from ourselves to notice our speech patterns or mannerisms to recreate them perfectly in a written script that is to be delivered in a way that does not sound read, staged and artificial.

Maintaining clarity, focus and the purpose of the scripted content minimises the danger of speaking off tangent or "waffling" unnecessarily. Include the following considerations when crafting your script to keep yourself within the boundaries: Who, what, where, when, why and how—the five Ws and one H.

3.5 THE RADIO PRODUCTION SCRIPT

- "Nar" indicates text for the narrator to deliver. A name may also be substituted in place of "Nar."
- "Con" or "Cons" indicates the insertion of an audio element that may be music, sound effects, or an edited pre-recorded interview. Here, it is important that if a commercially recorded song sound effect or music is used, the CD number and track will have to be quoted. These are for copyright purposes and to credit the source of the audio.
- "Vox Pop" is a pre-packaged series of faceless interviews with the man on the street. Literally, "Vox Pop" means voice of the people or "Vox Populi." Generally, these are edited and packaged as a montage reflecting a rapid-fire delivery of opinions from the public that present an "overview" of perceptions from "the ground." The opinions are included on their own merit with no reference to the individuals who have contributed them. Vox pops:

  - Should enhance the programme by adding to the pace, not slow it down.
  - Get the introductions out of the way quickly and get to the point at hand.

Link all relevant sources together and let them explain themselves.
You don't have to hand-hold the listener through everything.
Some examples of *Vox Pop*:

Never thought of it ... I think it stinks ...
It never bothered me ... They should all look at themselves first and
lead by example ...
How will this solve the problem? ...
You know it's already so difficult to manage, and with the economy
like that, I don't know man, I don't know ...

FIGURE 3.4 Example of a Production Script

**Example of a script
(without cue-points and timings)**

Radio Station   **Date of TX:**
                                               Time of TX:
                                               Producer(s):

Title

Nar: ("**Nar**"rator may be replaced with a name)
          The common fruit bat is about the size of a rat. It looks imposing sometimes
          because of its wing span that could reach as much as 3 feet.
Con: SFX (Wings flapping) CD SFX 378 Tr 29 (5 secs)
          (Please credit the sound source – quote number on the CD jacket spine)
          (Quote only the duration of the sound used) (Include any production
          action as well – eg. Fade down, fade up etc...)
Nar: (Voice over after 3 seconds) These bats are able to swoop down as fast as
          50 kilometres an hour and are often mistaken for ...
Con: Music (Title of music) CD AD 1117 Tr 5 (10 secs)
          (Same with all sound sources – credit the source)
Dr Lim: (This is an interview that has been included. The suggested practice is to
          transcribe the entire edited interview in the script) These creatures often
          feed on ...
James: How do you account for the fact that...
Vox Pop: ("voice of the people" This is normally a fast paced montage of short
          phrases or views taken from the public on a specific topic or person.)

2000 Rafael Oei

3.6 QUICK TIPS ON THE INTERVIEW

There are various ways to insert and frame an interview into the packaged programme. A straightforward introduction is usually done. For example the central narrator could introduce an interview to launch into a pre-edited interview:

> *Narrator*
> I was speaking to Dr. Robert Hanson of the Institute of Molecular Science, and he had this to say about the project:
> Dr Hanson (edited interview)
> My research has brought me ... etc ....

You may end the segment with:

> *Narrator*
> Dr Robert Hanson of the Institute of Molecular Science, speaking to me about his project.

In all these insertions, the pace and flow of the programme must not be disrupted. Just as a music performance is propelled by the score's tempo, a broadcast programme has a pace and rhythm that should not be disrupted. Editing out the normal niceties in a pre-packaged interview is fine. One does not have to pretend to be broadcasting a "live" interview when in actual fact it has been packaged. So "thank you for granting this interview" and "hello, good morning," and formalities like that can be edited out in the final product. Ask the first question and go straight into the interview with the answer.

When conducting an interview, preparation is key. One cannot stress research enough. Research is essential whether it is to interview a rocket scientist, politician, musician, rock-star or a child. As far as possible, put all the researched notes onto one sheet of paper. It may be organised in bullet-point form, or drawn as a mind-map. This list of notes not only serve to trigger points of interest during the interview. Having all the points on one sheet of paper dispenses with the need to rummage through heaps of paper for a particular fact. It also enables the interviewer to glance quickly for essential material without distracting the interviewee.

Questions are better written down, rather than remembered. These may be written out in full, or in point-form. While the questions are essential to the flow and direction of the interview, a good

119

interviewer LISTENS to the answers and takes the cue from what is being said. If the interview is being done live, body language and posture also contribute to what is being unsaid. As an interviewer you may or may not want to follow through with your intuition. Taking an unbiased and neutral position in an interview allows the listener to draw their own conclusions. This will reflect on the integrity and credibility of your radio station.

As a rule of thumb, the best answers are ones that have been unprepared. However, some politicians and personalities require questions to be provided up to a week in advance of the interview. I would always accommodate these requests out of goodwill and courtesy. Similarly, I would always package a copy of the edited interview and the finished programme, and send it to the interviewee after it has been broadcast. I find that this little gesture, if allowed by your radio station, is appreciated by the interviewee. It creates goodwill, again, and helps develop a relationship that may be advantageous in future projects.

It is courteous to call the interviewee the day before to reconfirm the interview date, day and time. On the appointed day, arrive well in advance of the appointment to prepare yourself mentally, sometimes emotionally, and to set up your equipment if necessary. Of course if the interview is assigned without prior warning, or in an emergency situation, then preparations are done "on-the-fly." Whatever the situation, with radio interviews, in person or over the telephone, all that is needed is a recording device and a microphone. Gone are the days when we had to lug around a huge open-reeled Nagra recorder. With digital recorders, everything can be held within the palm of one's hand.

When introduced to the interviewee, if it is the first time, have your identification ready, and prepare to present your business card.

When the interview is conducted at the interviewee's office or on location, selecting the best spot to conduct the interview is important. The first consideration is the editing of the interview, and to minimise as much unwanted ambient noise as possible so that edit points will not be as obvious.

1. Select a small, cosy and quiet carpeted room, if possible. The carpet helps to absorb sounds so that if the recording levels are correct (see next chapter), and the microphone technique

and positions are correct, the interview will be recorded clearly with "presence."

2. Stay away from air-conditioning vents or air vents. It may not seem as loud, but the sound of rushing air from these vents will be very noticeable after being recorded and can often drown out the entire interview.

3. Have a soft surface or curtain behind the interviewee and you. This absorbs sound and minimises "echo." Having a hard, or worse, a window or glass surface behind or facing you will cause your voices to reverberate off the surface resulting in metallic sounding voices and an echo-like effect.

4. Facing a large room during the interview will cause a recording that would have a large and roomy ambience. At worst, the interview will be unclear and hollow as if it had been conducted in a cave or in a large cathedral with loud ambient noise.

5. To minimise cable noise due to a loose microphone connection, loop the cable around your hand when holding the microphone.

6. The microphone should be held about six inches away from the mouth. Having said that, I would always advise my students to adjust to each person as everyone speaks and uses their breath differently. Putting on and listening to the interview through one's headphones helps in positioning the microphone to get the optimum position and minimise on microphone "pops."

7. When warming up and taking the recording levels before the interview, indicate that you are about to begin the recording to check the levels, and converse naturally as you would like to adjust the volume levels to the interviewee's natural speaking voice and volume. Before proceeding with the actual interview, give a short cue for the recording indicating the name of the interviewee, date, time and nature of the interview.

8. During the interview, maintain eye contact, and LISTEN to the answers. The purpose of having the interview is not to go through all your questions. Listen and lead the conversation. The questions help direct the flow of the conversation from one point of interest to another. Avoid repeating the answers back to the interviewee or telling them what they already know.

9. Avoid acknowledging and punctuating the replies verbally with "ah-huhs," "ehms" or similar vocal responses. These may make editing difficult later. The occasional nod, smile and eye contact will convey

your interest. Use visual cues and responses to put your interviewee at ease when recording the interview.

10. After the questions have been exhausted, if time permits, I would run the recording again for the interviewee to listen to what has been recorded. I may ask if there is anything more to be added and proceed to record it. I often find that when the questions have been asked, the interviewee is more relaxed. At this point, the best answers may occur as a more natural and sincere response is given.

11. During editing and packaging there may be the temptation to equalise the recorded interview to make it sound "warmer" or to make the interviewee sound "better." However, my opinion is an untreated voice always sounds warmer and sincere.

3.7 A WORD ABOUT MUSIC-BEDS

The better-packaged programmes would be produced to create a picture for the mind. Using interviews, sound bites, sound effects and music, the content of the programme and interview can be enhanced dramatically to sustain the listener's interest.

Paint a picture for your listener using words, SFX and music. Use music to punctuate and highlight. However, music droning in the background will irritate if it is not mixed well with the verbal content, or if the music selection is inappropriate. Unfortunately, many radio programmes and interviews are packaged with a music bed that is sometimes overpowering. Sure the music may be hard-hitting and upbeat, and these are often used because the producer and/or the presenter feel that it would enhance and make the interview or programme less boring. My response to that has always been, if the content is boring or uninteresting in the first place, it should not have been packaged or transmitted. Nothing done to an uninteresting recording, badly edited interview, or a "boring" production will make it more appealing or interesting. The listener may be distracted by the upbeat music, but they will not remember anything about the actual content of the programme or the interview.

A "Cue Sheet" would also have to be prepared. This "Cue Sheet" is for the duty or "On-Air" presenter to refer to when playing your programme for transmission. It would tell the Presenter:

FIGURE 3.5 Cue Sheet Example

Radio Station Name   **Date(s) of TX:**
                                                       Time(s) of TX:
                                                       Producer(s):

Title of Programme
Sub-title (if any)

Ann: Introduction to the programme to be presented by the duty announcer if
the programme is not self-contained.
If there is no need for the duty announcer to introduce the programme,
leave this segment out and play the Station ID if appropriate.

Cons: MD or Reel ID / Track no. if necessary: Title (as labelled) (Duration: of
programme).
      Begins: (Signature tune: if any) At least the first sentence of the
               programme...
      Ends : ... at least the last 1 or 2 sentences of the programme.
               (Signature Tune: if any.)
               (If Music is used, indicate if music ends cold or fades out –
               indicate length of fade in seconds.)

Ann: Include this only if necessary; this is a backsell for the preceding
programme.

Information: This section is important -
It includes information on the programme that can be used to
trail it during other air-shifts.

This section should include:
- Information on the content of the programme.
- Interviewee's names (if any)
- A summary of the programme, short enough to be the 'hook'
of the programme that the producer feels will interest and is
relevant to the listener.

Rafael Oei 2000

- What to say or do before and after the programme.
- Actual duration of the programme, not the assigned time (i.e., if the window for the programme is three minutes, the programme should be no more than 2:55 seconds maximum. A timing of 2:58 would be cutting it close to the next event to be broadcast.)
- Where the programme begins and how it ends.
- What to say if presenters wanted to trail for your programme.

A programme/capsule may have an initial proposal that may take the following form:

FIGURE 3.6   Proposal example.

Proposed title of programme:

Duration:

Proposed Time-belt:

Frequency of broadcast: (number of times to be aired per week)

Number of episodes: (If it is a series)

Some titles for each episode:

Presenter: (if you want someone specific)

Programme summary: (explain the rationale for the programme)

Target Audience:

Information Sources: (if any)

Possible Sponsors: (if any)

Rafael Oei 2000

In summary, if you subscribe to the idea that radio is a personal medium, and that it is basically an audio medium, then your scripts will reflect attributes that would contribute to delivering clear and focused information. The script must, after all, be easy on the listener's ear. It has to be "conversational." The listener has only one chance to understand what you're saying.

A way toward a more "conversational" script is to use:

- Active voice
- Present tense
- Short sentences
- Sentence fragments
- Contractions
- Simple words
- "Number rule"

3.8 THE "NUMBER RULE"

When writing a presentation script, numbers below 10 and above hundred are normally spelled:

- one, two, 15, 31, 42, ...
- One hundred and twenty, 23 thousand dollars
- 13 million US dollars not US$13 million

Generally, broadcast copy-style also suggests that abbreviations are not used; that titles are placed before names; and initials are not used in names unless the person is widely known.

Verbal simplicity is the mark of a good broadcaster. Relate in simple terms to the listener as the listener has only one chance to catch your meaning to understand you. Use everyday language that even a child can understand. This makes your presentation palatable and universal. That's the art of writing for broadcast.

To be verbose in order to impress is not advisable. For instance, try to identify these songs:

- Colourless Yuletide
- Castaneous-coloured Seed Vesicated in a Conflagration
- Righteous Darkness

- Arrival Time: 2400hrs: Weather: Cloudless
- Far off in a feeder
- Array the corridors
- Jehovah Deactivate Blithe Chevaliers

(If you need the answers, you may email me at rafoei@shaw.ca although I am sure you can figure them out).

And so, when scripting:

- Ask yourself if what you are planning to say is relevant to the listener.
- Give your information the "So what?" test, or the "Why?" test. Ask it enough times and the essence or focal point of the content will become evident.
- Keep the content of what you want to say focused.
- If you are doing a live presentation, use *One Idea* per *Talk Break* if possible. Saying too much, or a laundry list of items, is counter-productive.
- Write for speech.
- Keep your sentences short.
- Use descriptive words, adjectives, the present tense and the "active voice."
- Think three dimensionally.
- Read your script aloud to test it.
- If you feel uncomfortable with it, rewrite it until it feels natural.
- Script everything you are going to do or say.
- If there's nothing to say, don't say anything.
- Even the best ad-libbers have their content drawn out in point form.
- Your listener is probably engaged with some other activity, so script to allow your listener to grasp what you're saying *the first time round*.

3.9 SOME WORDS TO THINK ABOUT

Listed below are some commonly-written phrases that are best replaced with simpler ones.

Abrasions and contusions	Give rise to	Resuscitate
Accede to	In addition	Retain his position as
Adequate bus transportation	In attendance	Retired for the night

A large proportion of

Ascertain

At an early date

At the present time
Best of health
Attired in

Behind schedule
Beverage

Called a halt

Caused injuries to

Continued to remain
Deceased

Dispute the fact
Discontinue
En route
Exceeding the speed limit

Filled to capacity
Gained entrance to

In consequence of

In many cases

In order to

In the course of
In the direction of
In the majority of
   instances
Less expensive
Leaving much to be
   desired
Made an approach to

Made good the escape

Occasioned by
On account of the
   fact that
Pay tribute to
Placed under arrest
Prior to
Put in an appearance

Residence
Rendered assistance to

Submitted his
   resignation
Succeeded in
   defending
Succumbed to his
   injuries
Sustained injuries
Take action on the issue
Terminate

This day and age
Took into
   consideration
Took up the cudgels on
   behalf of
Under active
   consideration
Utilise
Voiced approval

Was a witness of / to
Will be the speaker at
With exception of
With the minimum of
   delay

CHAPTER 4

Think "Radio"

"Begin with the end in mind." This simple phrase has been used to cover areas that range from business processes to creative pursuits. As clichéd as the phrase may have become, its simple truth still resonates. The same applies to radio productions. It all begins with an idea and the concept. If the end product can be "seen" or "heard," then deconstructing the product to its elements would be an easy task. When a production is broken down to its elements, the producer is able to identify specific components to obtain, record, research, source for, and prepare. Having the end in mind, taking it apart and then piecing it together in the studio cuts down on production time and streamlines the packaging process of any production.

An earlier chapter traced the evolution of radio as a service to the listener. What became clear were the way presentation and production methods evolved as the purpose and function of radio transformed. These eventually became institutionalised into approaches, practices and expectations currently held by broadcasters and listeners about the business of radio broadcasting. It was a brief outline to set the tone for subsequent chapters on production and presentation in this book.

Even the radio listener has evolved into a media participant—more so in recent times as a "consumer-user," with advancements in digital technology that have made consumers frequent and familiar digital media users. Digital radio, based on a digital technological infrastructure, presents the potential for including text and graphics along with the traditional audio expected in radio programming. And so, to conceive digital radio programme content is to include the design and inclusion of text and data that will be a visual option to the transmitted audio. Before proceeding into the realm of extended data content for audio files, this chapter first begins with a brief outline of basic production approaches before exploring the inclusion of visual content to traditionally audio programming in the next chapter. I will begin with descriptions of traditional editing and production processes, developing into a discussion about what may be utilised and offered in a digital radio environment, covering both the production of content for Internet web streaming and for digital radio on a Eureka 147-DAB platform. This discussion will flow into the final chapter where we address the issues facing radio producers and presenters in digital radio. I have placed importance on audio production first as this remains the backbone of radio broadcasts. It is essential that the radio student is able to edit and produce compelling audio productions before thinking of visual content that should only really serve to enhance and supplement audio programming. Having text, graphics and data accompany music and audio-information content, in my mind, is the value-added enhancement available to the listener through digital radio receivers and the personal computer through webcasts. Primarily, radio is still considered an audio medium.

For a description of the structure of Eureka 147-DAB digital radio, you may refer to my book *Borderless Bandwidth: DNA of Digital Radio* (Oei 2002), Robin Blair's (1999) *Digital Techniques in Broadcasting Transmission*, or *Digital Audio Broadcasting, Principles and Applications*, edited by Wolfgang Hoeg and Thomas Lauterbach (2001). In order to understand the concept behind the designing of content for digital radio, not confined to online Internet webcasting, one needs to understand what is available in the technology and its potential. This is essential to the radio producer-presenter of today. By being aware of the enhancements available in digital radio, producer–presenters will be better prepared to manage digital radio services in the future.

Many would argue that living in the digital information age, broadcast students should only be trained in the essential digital disciplines. From a developmental perspective, basic approaches to the production and presentation process provide a foundation that includes a sense of history, an understanding of the origins of basic radio assumptions and the source from which present production techniques evolved. For instance, in Ngee Ann Polytechnic's School of Film and Media Studies, the radio curriculum was designed in such a way as to ensure that first-year radio students go through the experience of dub and splice editing analogue tape using open reel tape machines. The experience of recording onto, editing and manipulating magnetic tape is to allow the radio student to experience that process kinesthetically, to acquire basic editing skills in a tangible editing environment before moving on to a virtual digital editing environment. If the student were able to comprehend and systematise an approach to produce a complex production using a two-channel analogue open reel tape, a sound source, a microphone and a splice-kit, then putting together a production in a virtual multi-track digital environment that presents an infinite number of possibilities will be relatively easy. The benefit of working with an audiotape in acquiring a systematic approach to editing and producing aural-radio content is immense.

Radio is transient and its content is often time-sensitive. This means that radio programmes, content and productions would have to be researched, acquired, packaged and transmitted within the least amount of time. With that in mind, being skilled at analogue editing is an asset, especially in a digital environment that is prone to data loss and hard-disk crashes. Programmes and interviews will still be expected to be broadcast, even if a digital editing workstation has a virus or has crashed due to various reasons. When these unfortunate occasions arise, the analogue open reel would be a welcome ally.

Here are the basic attributes of radio as a broadcast medium:

TABLE 4.1 Attributes of Radio as a Medium

Audio	Raises issues	Informs	Reflects the community
Personal	Provokes	Educates	Entertains
Companionship	Discusses	Friendly	Serves the community
Immediate	Challenges	Mobile	Influences

This book will not explore the relevance of specific radio content. My intention is to provide a spectrum of considerations and production techniques that may be used in approaching your own production for whatever purpose, radio format or genre you may be in. The best hardware, software, microphones or sound processors that should be purchased will not be discussed. That is not the intention of this book. The concern is not in external tools. This book presents and shares internal approaches and thought processes behind production and presentation methods that will eventually emerge as intuition or production instinct when practised consistently. These go beyond software and hardware that will become obsolete very quickly anyway.

4.1 THE "END" PRODUCT

Radio programming content evolved from a combination of spoken word services, news and commentary along with musical interludes to a more popular scheduled-music-programming jukebox approach. During World War II, community reports and news coverage became more extensive as listeners craved to know more about the world around them. As radio technologies and creativity matured, radio productions became more elaborate, producing results like the infamous Mercury Theatre production of H. G. Wells' classic *War of the Worlds*, developing into production aesthetics that have in turn enhanced production values that have created very compelling complex documentaries, features and commentaries.

In all radio productions you will find the same elements put together in various combinations, whether it is in a pre-packaged production or a "live" broadcast. Assuming that research into the feasibility of the project has already been done and approved, the elements in the production process may be broadly represented using the following diagram, Figure 4.1.

In exploring the process of putting together a pre-packaged programme for radio broadcast, let us use the fairly complex production framework that may be applied to the production of the radio feature or documentary. In considering and reflecting upon the elements that go into such a multi-layered and multi-faceted production, you will appreciate the process and will be able to apply a similar approach to less layered and complex productions. It is the integration of diverse elements into a discernible and comprehensible form within a context, whether it is information in the news to be taken seriously, a music talk show to be taken as entertainment or the documentary or feature where the

FIGURE 4.1 Production Elements

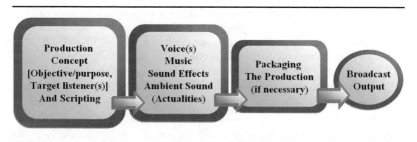

Rafael Oei 2003

131

information and experience is digested cerebrally. The listener will decode these accordingly.

As has been established in Chapter One, and will be explored in this and in the next chapter, "key to the meaning of the sounds, music and silences of radio—and the means by which the context is established is at bottom *verbal*" (Crisell 1994, p. 53). Roman Jakobson's communication model describes it thus:

FIGURE 4.2   Roman Jakobson's Communication Model

SOURCE: Crisell 1994, p. 60.

4.2 THE DOCUMENTARY/FEATURE

David Hendy, in *Radio in the Global Age*, states that in the radio production process "to capture physically images that convey meaning—radio requires its producers to embody their ideas through sounds" (Hendy 2000, p. 74).

> Ideas need to find their *voice*—and it is the producers who have to find it. Very often these producers look to the real world and its "raw" sound, and seek to let this sound "speak for itself." In so doing, they owe something to the pioneers of the 'realist' documentary film movment of the 1930s who first argued that more should be made of the film-camera's ability "for getting around, for observing and selecting from life itself" (Ibid.).

The phrase "if you can see it, you can achieve it" applies similarly to the audio production. If you can hear the completed production in your mind, you would be able to visualise the elements that make up the programme. Andrew Crisell in *Understanding Radio* (Crisell 1994) describes it this way:

> Sounds on the radio may also carry what I have termed an extended signification. An owl-hoot, for instance, may open a documentary about feathered predators or it may evoke not merely an owl but an entire setting – an eerie, nocturnal atmosphere, as it would in a melodrama or a programme about the occult (Crisell 1994, p46).

By beginning with the notion of visualising the "end product," and using the example of producing a radio documentary or feature, the first consideration in approaching the production may be about ones understanding of the terms "radio documentary" and the "radio feature."

Whilst many texts offer various explanations for each (Keith 2000, Mencher 1999, McLeish 1994, Siegel 1992), these texts also acknowledge that the terms are interchangeable and broadly used. McLeish considers both "exciting and creative areas of radio" that covers a huge range of content and subject matter (McLeish 1994, p. 239).

In considering the differences between the radio documentary and the radio feature, a rough comparison may be made between the documentary and the feature in the following manner. These are some of my ex-students' comments taken from *Advanced Radio Production* documentary/feature workshop:

TABLE 4.2   Differences between the Radio Documentary
and the Radio Feature

Radio Documentary	Radio Feature
1. Subject matter is broadly researched researched and presented with multiple perspectives based on available evidence, fact and artefacts.	Selective subject matter researched for specific programming objectives: • As part of a radio promotion • Supporting/complementing an event (e.g., a feature on a stage musical or a feature film screening sponsored by the radio station).

133

TABLE 4.2 Differences between the Radio Documentary
and the Radio Feature (cont'd)

Radio Documentary	Radio Feature
2. Timeless and has no "shelf life." An audio documentation of the subject that can be archived and re-broadcast because the information and data are historical fact.	May be time-specific and relevant only within a particular time frame, e.g., a feature on a band or an artiste that may be performing during that weekend.
3. Boring.	Entertaining.
4. Wholly based on fact.	May be loosely based on fact.
5. Objective.	Subjective, sometimes speculative.
6. Generally non-commercial.	Commercial.

While these are opinions shared by radio students, there are some challenges present, and some aspects that may be interchangeable between the two. For example, it is unfortunate that documentaries are labeled as boring. While keeping the listeners' interest may be a challenge to documentary producers, it is certainly not true of all documentaries. What is common to both is that when one refers o a documentary or a feature, one generally refers to a production tha¹ may be fairly elaborate and complex, rich in content, and lasting anything from 30 minutes to one hour or more.

Issues that spring to mind for such productions are the relevance of the subject matter, access to content and the ability to sustain the listeners' attention over such a long span of time. Whilst students generally consider documentaries slow, educational and boring, my challenge to them is always to bring the information and content to life through various audio devices such as re-enactments, dramatisations and multi-layered story-presentations which provide opportunities to present the subject from different perspectives using a combination of interviews, *vox-pops*, music, actualities, narratives and sound-effects.

A first approach to the production is to consider the following:

FIGURE 4.3 Feature/Documentary Proposal

Proposed title of programme:

Duration:

Proposed Time-belt:

Frequency of broadcast: (number of times to be aired per week)

Presenter: (if you want someone specific)

Talent: (names of people you want voicing your programme)

Programme summary: (explain the rationale for the programme)

Target Audience:

Interviewees:

Possible questions:

Information Sources:

Sound-bite sources:

Possible Sponsors: (if any)

Rafael Oei 1997

1. Be clear about the purpose for producing the documentary or feature. Good intentions to put together content to inform and educate is not enough to justify a programme's production. Being an evangelist for causes or pet subjects is not good radio nor the purpose for a producer's existence.
2. The objectives in putting together information and resources into a broadcast programme are important:
    *   If it is for a social commentary, why is that needed?

- If it is to present archived historical information, why is that important to your listener?
- Who are the targeted listeners for the programme?
- If the focus is on a culture, race, neighbour, society, country, musical genre, art-form, literature, movie, personality or artiste then what impact does it have on the radio–listener, the community, the nation, the radio station or your reputation?
- What is the intended impression on the listener?

3. Will it be a call to action or do you want empathy with the subject, situation, protagonist, issue, story, content or information?

- Is the programme meant to uplift, motivate, depress, cause reflection, question, challenge or tease your listener?

The value and benefit wrought from a broadcast of the completed documentary or feature should be an objective exercise that produces tangible outcomes for both the listener and the radio station. Here is a template that roughly draws out some considerations in formulating a proposal for such a production.

The fundamental purpose and "why" to a production often inherently moulds the framework and approach to the production that will include an appropriate treatment of the subject matter. The question of form brings with it problems such as determining the appropriate medium to "tell the story".

4.3 NARRATIVES

The narrative, in the form of pages and pages of first or third person written text to be voiced, often becomes the backbone of the documentary or feature. While this form of "telling the story" in a one-person linear manner—much like reading a storybook to a willing audience—is not intrinsically ineffective, it does not utilise the multidimensional potential available in an aural medium such as radio. In defining narratives and identifying a useful framework to adopt in one's production, we may consider, amongst various approaches, what Hendy describes as "hierarchical" and "linear" narratives (Hendy 2000, p. 78).

Hendy describes "hierarchical narratives" as using various voices and sounds that are given dominance and prominence over other elements at any given point in a radio programme to "frame" these other elements (ibid., pp. 78–79). The "hierarchy" of voices reflects the position or status of the narrator or an organisation in relation to the subject in question; contrasted against or framing input from the general public that may take the form of "vox pop" or "vox populi" (voice of the people) insertions, interviews or commentary. This form of narrative may be seen in the example of a programme that has the main narrator, perhaps a newsreader, journalist or reporter, who has a detached "discursive control" of the content that ties the story together with an introduction, intermediary links and a conclusion. Actualities and reporters form the next level in this storytelling, and so on down the layers being presented in that story. The tying and binding the story together with the main narrative is what wraps the entire story in a package—giving rise to the phrase "wrapping it up" when a presenter is asked to conclude a presentation.

If we were to make a graphical representation of what is involved, we may put together a model that may look something like Figure 4.4. To be able to visualise the flow of the elements within a production in a similar fashion helps in formulating the approach to producing the programme, especially if the production is to be done solo by the producer–presenter, in a one-man-operated production studio or editing workstation. The ability to visualise the completed production and its elements can be usefully applied to both dub and splice editing techniques and the virtual digital multi-track editing environment.

In this graphical representation, the programme begins with an easily identifiable "programme signature tune" (Sig. Tune) that cross-fades into the programme introduction by the central narrator. The significance of the "signature tune" is in its function as a herald that a particular programme is beginning. As a signifier, it becomes a coded trigger for the listener, and its influence can be heard whenever we hear a programme's signature tune being hummed or sung by the media user; for example singing the Davy Crockett theme song from Walt Disney's production of *The Adventures of Davy Crockett* in the 1950s. Crisell comments on the effectiveness of the "signature tune" using the example of the news:

> The broad function of the music is to identify the genre of the programme, to remind us that what we are hearing is "the news" as distinct from records or chat; and it does this by being staccato and repetitive, acting as an iconic index of various kinds of information technology—a typewriter, Morse telegraph, computer or teleprinter. Moreover there are other aspects of the music which declare that the news we are listening to is of *popular* rather than "quality" appeal (Crisell 1994, p. 114).

137

FIGURE 4.4 Hierarchical Narrative

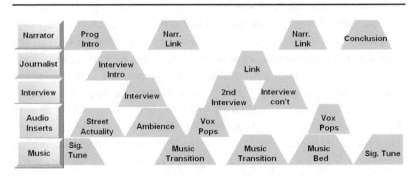

This is the direction of the programme.

The gradients indicate
fade-ins and fade-outs.

Rafael Oei 2003

So the selection of an appropriate musical or aural signifier is important to the production as it sets the tone of the entire programme.

Continuing our discussion of the "hierarchical narrative," we see this example is told in multilayered narratives consisting of the "central narrator," the "journalist," the two "interviews," the "vox pops," the actualities and ambience, and the music.

After introducing the programme, the central narrator leads the listeners to the next layer presented by the "journalist." The "journalist," in turn, illustrates the story with an interview, backed by ambient sound. The central narrator continues the narrative with a link to the next segment of the story that is punctuated by a montage of voices from the public called the "vox pop" or voice of the people. Having the general public commenting on a person or a subject occasionally adds width to the content, giving a flavour of the peoples' general perception of the subject matter. The "vox pop" leads the listener into the next interview that the "journalist" complements with supporting material, linking that to the next interview.

Music transitions are used to allow the listeners time to digest the content and to flow from one point to the next in the story. In this diagram, the central narrator then takes up the story from the interview and leads us to another "vox pop" that is blended with a music bed to link that

138

FIGURE 4.5 Linear Narrative

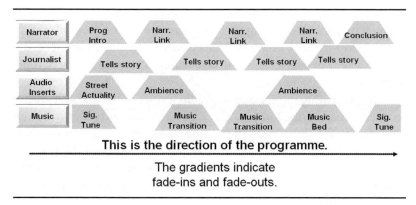

This is the direction of the programme.

The gradients indicate
fade-ins and fade-outs.

Rafael Oei 2003

segment to the concluding remarks by the central narrator. As the central narrator "wraps up" the programme with a summary of the content, the signature tune fades in from the background and takes over from the narrator as the last words are delivered.

"Linear narratives," on the other hand, have a juxtaposition of one or two voices and sounds that convey the story to the listener (ibid., p. 79). The narrative in this instance follows a singular path drawn by these voices and sounds that lead the listener across the story without providing layers of other voices or actualities to illustrate the subject's depth or other related perspectives. Using another graphical representation, we see at least two layers are removed in the narrative framework.

Other forms of narrative include using the "montage." In this form, sounds and actualities are juxtaposed to propel and tell the story. These may be a combination of interviews, "vox pops," ambient sounds, and anecdotes. To some producers, having a montage of perspectives and anecdotes provides an added authenticity to the documentary or feature that third party or institutionalised narratives cannot provide. Hendy considers this form of narrative "elliptical" in nature, with "no conclusions spelled out, and it is commonly used to explore more abstract ideas" (Hendy 2000, p. 80). This is where "an *unspoken* narrative order has been produced, that sounds, and words, and music and silence can often tell a story without the need to 'point the finger'" (ibid., p. 81).

As simplistic as it may seem, one more approach may be to use a framework that is similar to musical form. The simple "A:B" where one subject or supporting information leads to another; "A:B:A" where the first subject is repeated at the end as a reinforcement of that point. Of course it may become as complex as to go into an "A:B:A:C:A:D" format, the "rondo form" or even the "sonata form." In these instances, the musical theme or subject is substituted with the intended research topic or theme.

By presenting the content of a radio feature or documentary using an approach described above, the suggested framework provides an opportunity for the scriptwriter and/or producer to manipulate the content and data in a manner that may be appealing to the listener. Considering that framework within which to work also allows the producer to focus on streamlining the production process and information gathering.

Whatever the case, the importance of having a strategy, a blueprint and a plan with which to present the story or subject is essential. Immediately gaps will surface and suggestions to acquire information from specific sources will present themselves.

4.4 RECORDING LEVELS

The first phase of the production process is to be able to record all the audio material at a good strong input level. To ensure recording levels

FIGURE 4.6 Input Levels

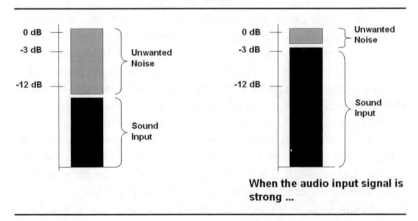

Rafael Oei 1998

140

are consistent, the input levels on the multi-channel mixer, or the "target" recording machine, must be calibrated to around -6 dB using a tone oscillating at 1 k. This would ensure that the recorded audio is clear and strong, leaving enough headroom for sudden peaks to minimise distortion in the input recording. If the recording level is too low, say -12 dB or more, there will be a "hiss" or noise that will be evident in the recording as well. Although the environment or room may be "silent", this noise is the movement of air-particles that have been recorded along with the audio that you want. Digital recordings also have a similar problem if the audio is recorded too low.

In the absence of a mixer, or should the sound source be connected directly into the recording machine, then input levels are taken based on the volume of the source—assuming that the source material is not distorted and is of a reasonably good quality, a highly subjective phrase to use. I will leave it to the reader's discretion as to what constitutes "reasonably good quality" as that can only be determined through actually listening to the sample to be recorded. I will say that if the sample sounds "strong," clear, undistorted, almost "in your face" with "presence," and that sounds as close to the original upon playback, that would be a good indication of "reasonably good quality."

The illustration above (Figure 4.6) shows just how much unwanted noise would be recorded based on the recording levels set.

Once the "ideal" input level is set, the input faders are not altered throughout the entire recording or editing session. Any alteration would be done on the output levels of the source machine(s) or faders. This is to ensure integrity in recording levels from all possible sources. It would enable editing to be done without having inconsistencies occur between different recorded sources or between different recording sessions. All too often, I have witnessed new producers and radio students altering the output level, then the input level, and then compensating on one or the other to get the meter on the recording machine to kick up to the -6 dB to -3 dB levels whenever there is a change in the quality of the source material. Then upon playing back the recorded material, they find that the recording levels are inconsistent from recording to recording; even though it was all done within the same recording session. When the input levels are set, leave it alone during the entire recording session! Once again, the first phase of the production process is to record all the audio source material at a good strong input level. Post-production or mixing is a different process from this stage of the production. Once all the material has been recorded clearly, these can then be blended in easily.

4.5 DUB AND SPLICE EDITING

When all the information and material have been prepared, and the producer has decided on a treatment or approach to the subject, the next step is to put it all together in the editing studio or workstation.

In analogue recordings, and in what has been termed dub editing and splice editing, the magnetic tape is used, normally available in 15-minute, 30-minute and 1-hour tape reels. These tapes consist of three layers, the magnetic layer, the plastic base and the backing layer.

The common metallic compounds for the magnetic particles used on the "magnetic layer" are:

- Ferric Oxide (rust in its natural form) for Type I category tapes
- Chromium-dioxide for Type II
- A dual-layer Ferri-chrome for Type III (not available anymore)
- Pure metal magnetic material for Type IV

"Dub editing" consists of recording selected portions of audio and discarding the rest. This "selective recording" generally occurs between two audio machines, whether it is between "Open Reel" tape machines, a cassette player and an "Open Reel" tape machine, or between a compact-disc player and an "Open Reel" tape machine. Analogue tape reels are often referred to as "open reels" because the reels of tape are not enclosed in casing, as are cassettes or digital audiotapes (DATs).

FIGURE 4.7 The Analogue Tape

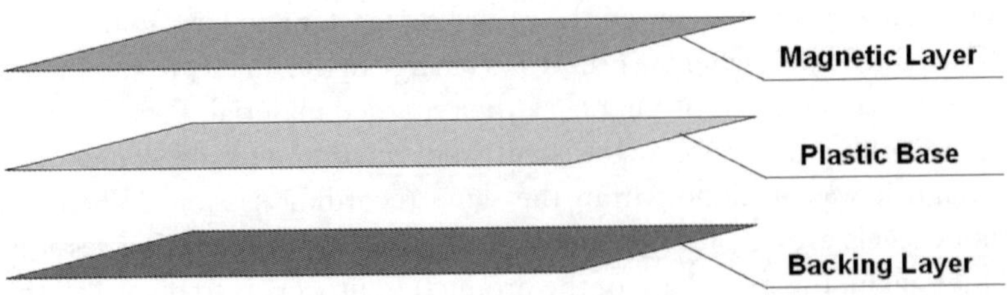

Magnetic Layer

Plastic Base

Backing Layer

Simply put, selective recording is done by recording relevant segments of audio from a "source," whether it is a tape, cassette, CD or any other audio device, to a "target tape" which may end up the Master Tape to be used in broadcasts. I will not attempt to go into further detail of dub editing as this has to be shown and experienced in order to perfect the skill. Accuracy in "fusing" together different parts of a recording or different recordings through this technique will include blending the principal audio element, background elements and ambient sound to create smooth, seamless edits. From experience, the speed at which the tape machine activates the "punched in" recording during the dub process is also critical—and that is where a book is unable to fully extend that experience.

"Splice Editing" involves cutting up the tape and "splicing" it together. Splice editing is often used to "clean up" edits due to its ability to achieve "fine edits."

FIGURE 4.8   Dub Editing Examples

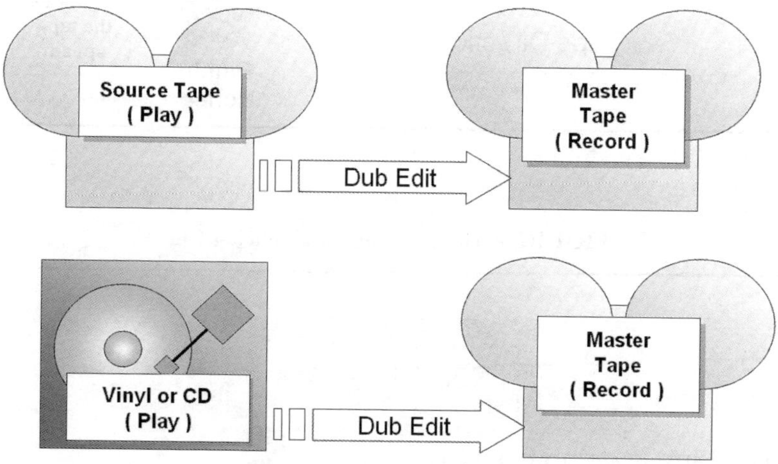

Rafael Oei 2002

143

When an analogue tape is to be "spliced," the editor first searches for the "edit points." These points are the silent gaps between recorded audio where the editor can safely cut the tape without cutting off essential portions of recording. In searching for these gaps, the editor stops the tape at the potential edit point, then listens to the tape by manually joggling the tape reels with both hands—scrubbing back and forth until the gap is "found." This is determined by locating the "sound" against the "play head" of the tape machine; after all, sound is only reproduced when the magnetic particles pass over this "play head." So when all you hear is silence, or the gap, invariably this silent gap on the magnetic tape is now positioned over the "play head."

FIGURE 4.9 Tape Machine Heads

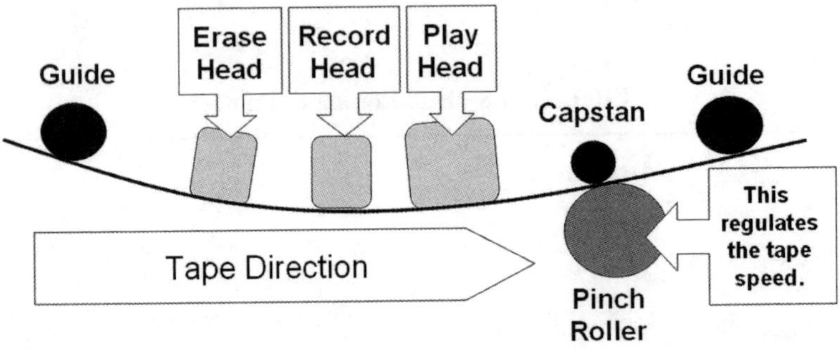

Erase Head
Record Head
Play Head
Guide
Guide
Capstan
This regulates the tape speed.
Tape Direction
Pinch Roller

Rafael Oei 1998

FIGURE 4.10 Marking for a Splicing Cut

Erase
Record
Play
The tape is going this way... >>
... say to trying I'm what
...eh ... What

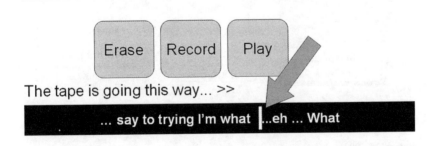

Rafael Oei 1998

Once the gap is found, the editor then uses a "china-graph," or wax marker, to draw a line on the backing layer of the tape. The words in the diagram below represent what has been recorded, in the sequence it appears on the tape.

To cut out the offending "eh," in this example, two marks must be drawn on either side of the "eh." Using the same manual method, the editor would then joggle the tape once again to locate the gap before the "eh" to draw another wax marking there.

FIGURE 4.11 Splice Cut

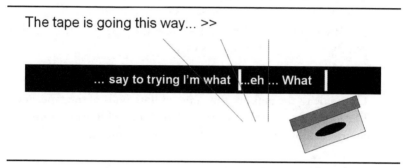

Rafael Oei 1998

FIGURE 4.12 Labelled Tape

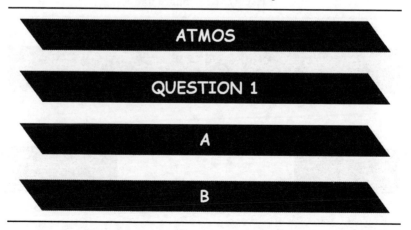

Rafael Oei 1998

Once there are two markings on the tape, the editor can be sure that the "eh" resides between the two. The cuts can now be made. This may be done using a blade over a "splice block" that has pre-cut grooves to guide the blade across an angled cut, or a "guillotine-type" splice block.

When the cuts have been made, it is always a good idea to mark the tape. This is because unlike a digital environment where each recorded region or segment can be labelled with a nametag on screen, one cannot see the configuration of the magnetic particles that produces the recorded sound. In fact, after just 10 to 15 minutes of splice editing, there will surely be a spaghetti of tape beside you. And one word recorded on analogue tape may be about a metre in length after it is cut from the spool.

After the "offending" portion is removed, the editor will now have to join the two ends of the tape. Positioning the tapes within the splice block once again, the editor ensures that:

- The tape has been placed with the backing layer facing upwards,
- The angle of the cuts are the same on both ends of the tape, and
- The tapes accurately meets end-to-end. This can simply be determined by running one's fingernail over the tape.

Notice from the diagram that when the ends of the tape are joined, the wax marking forms a line once again.

FIGURE 4.13 Splice Join

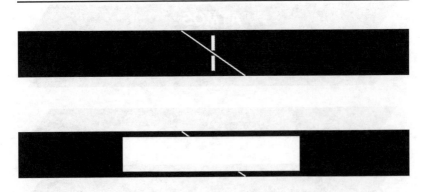

Rafael Oei 1998

Then, about an inch of splicing tape is cut and pasted over the join. The length of the splicing tape is important: too short and the join will snap during playback. The fingernail is once more passed over the spliced tape to ensure that the adhesive is secure and to remove air-bubbles that may have gathered under the splicing tape.

Having described dub and splice editing, it is quite obvious that some thought and planning must go into putting elaborate productions together.

So when putting a programme together using dub and splice editing methods, my practice has always been to lay down and edit the "backbone" of the programme on one open reel. This is often the narrative or the edited interview. This is then set up on one open reel machine ready to be "punched" into the master tape, interspersed with content from other audio sources. With the production script as a guide, audio elements are pieced together from various sources by recording each onto the machine running the master tape, slotted into the appropriate spaces. In the case of the narrative examples described above for the documentary or feature, the "backbone" of the programme is the "central narrator" which is the one constant in the story. The gaps between the paragraphs or sections seen in the diagram represent spaces that can be filled with appropriate music, interviews, "vox pops," or commentaries.

For instance, in preparing the narration-reel, already recorded on one open reel, my practice has been to have 5-second gaps of silence where an audio insertion is to take place. These 5-second gaps allow the producer or recording engineer to stop that tape and set the narration to begin with the next portion, while the audio insertion is being recorded into that gap from another source, without running into the next phrase, sentence or paragraph. In "dub editing," other audio elements are recorded into these gaps by using the "punch-in" technique that inserts these elements played from either another open reel machine, a turn-table, cassette player, compact disc player or other audio sources.

Recording layers of material and cross-fading each using "dub and splice editing" techniques is always a challenge as most of the over-dubs are done in real time. One mistake, one miscue or telements out of sync may mean re-recording the entire sequence and starting from the beginning again. Splicing is later used to "clean up" the edits to produce a seamless edited product.

147

FIGURE 4.14 Dub & Splice Editing Approach

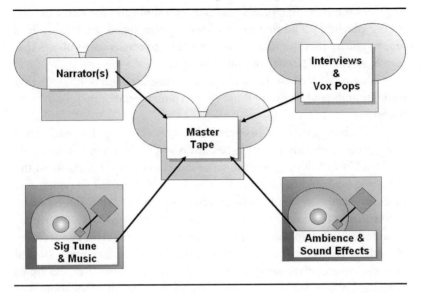

Rafael Oei 2002

While the above techniques seem ancient by digital standards, having our radio-students trudge through the planning process of dub and splice editing hones their skills in piecing together material for a virtual digital editing environment. And so in using the dub and splice editing techniques, production strategies are a little more sophisticated because the producer or recording engineer is confronted with the problem of configuring the editing process using conventional analogue hardware. At the risk of sounding simplistic, I suggest that this production process may be made easier if a mental picture of the sequence of the recording/ editing process can be visualised, similar to the diagram above, using the production script as the base. Knowing and visualising the sequence in layering the recordings provides a clear plan of action during the production process.

4.6 THE STEREO EXPERIENCE

Once the above production process is experienced, virtual digital multi-track editing and production becomes an easier skill to develop within a radio student.

Clearly, for purposes of maintaining credibility, radio content largely consists of a mix of music and spoken word programming, with the emphasis on obtaining authentic natural audio recordings (especially for documentary features and news content) for broadcast with minimal sound processing. While straightforward recording and broadcast of "actuality" is preferred, the ability to skilfully construct and produce programmes using digital editing/multi-track software brings with it an added dimension to just putting on tape the sounds that are around us.

Being able to manipulate audio content within this virtual editing environment has become more widespread amongst the youth due to the competitive pricing of digital editing software. What the radio lecturers from Ngee Ann Polytechnic's School of Film and Media observed was that while some students possessed the basic skills and technical knowledge necessary to navigate through the digital environment, the ability to apply these skills to specific productions for specific outcomes was limited. Students were weak in formulating and constructing aural arguments, reviews or "storytelling" using available data, information, artefacts and evidence. The question of applying the formulation of arguments, constructing stories and delivering polished programmes is a separate subject that will not be pursued here. This section continues the example of the documentary or feature already described above, but this time within a digital audio multi-track environment beginning with understanding and constructing a virtual aural stereo experience for the listener.

In the digital multi-track environment, an understanding of creating a virtual "stereo" environment is important. This includes the understanding of how the placement of sound within the virtual audio space affects the aural experience of the listener. Often when asked, the layman and even radio students take the stereo reproduction from pre-recorded music compact discs for granted. Pre-recorded music burnt on compact discs are accepted as already divided into its component instruments and automatically placed in specific positions within the left and right stereo spectrum to create the experience of music being played in an active, living space, the "stereo" environment being limited to the space between two speakers, left and right.

The need to bring the radio student through the mechanics of creating stereo productions lies in the ability to actually conceive of and produce these stereo productions from scratch. As mentioned above, all too often, stereophonic and even surround sound reproductions are taken

FIGURE 4.15 The Stereo Space

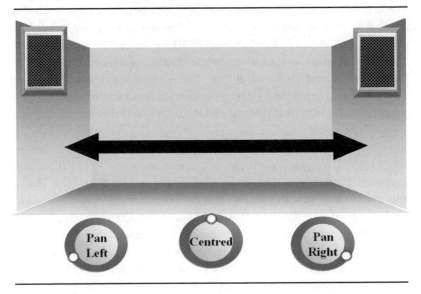

Rafael Oei 1998

FIGURE 4.16 180-degrees in Front

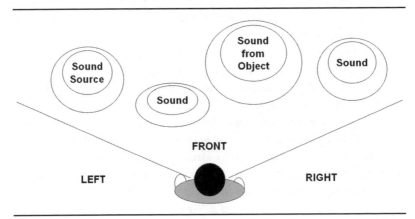

Rafael Oei 1998

for granted by listeners. Broadcasters of the future, working in a digital domain, would also benefit from learning the art of creating stereophonic audio images. Of course, in a few years, this may expand into the art of creating an audio image that surrounds the listener.

The frequent argument is the presence of computer software that can split the left and right inputs/outputs of audio material. This is not enough to constitute the ability to create stereophonic imagery. Even monophonic audio can be played through left- and right-outputs and still remain a monophonic experience to the listener. Stereo imaging consists of a combination of audio elements strategically-placed within the left and right stereo spectrum to create a total stereo image of what was intended. Most software are not sophisticated enough yet to automatically place a saxophone to the left of the stereo image to avoid a clash with the trumpet section. The producer or sound engineer would still have to manually tweak the pan-pot, or programme the orientation into the software.

This virtual space occupies a 180-degree perspective that is an aural experience occupying a "forward" orientation between the left and right speakers (Figure 4.16). The experience of the listener listening to audio produced in "stereo" in this manner would hear the different audio elements emerge between the left and right speakers limited to the field directly "in front" of the listener.

A three-dimensional depiction of the "stereo experience" is given below (Figure 4.17).

FIGURE 4.17 Sound Image in Front

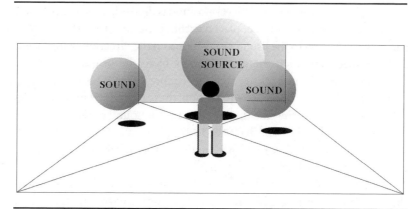

Rafael Oei 1998

FIGURE 4.18 Panoramic Pots

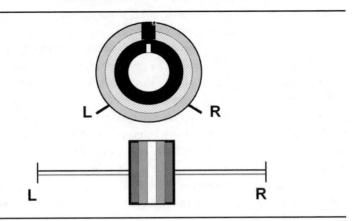

Rafael Oei 1998

This stereo imaging is achieved by simply tweaking the pan-pot, or panoramic pot, on the multi-channel mixer of each audio element. This act places these aural "objects" within the stereo spectrum depending on the degree in which the pot is turned or shifted between the "left," "centre" and "right" positions of the pan pot. Even "live" interviews in the broadcast studio can be configured in this way using the pan-pots available in most broadcast consoles. In a production situation, the pre-packaged programme can be produced using digital editing software to enable the producer to create aural "space" in a number of ways.

For example, in the figure above, "L" refers to "left" and "R" refers to "right." The illusion of an object's position is dependent on the position and angle of the sound source, placed within time and space through the pan-pot, in relation to the listener's position and the direction being faced, and the speed in which the sound travels from the originating sound source and the time it takes to reach the listener's ears. This is artificially recreated using the pan-pots to position these sounds. The illusion is achieved by reproducing the time it takes for the sound to reach each ear or what Michael Talbot-smith (1998, 1997, 1995) calls "Time of Arrival."

With "surround sound" productions, the aural environment is extended to a 360-degree sensory experience.

The aural experience in this case would be of the listener being in the midst of the "artificially" created virtual aural environment. Again, a three-dimensional depiction of the same experience is presented below.

FIGURE 4.19   Time of Arrival

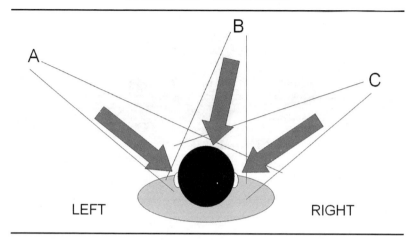

Rafael Oei 1998

FIGURE 4.20   360-Degree Around

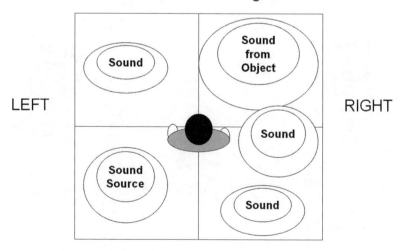

Rafael Oei 1998

FIGURE 4.21 Within the Sound Image

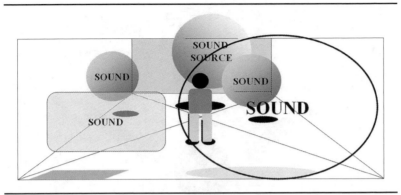

Rafael Oei 1998

Placing audio elements within the "left and right" limits of the stereo spectrum is only one dimension of the process. With volume manipulation, increasing or decreasing the volume level of that sound within this virtual environment can recreate the illusion of "spatial depth" or distance of that object from the listener.

FIGURE 4.22 Creating the Spatial Depth

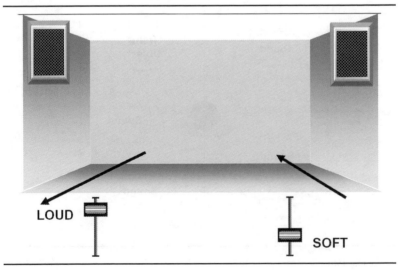

Rafael Oei 1998

FIGURE 4.23   Placing Audio Objects

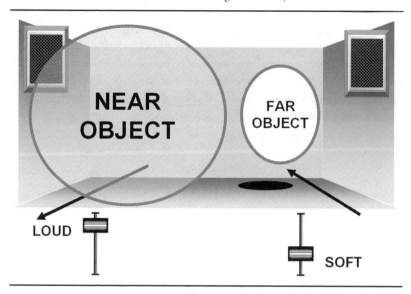

Rafael Oei 1998

FIGURE 4.24   Talk Shows in Stereo

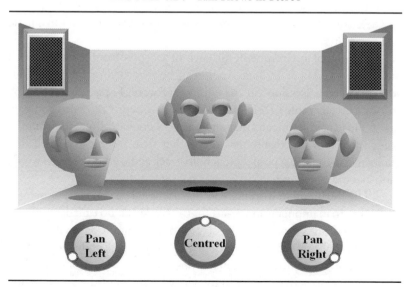

Rafael Oei 2003

This enables sounds and "objects" to be placed in specific positions within the stereo environment, making the listening experience more dynamic.

The orientating of people within this virtual environment, for instance, in a radio interview segment is not often used. Imagine how interesting a two- or three-person interview can be if they were placed to the left, right or centre for the listener to experience their "presence" in this virtual "room" during that interview. Increasing or decreasing the volume levels for any one of these aural objects then brings it closer or further away in the aural image that is created for the listener.

4.7 DIGITAL MULTI-TRACK EDITING

When the concept of "stereo imaging" is understood and the producer/editor is able to manipulate the sound to remain either in a fixed position or move about in a predetermined fashion, using one track of the multi-track editor, layers of sounds over a number of tracks can then be included. In this multi-track environment, the ability to work with, blend or contrast each sound to produce a specific impression or output is then explored. This is a long way from the radio productions of the 1940s or 1950s where multi-track recordings were unheard of. Even if there were multi-layered audio productions at the time, these suffered from "drop-out" and deteriorating sound quality due to multiple recordings over magnetic analogue tape.

In a digital environment, the current accepted sample for recorded audio is 44.1 kHz at 16 bits. Audio can be recorded or imported into what is called a "session" in the editing software. Latest digital editing software are also able to "rip" audio directly from pre-recorded compact discs. This basically means that audio can be copied wholesale from the compact disc in practically no time, rather than having to record that audio in real-time. A typical digital multi-track audio editing screen would look like the following.

The flexibility in working within this digital virtual environment is the ability to manipulate and re-arrange recorded audio called "regions." Cutting, pasting, re-ordering, re-sizing, and fading the audio in and out within the "edit screen" of a typical digital multi-track audio editor adds to the versatility of editing within a "non-destructive" environment. The term "non-destructive" refers to the virtual altering of the audio region leaving the originally recorded material unchanged no matter how the

FIGURE 4.25   Digital Audio Editing Screen

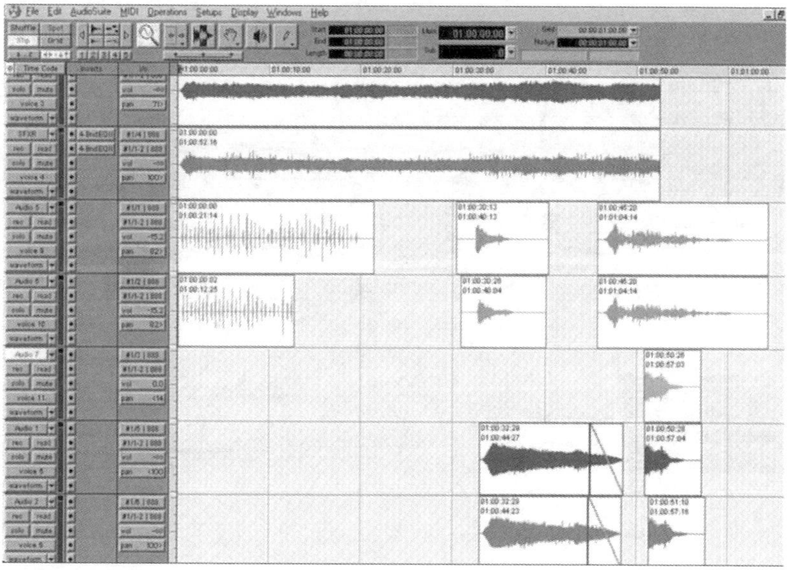

Screen shot taken from author's PC.

recorded region is manipulated within the editing screen. Audio manipulation also includes being able to texture the sounds using audio "equalisation" plug-ins that alter the brightness or dimness of the audio. Other sound processing capabilities available in typical digital editing software include compression, limiting amplitude peaks, adding audio "gates," phasing, adding chorusing, and a myriad of other sound processing plug-ins.

Volume and panning controls in this virtual editing environment can be automated, making mixing and post-production processes more convenient. These are activated using linear grids that can be moved, increasing or decreasing the volume levels by simply increasing or decreasing the gradient of the line, as shown in the following diagram.

The work capacity of these editing software is limited only by the number of input channels available on the computer's sound card or the proprietary sound processor card that comes with some software packages, and the processing speed of the central processing unit (CPU) of the computer.

FIGURE 4.26 Automated Volume and Pan Controls

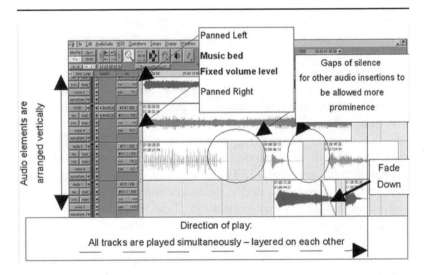

Screen shot taken from author's PC.

FIGURE 4.27 Multi-Track Edit Screen

Screen shot taken from author's PC.

FIGURE 4.28 Visual Representation of the Production Script

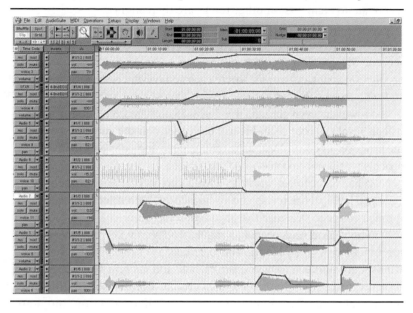

Screen shot taken from author's PC.

What can be implied from the above screen shots is that the work ethic and production process is vastly different from the dub and splice editing techniques described earlier. Immediately what is evident is that the production process is now non-linear. In this environment, it does not matter which audio is recorded first. And making an object move aurally from left to right within the stereo spectrum is a simple process.

Having said that, however, being disciplined in one's approach to the production process in such a versatile environment greatly influences the speed and quality of the production. This is the reason that radio students in the School of Film and Media Studies at Ngee Ann Polytechnic, Singapore, must first experience the dub and splice editing process. The experience eventually creates a clear process in the mind of the student as to how to proceed with the audio production.

Taking the documentary/feature example already related above, a starting point, even within this digital virtual environment, is to record the narrative first. This will serve as the backbone of the production. Based on the production script, that audio is then edited and separated into individual regions within that same track, leaving gaps of silence where audio elements on other tracks are then aligned.

Unlike using analogue tape, the audio can now be "seen" in the form of rendered waveforms. Aligning each element within the editing screen, the producer/editor now has a visual representation of the production script and can see where each audio event occurs in the context and sequence of the script.

However, even though the audio is now "visible," the product is still an aural experience and is still dependent on the aural judgement of the producer or editor. And so, listening and using one's ears in the editing process is still important.

What is useful in working within this virtual environment is the ability to label all the tracks and audio regions with discernible names. It is much easier to organise the production environment, with each track and audio region now bearing a name. And so, by keeping to a system, for instance when placing audio tracks for background music or atmosphere, immediately you can "label" and assign two tracks to each actuality, background music and background ambient sounds. In setting these background elements, by virtue of their function and static characteristic, volume levels can be set accordingly and each set of two tracks can be permanently panned to the left or right orientations.

FIGURE 4.29 Volume & Pan Examples

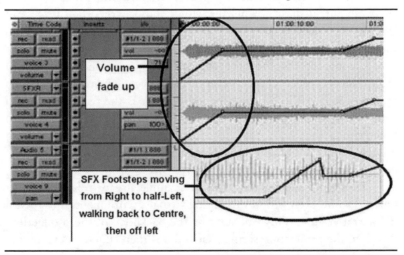

For spoken word elements, and singular monophonic sounds like the sound-effect of footsteps in the example below, that are to be moved using the automated functions, assigning these to one track is sufficient. These can then be assigned to the appropriate panned-orientation to reproduce an object moving about between the "left and right" extremes of the stereo spectrum. In most digital multi-track editing software, automating volume levels and audio panning is affected using grid lines like these.

The automation feature is useful in that multiple audio events may be set up and left to execute on their own while the engineer or producer mixes-down, not needing to worry too much about audio events not taking place. For instance, two tracks with the left and right of the background music is configured to fade-up in stereo, the pan-pots of both tracks already panned left and right respectively; a character may be speaking, moving from left to right using the recorded voice on one track and dragging the pan pots, via the grid-line, to place the audio from left to right accordingly to create the illusion of movement. To further enhance this movement, the appropriate sound of footsteps recorded onto a single track is similarly panned from left to right in synch with the moving voice—completing the illusion that a person is speaking and walking from left to right of the stereo landscape, accompanied by the appropriate "mood" music.

Once the audio recording has been mixed-down and saved as a digital audio file, this file is then uploaded onto a database of songs, saved on a diskette or burned onto a compact disc to be programmed, scheduled or archived for future transmission. With present digital technology, this recorded audio can be further enhanced by adding other elements that have not been traditionally associated with an audio medium like radio. This is adding text, data and graphics to audio files. This may be done within the framework of the compressed audio file, or separately with audio files residing in one database, and the data, text and graphics residing in another database—integrated by a multiplexer at source transmission and received by an appropriate decoder that would play both audio and data.

In the next chapter, we will look at the environment that faces the radio producer/presenter. Going beyond the need to understand the differences between analogue and digital methods of recording and production, or producing using digital software and recording in digital format onto virtual disks in the form of memory chips or fixed-disks, we will look at the features of the European Eureka 147 Digital Audio Broadcasting standard (DAB) along with web-casting. In providing information on the architecture of digital receivers, producer/presenters will be drawn to aspects to consider when producing data, graphic and text content for transmission along with traditional audio content through digital broadcast systems.

CHAPTER **5**

The Face of the Digital Radio Broadcaster

> Radio provides a speed-up of information that also causes acceleration
> in other media. It certainly contracts the world to village size, and
> creates insatiable village tastes for gossip, rumor, and personal malice.
> But while radio contracts the world to village dimensions, it hasn't
> the effect of homogenizing the village quarters. Quite the contrary.
> In India, where radio is the supreme form of communication, there
> are more than a dozen official languages and the same number of
> official radio networks. (McLuhan 1994, p. 306)

McLuhan's statement draws us to the misconception that media technology
would one day unify or at least influence the masses into homogeneity.
While digital technology has, in effect, changed our lifestyle and has opened
the masses to a massive ability to access anything at anytime, it has amplified
the individual-ness of the listener. Digital media now possess the ability to
"narrowcast" and provide individualised services for its user/listener on
demand. Marshall McLuhan had already observed what has become a
reality—that users will simultaneously become active producers and
consumers. The paradigm shift slowly took root in the early 1990s with
the emergence of the personal computer and the Internet. The implications
for broadcasters were not yet known. In many ways, die-hard radio
broadcasters are still adamant about the nature of radio and have caused
the transition into digital radio to extend over a decade, and still institutional
radio stations around the world are not organised and structured to deliver
digital services optimally. We see it throughout history.

> At first, radio might seem like a threat to the recorded music industry.
> After all, they play the *entire* song, not just a few notes. And if it's a
> hit song, you can hear it night and day on the radio every few minutes
> if you're so inclined.
>
> For a while, the music business fought the idea of radio stations
> playing songs for little or no compensation. Then, in the 1950s,

they realized how valuable airplay was—so valuable that a congressional inquiry discovered that music labels were bribing disk jockeys to play their records. Fast forward a few decades to MTV. Once again, the music labels balked at supporting MTV's insistence that they provide expensively produced music videos—for free! It took a year or two for them to discover that MTV *made* hits—that giving away the music for free turned out to be the best way to sell the music (Godin 2000, pp. 134–135).

Media professionals are just coming to grips with the digital technology that has practically overwhelmed and all but reinvented approaches to mass communication. This chapter will take us through the digital architecture that faces the radio broadcaster.

5.1 ADDING DATA, TEXT AND GRAPHICS

Media experiences are now on multiple planes. The human senses are bombarded on different levels by audio, colour, text, graphics, animation, and information all at once. As seen above, in a preceding chapter, the media consumer–users of today are living in a culture of access. The digital domain is second nature, and the assumptions navigating through a digital environment is a pre-conceived expectation. When viewing a digital television programme, the ability to click on commentary or visual captions for the hearing impaired is an expectation. To be able to click into the bio-data of the presenters or actors, and to find out more about the history or background of some element in the television video or programme is a feature that is expected. The *Matrix* series of Digital Video Disks (DVDs), with its multilayered access to content from any part of the movie using hidden and obvious icons, is a prime example of a dynamic digital environment within a traditional communication format—story-telling through the motion picture. Consumers expect these added multilayered features to be present in DVD format movies, otherwise the value of that DVD package and movie decreases.

Similarly, for a web-cast or digital radio programming, the ability to access the bio-data of the programme or singer is an expected feature; as is the ability to click on the song to purchase the song album or the song, or to navigate through the recording label and singer's website. When digital radio becomes more ubiquitous and integral in daily life, the same demands will evolve into normal expectations in that digital medium. As a radio producer, producing for a multimedia experience on digital radio, production considerations will now extend into conceptualising and designing visual content to accompany the traditional audio content transmitted in radio broadcasts. Programming issues are discussed in my book *Borderless Bandwidth: DNA of Digital Radio* (Oei 2002).

Most multi-track software allows for the exporting of the entire session as a stereo wave-file that will be "mixed down" automatically. After the production is completed and the output has been balanced and "mixed-down", the result is a stereo wave file that can be transported or archived within the digital domain. Common wave formats include the Windows "wave" format, MPEG (Motion Pictures Experts Group), Apple's Quicktime format or streaming formats.

Data and text can be added onto the wave file through Windows media encoding and authoring software. This software converts the wave-file into a stream file. Text and graphics can then be added on

FIGURE 5.1   Webcast of Radio Heatwave

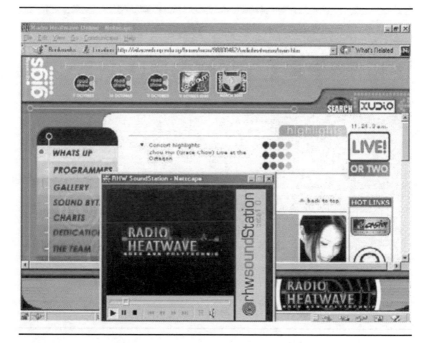

Screen shot from author's PC.

just by dragging and dropping the appropriate screen captures, graphic files or text converted to a graphic file. Once packaged, the audio is then streamed through the Internet along with the attached text and graphics appearing along with the audio. The screen shot (Figure 5.1) of a web cast from Ngee Ann Polytechnic School of Film and Media Studies' campus radio station, Radio Heatwave, has the logo of the station appearing along with the audio. The campus radio station uses Windows media to stream the station's daily output from the broadcast studio on campus.

Here is a screen shot of an earlier version of the Windows media-authoring tool.

Whilst this provides the producer/editor with a way to transmit text and graphics along with the audio over the Internet, transmitting content over Eureka-147 DAB is slightly more complicated.

FIGURE 5.2 Windows Media Authoring Screen

Screen shot from author's PC.

Specifications of screen sizes will vary, depending on the DAB monitor being used and if transmission is to a DAB PC receiver. Obviously, creating a screen for PC reception would call for a wider frame, a specific font size, and greater potential for providing interactive content. The question of scalable screens has not been resolved yet, the ideal being to have a Macromedia Flash-type capability to enable convenience in configuring data and graphic content for DAB transmission.

Currently, the Short Message Service (SMS) available on mobile telephones is the rage. Even radio stations have begun to have promotional campaigns and contests that utilise SMS. Interactivity over the Internet through websites and packed DAB data content allow listeners the two-way communication described by Brecht (Hendy 2000, p. 195). While text, data and audio synchronisation is not a problem in web streaming, configuring and synchronisation through DAB encoders pose a slight challenge. While there are broadcast systems providers who claim to have fused audio to data content for DAB transmission, the basic system still has encoding for data and audio going through separate modules in the DAB configuration.

FIGURE 5.3   PAD & Audio Encoding

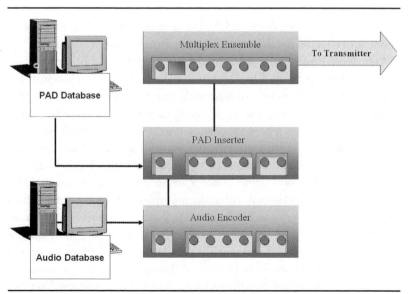

Rafael Oei 2002

FIGURE 5.4 Production/Broadcast Chain

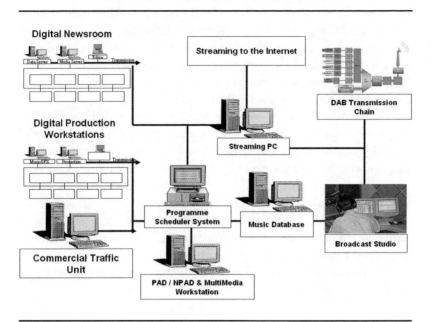

Rafael Oei 2002

In the example above (Figure 5.3), the data content and audio content reside in separate databases. While the Programme Associated Data (PAD), Non-Programme Associated Data (NPAD) and other graphics files are being generated by the multimedia workstation shown in the diagram, these are synchronised with the appropriate audio within broadcast automated software provided by companies like Dalet or Radio Computing Services. These are channelled through the broadcast studio into the encoder via separate streams, routing audio and data content through different channels into the audio and data encoders respectively (Figure 5.4). Data and audio content being channelled through DAB encoders are split and joined within the multiplex. This is then channelled through both the web and DAB encoding systems out onto the Internet and the digital transmitter. For DAB signals, these are split during decoding within a DAB receiver for the data to be displayed over the monitor and for the audio to be blasted through the audio speakers.

Programming issues will not be explored in this volume. Do refer to *Borderless Bandwidth: DNA of Digital Radio* (Oei 2002) where I discuss screen layouts and possible content design and programming for an on-demand non-linear environment. More fundamental to all these is the ability of the radio programme director to craft and design a digital radio listening experience that is flexible, convenient, mobile, interactive and on demand. This means having audio programme archives being made available to the listening public to enable unrestrained radio listening beyond the normal linear, time-based "news at noon" convention. The consumer-user would typically want information, news, promotions, entertainment and music anytime, anywhere. The implications include the tagging of data content to every song that is on the music playlist, for instance, for broadcast. This will enable an automatic refresh of DAB monitors accompanying the music output.

In terms of digital services, having brought my former radio students through the architecture of Eureka 147-DAB, and the implications of having to programme for digital radio, the campus radio station management team is expected to produce and manage their own website. Students were required to design the website with a view that radio services are now interactive and supportive of the audio output from the broadcast studio. Although commonplace in most websites, here are some examples from the campus radio station's website targeted at increasing interaction with listeners and obtaining information for the listener's database. These artefacts also show that the radio students' output included visualising relevant data and graphics to support the audio content being transmitted.

Apart from the normal background history of the radio station pages and management team bio-data, here in Figure 5.5 is what is typical to most radio sites—the Programme Schedule. Whilst the above is for the PC monitor, this information, or graphic could be streamed through the NPAD (non-programme associated data) channel on a DAB receiver. Considerations for a smaller DAB monitor would include the layout of the programme schedule, the image format (i.e., TIFF, JPEG, PNG, using HTML, XML, etc.), image size (150 × 150 pixels, 200 × 150 pixels, etc.) and font size. Considerations for graphics streamed through the Internet will include the size of the image file, the number of colours used, and the type of palette the image relies on as these would affect download and screen refresh time for the image and webpage.

FIGURE 5.5 Radio Heatwave Programme Schedule

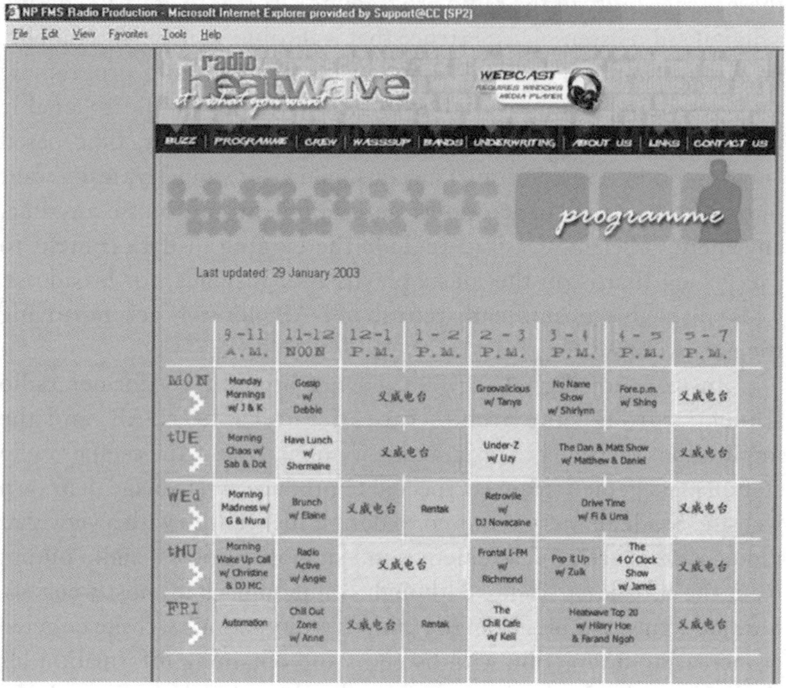

Screen shot from author's PC.

In this series of screen shots, what you see is information pertaining to a radio DJ competition organised by the campus radio station. During the promotion running up to the finals of the competition, the performance of each contestant was transmitted daily to garner listeners' votes and to provide an avenue for listener feedback on the contestants. As each competitor presented "on-air," relevant data on each contestant accompanied the audio transmission. This level of interactivity, being a product of student broadcasters functioning in a learning laboratory, was excellent. The competitors, who were students from secondary or high school level, were thrilled with the interaction. The response generated from the participating schools, with students supporting their friends, provided a rallying point amongst students within those schools. At the same time, it provided exposure for the campus radio students and the

FIGURE 5.6 Radio Heatwave DJ Competition Website

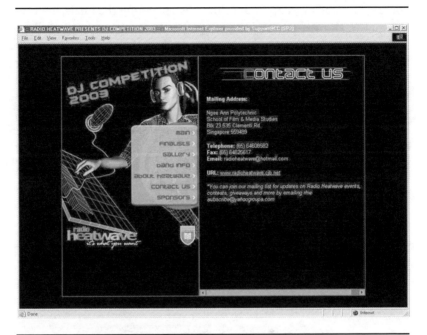

Screen shot from author's PC.

radio course within the School of Film and Media Studies—raising the programme's profile to top-of-the-mind awareness in those secondary and high school students wishing to enrol into a broadcast media programme after graduation. Here's the site for the DJ competition (Figure 5.6).

The information being transmitted along with the DJ's performance would be similar to the following screen (Figure 5.7). That is followed by the feedback screen to allow students to input their comments and votes (Figure 5.8). The ideas generated that conceived the structure of this section of the campus radio website is the result of knowledge acquired from various modules on web-design, webpage authoring, radio writing and production, marketing, promotions and communications theory. Are these the skills that digital radio broadcasters must now possess? In short, the third-year radio management team of the campus radio station dreamt the entire concept and put it all together—including the competition itself, organising the schools and contestants (including providing crash courses on radio presentation techniques), planning the finals, inviting the guests and judges, and sourcing for prizes. It was an excellent realtime radio/webcasting promotional event that would have been effective for major radio stations in boosting their image, associating themselves with the community at large, interacting with the community, and building their database of listeners and possible candidates that may be added to the DJ/radio presentation pool.

The campus radio management team designed the feedback mechanism, as well as a music chart voting system, receiving input from the listener apart from the regular means of communication via email services and now the Short Messaging System (SMS).

FIGURE 5.7 DJ's Information on Website

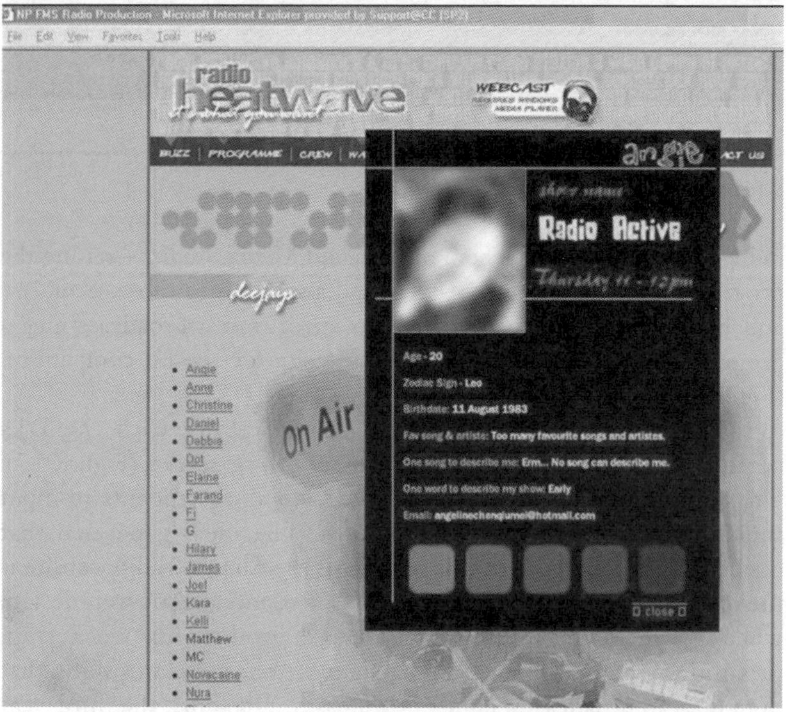

Screen shot from author's PC.

FIGURE 5.8   Radio Heatwave Feedback Form

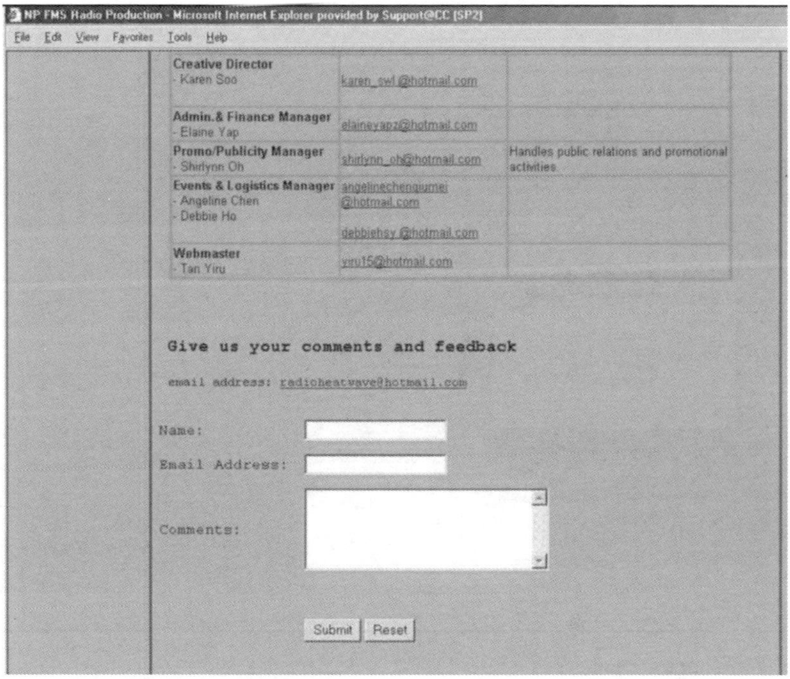

Screen shot from author's PC.

Regular content and the daily broadcasts from the campus radio station were streamed through the Internet using a live streaming software. Student producers and presenters were expected to produce text and graphical content to accompany their audio programmes. Here (Figure 5.9) is one example of a student-produced food programme streamed through the campus website. "Makan" is the Malay word for "eat".

While the above examples are ostensibly web-based and familiar to web-savvy surfers and authors, in the context of traditional radio broadcasting it differs from its typical linear radio-programming model. Radio services now extend beyond a linear timeline. It is multi-dimensional (Oei 2002). Radio broadcasting in this model must satisfy the demands of the listener over the linear time-continuum as well as across the services provided by the radio station, and the depth of graphic and textual information that can now be included with the

FIGURE 5.9 "Makan" Programme Streamed

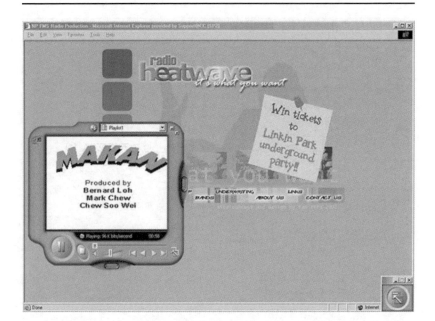

Screen shot from author's PC.

audio transmission. These components are graphically depicted below (Figure 5.10) as an integrated whole that contributes to the digital radio experience. The "time-line" arrow only points one-way as that is the nature of time, progressing linearly in one direction. The vertical and horizontal arrows that point in two directions represent services and visual-data content that have unlimited potential.

Conceptually, this implies that radio programming be approached to consider both the static and the fluid. A longer discussion and suggested templates to spark the conceptualising process for digital radio services can be found in *Borderless Bandwidth: DNA of Digital Radio* (ibid.).

As the students build upon providing interactive services for the Internet, and the DAB receiver, we will find a more versatile radio service with a mix of archived, interactive and traditional "live" radio presenting. Four-hour shifts may be a thing of the past with digital radio. Producer-presenters or disc jockeys will be more specialised and focused, producing and presenting for specific programmes that may only last one hour. In

174

FIGURE 5.10 Multidimensional Digital Radio Content

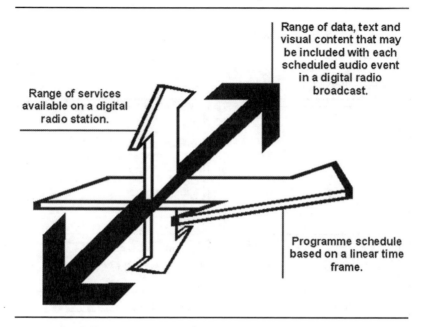

Range of data, text and visual content that may be included with each scheduled audio event in a digital radio broadcast.

Range of services available on a digital radio station.

Programme schedule based on a linear time frame.

Rafael Oei 2002

fact, presenters frequently pre-record what are called voice-tracks that are sequenced into a programme schedule. A music scheduler, such as Radio Computing Service's *Master Control* or Dalet's *5.1* would then play the scheduled music and programmes automatically, and the voice-tracks would be activated at the appropriate times simulating the presence of a deejay where there is none. Radio stations employ this device over weekends or on public holidays. And so, producing for digital radio transmission, the producer has to consider what could best accompany a completed audio programme such as the documentary or feature. Once the content for the data screens has been laid out and more or less been decided on, research to "beef-up" the information on these screens continue, while content is sorted and organised according to the audio sequence it is to be displayed. A suggested template for organising Programme Associated Data (PAD) screens may be the following (Figure 5.11).

These screens are then created and captured (with text and graphics) into an image file, if no interaction has been built into it. The screens would then be displayed either via a carousal method where all the screens

FIGURE 5.11 A PAD/NPAD Organiser Template

Audio / Data Service Name: _____

Ensemble No.: _____ Total no. of screens: _____

Time or Mode of Transmission: _____

Screen:_____

HTML / Graphic   PAD / NPAD

File Name: _____

Client's Name: _____

Screen:_____

HTML / Graphic   PAD / NPAD

File Name: _____

Client's Name: _____

Screen:_____

HTML / Graphic   PAD / NPAD

File Name: _____

Client's Name: _____

Screen:_____

HTML / Graphic   PAD / NPAD

File Name: _____

Client's Name: _____

are transmitted in rotation, or triggered by key audio points pre-programmed and flagged using software like the Windows Media Authoring package or even Macromedia Flash files. Of course the latter method is specific to the assigned programme and would therefore be a better value-enhancement for the programme. As discussed in *Borderless Bandwidth: DNA of Digital Radio* (Oei 2002), these create "depth" in the content that accompanies the transmitted digital audio. As to how these may be achieved will be presented below as the nature of programme associated data is described.

Predetermined screen files may be set aside as commercial spaces to be bought. All these, once packaged and downloaded onto the data-server, would then be attached to the mixed-down documentary wave-file and transmitted along with the audio on the scheduled broadcast day and time. Thereafter, whenever the documentary is streamed or transmitted, the accompanying screens will be flashed either on the PC monitor, or the DAB monitor attached to a DAB receiver.

FIGURE 5.12 Data Screens with Audio Frames

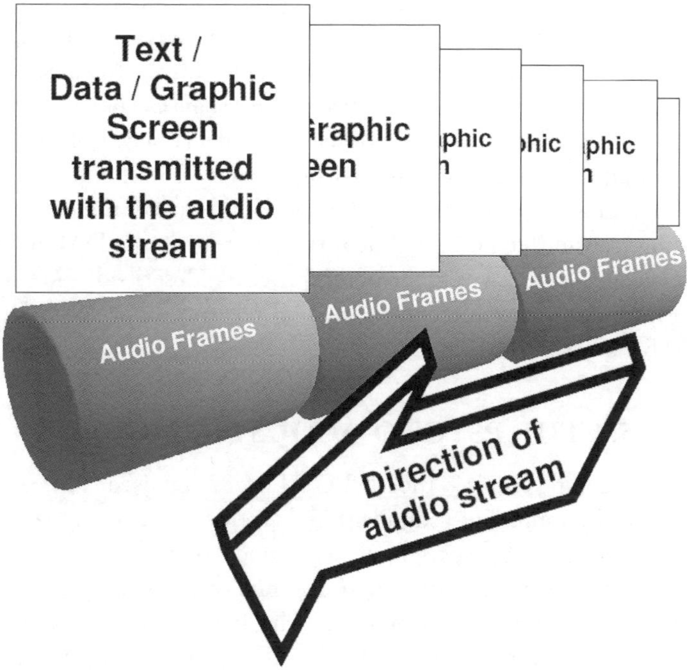

Rafael Oei 2004

177

There are no specific layouts for putting together a screen for DAB transmission to accompany the audio. Screens received by personal computers are limited to the size of the computer monitor or the limitations of the digital radio receiver software. When we consider configuring content for DAB, for instance, XML scripting is required for scalable screens. Until DAB monitors are able to decode Flash scripts, screen grabs and sizes are limited to the size of the optional monitors available to portable DAB receivers.

Choice of colours, font size and font type are important, especially for screens that are only, for instance, 3 by 2 inches to 5 by 5 inches. A rule of thumb, then, would be not to clutter the screen. Font and images would have to be scalable, or at least discernible enough (e.g., at least a 12 point for fonts) to ensure integrity in decoding the information and in displaying the information and graphics accurately, legibly and in sync with the transmitted audio.

The present DAB system transmits the data and audio components in a radio programme separately. Having the data and audio streamed through to the DAB multiplexer to be encoded for transmission separately has presented challenges in synchronising audio content to its associated data, text and graphical content. Transmission of data can be set according to a specifically scheduled time in order for the data to be displayed along with the audio or programmed to be displayed immediately upon decoding. This has to be calculated based on the size of the data screen file being transmitted and the time it takes to refresh the DAB monitor on the receiver-end. An example of this process is described below under a description of the architecture of a DAB receiver. First, let us look at the DAB carrier bit-stream.

5.2 THE PSYCHO-ACOUSTIC MODEL

The source coding employs the MPEG 1 Layer 2 standard. This reduces the bit rate by removing redundant and irrelevant audio signals from transmitted audio using a psycho-acoustic model based on the limitations of the human ear in detecting the full range of audio frequencies and frequencies that have been masked. The listener will only discern transmitted audio that is perceived to be CD-quality. Briefly, this is how that is achieved:

A CD signal is normally quantised at 16 bits per sample. The signal to quantisation noise ratio is 96 dB measured against 0 dBFS (full scale digital coding limit = 0). Reducing the quantisation step-size increases the quantisation noise relative to the audio signal. However, when a tone is perceived by the human ear, signals that are close in frequency to that tone remains inaudible, or "masked". The human ear also has a hearing threshold beyond which, it is unable to detect further audio signals. This has been called "perceptual coding" (Hoeg and Lauterbach 2001, pp. 75–76).

To use this phenomenon to good effect, the signal is split into small frequency regions. Within each region, as the bit rate is reduced, the quantisation noise increases. However, it remains masked and below the frequency signal. This minimum masked threshold is calculated to determine the maximum possible noise level for each band. It is the difference between the maximum signal level and the minimum masked threshold that is used to determine the quantised level in each sub-band. In the case of MPEG audio codec, each signal is split into 32 sub-bands before the quantisation step-size is reduced.

While there are two basic psycho-acoustic models that may be applied to various levels of the MPEG codec, this formula has been applied to the MPEG-1 standard for both layers 1 and 2 (ibid., pp. 77–78). This provides the efficient transmission mode used in the Eureka-147 DAB standard, with a block length of 36 sub-band samples corresponding to 1,152 input-audio Pulse Code Modulation (PCM) samples, as shown below, located in the "sub-band samples" segment of the bit-stream structure depicted in the following diagram:

FIGURE 5.13   MPEG 1 Layer 2 Bit-Stream Structure

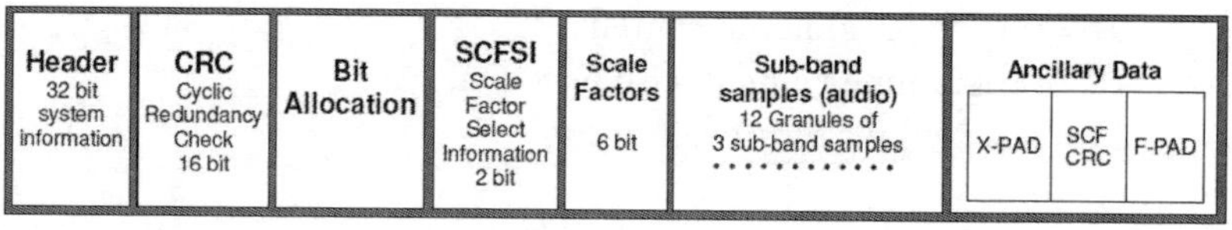

Header	CRC	Bit	SCFSI	Scale	Sub-band	Ancillary Data		
32 bit system information	Cyclic Redundancy Check 16 bit	Allocation	Scale Factor Select Information 2 bit	Factors 6 bit	samples (audio) 12 Granules of 3 sub-band samples ● ● ● ● ● ● ● ● ● ● ● ●	X-PAD	SCF CRC	F-PAD

Based on Hoeg and Lauterbach 2001, pp. 80–83.

The MPEG-1 Layer 2 audio frame used as the DAB audio frame carries all the information necessary for the DAB receiver's decoder to produce an audio signal at its output. Generally, the audio mode supports:

179

- One-channel mono mode.
- Two-channel stereo mode.
- Dual-channel mode that allows the listener the option of listening to the same programme in two different languages.
- Joint stereo mode that preserves the stereo audio output while reducing the transmitted data further. Of course this also takes up channel-space that may be used for other services.

5.3 PROGRAMME ASSOCIATED DATA (PAD)

Each frame also carries bytes that may be used for Programme Associated Data (PAD) that relates to the transmitted audio. The PAD consists of the Fixed Programme Associated Data (F-PAD) control channel at a data rate of 0.7 kbit/s, and the optional Extended Programme Associated Data (X-PAD) with capacities of up to 64 kbit/s. Added capacity to carry independent data or information pertaining to text, still images or video packets is transported through the Multimedia Object Transfer (MOT) protocol described below.

Information for Dynamic Range Control (DRC) is carried within the F-PAD segment of the Ancillary Data area of the structure. This controls the range between the highest and lowest signal level of the audio programme. A gain variation of 15 dB is coded in a 6-bit digital word within each 24 ms audio signal frame linearly. Music and Speech (M/S) Control information is also located within this segment, allowing the listener to balance the volume levels of music or spoken-word programming. Four modes are provided for:

00 = music programme content
01 = speech programme content
10 = programme content with no signal
11 = reserved for future definition

Apart from carrying data and information to accompany the audio programme, the F-PAD also carries information about the size of the extended data transport channel or Extended Programme Associated Data (X-PAD).

The X-PAD itself carries extra information and data that may be used for Dynamic Label or "DAB Radiotext." This is text information and control characters with a length of up to 128 characters within the

PAD channel. Information about the Multimedia Object Transfer (MOT) protocol also resides in this section of the bit-stream structure. As will be discussed in the next section, this includes data for still images, HTML content, services transported in packet mode and even video files compressed into packets.

5.4 MULTIMEDIA OBJECT TRANSFER PROTOCOL

The Multimedia Object Transfer (MOT) protocol is a transport protocol. This vehicle enables the transmission of multimedia content in DAB data channels to various receivers with multimedia capabilities. The general structure of the MOT object frame is shown below:

FIGURE 5.14   Structure of the MOT object frame

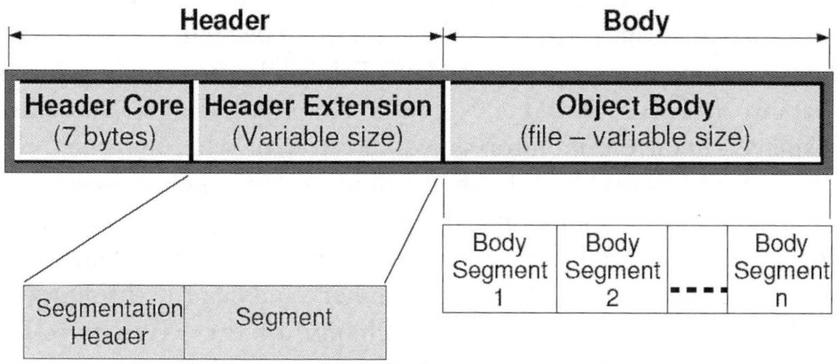

Based on Hoeg and Lauterbach 2001, p. 102.

The maximum object length is 255 Mbytes. The Object Body contains the object to be transported, which may be HTML, JPEG, MPEG audio or video, TIFF or XML files. During transportation, the object is divided into segments small enough to lower the probability of error within each segment during transport. These segments are continuously transmitted to ensure integrity of the transported object, especially large objects, when it is reassembled at receiver-side.

As noted in the figure above, the Header Core is fixed while the Header Extension is variable in size as this is the segment that carries all the information required to identify an attached object. During transmission of the object, the header information is separated from the body of the frame to allow that information to be compared against the segmented content data of the object being transmitted numerous times, during the decoding process, to establish the integrity of the reintegrated content at the receiver-end. This reduces error and maintains the integrity of the object transfer.

Among the parameters within the Header Extension is the "ContentName." This contains the unique name or identifier of the object. Next is the "TriggerTime" parameter. This specifies the time, coded in short or long UTC (Coordinated Universal Time) format. The setting of zero means "now," specifically instructing that the object be displayed immediately after it has been completely received. Otherwise, the object would be displayed according to the set time—in synchrony with the audio event, or as a space-time event within an audio broadcast.

When the TriggerTime parameter is set to zero or "now," it immediately displays the object content upon decoding. If the object body consists of a sequence of JPEG (Joint Photographic Experts Group) or PNG (Portable Network Graphics) images, these are displayed upon the monitor as a slide show or what is termed the "Asynchronous MOT Slide Show" (ibid. p. 106). This presentation of images may be done cyclically or in a single sequence. To change the object, the producer or content editor will either change the "ContentName" or the "VersionNumber" and send it through the multiplex again. This triggers a change of the "TransportID" (transport identity) to enable the DAB receiver, DAB terminal or PC to receive the new incoming object. The decoding delay for JPEG images is from two to 20 seconds depending on the size and complexity of the image.

For the object to be displayed at a predetermined time in sync with the audio, a predefined time is specified by the TriggerTime. To ensure that both the audio event and, for instance, the displayed image are synchronised, check that the time transmitted within the Fast Information Channel (FIC) of the DAB transmission system is the same as the time reference used for the service generation. Due to the delay during decoding, the object images of the timed MOT image or slide show should be broadcast in advance of the trigger time. At the moment, to generate a "smooth" slide show of images, each object should be 30 to 60 seconds apart. The reason for delays to the synchronised and asynchronous slide shows may become apparent as the mechanics of a DAB receiver are explained in the next section.

In summary, as time synchronisation of audio signals to associated data is crucial, PAD insertion should be done by the producer or content manager. The possible services that may be provided through the PAD are:

- The alphanumeric Dynamic Label. DAB receivers are typically able to display 32 characters per two lines of 64 characters per four lines.
- Multimedia Object Transport (MOT) protocol which allows audio-visual information to be transported (including image files and HTML content) either in PAD or packet mode.
- Broadcasting websites.
- Synchronised or asynchronous slide shows. Based on Hoeg and Lauterbach (2001), transmission times of MOT services are as follows:

TABLE 5.1   Examples of MOT Transmission Times

Content	No. of files	File Size	Transmission Time*	
			PAD	Packet Mode
		kbytes	*seconds*	*seconds*
CD Cover (JPEG) *Resolution: 320X240 pixels*	1	14	7	7
CD Cover (JPEG) *Resolution: 640X480 pixels*	1	42	22	22
HTML file (Text only)	1	1	0.5	0.5
HTML files 37	129	66	63	

*Data rate = 16 kbit/s
SOURCE: Hoeg & Lauterbach 2001, p. 124

For a full discussion of the mechanics and workflow of generating audio and content for digital transmission within a modified radio broadcast environment, see *Borderless Bandwidth: DNA of Digital Radio* (Oei 2002).

Having outlined some of the considerations of content generation through an explanation of the general architecture of Eureka 147-DAB, a basic schematic of the production workflow between Programmer, Producer/Presenter and Music Director, who formulates the daily broadcast playlist, would look like the following:

FIGURE 5.15 Production/Content Generation Workflow

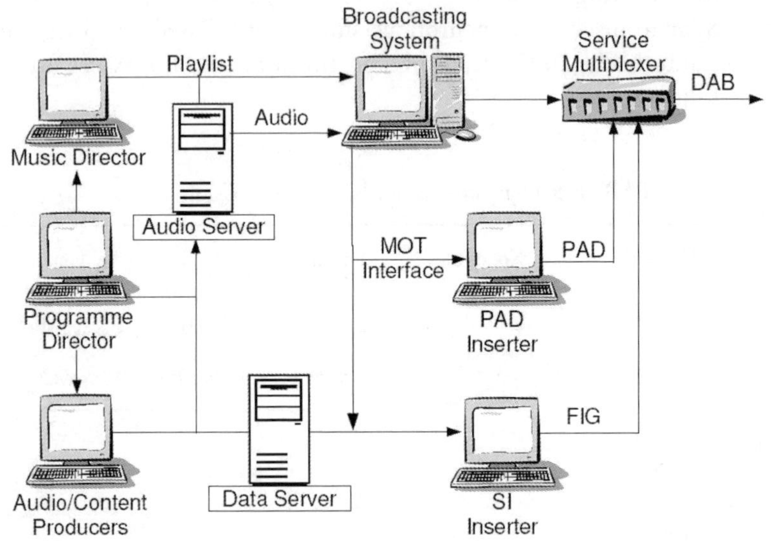

Rafael Oei 2004

5.5 ARCHITECTURE OF A DAB RECEIVER

Information on real time decoding and streaming of DAB audio through a personal computer environment is from the team of Darran Nathan, Berhard Sputh, Oliver Faust and Chua Beng Koon in their research paper presented to IEEE Transactions on Consumer Electronics (2002). This team at Ngee Ann Polytechnic's Digital Signal Processing/Digital Audio Broadcasting Technology Centre (DSP/DAB Technology Centre) is one

FIGURE 5.16 NP-DWS-USB-DAB Receiver

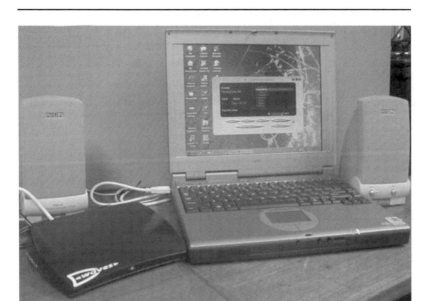

of the foremost digital media research teams in Southeast Asia. This was the same team that produced the then NP-DWS-USB-DAB (Ngee Ann Polytechnic, Digital Wireless Systems Pte Ltd, Universal Serial Bus, Digital Audio Broadcasting) Receiver in 2000/2001. Their present research delves into software-driven digital media that extends into Digital Video Broadcasting and other digital transmission systems. At the time of writing, the team had developed two data service decoding software packages for decoding stream Dynamic Label Segments, and Slide Show and Packet mode for the broadcast website. The two software programmes were written in Java language and can easily be adapted for use with any commercial DAB receiver module. For the moment, the off-air decoding feature is designed for educational purposes, and is intended for use with archive test file streams.

For the purpose of producing data content by radio producers and presenters, this section will now explain the process behind data and audio decoding through a DAB receiver linked to a personal computer. This enables a wide range of data processing utilising inherent PC operating system technology. By understanding the process behind data and audio decoding on the DAB receiver end, producers may have a better idea of how to conceptualise and provide data for their audio programmes. Figure 5.17 is a simplified block diagram of the USB-DAB receiver, the structure of the above NP-DWS-USB-DAB Receiver (for personal computers).

The USB-DAB receiver complies with the European Eureka 147 DAB standard that offers a multi-carrier Orthogonal Frequency Division Multiplexing (OFDM) modulation scheme. DAB frames within this scheme have fields defined for both data and audio. This system uses the Single Frequency Network (SFN) model that utilises converging broadcast signals to create redundancies in the signal to maintain a robust reception in the DAB receiver at all times. Advanced source and channel coding, along with spectral efficiency of the modulation scheme, makes this superior to the FM (Frequency Modulation) scheme in place for over 40 years.

Being attached to a computer, the receiver depends on the PC to perform all the control, decoding, and applications. All the DAB receiver does, in this instance, is perform the Radio Frequency (RF) conversion and channel decoding (Nathan, Sputh, Faust & Chua 2001).

FIGURE 5.17 USB-DAB Receiver Diagram

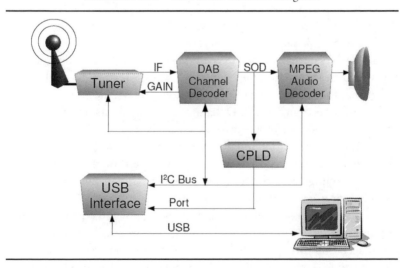

Based on Nathan, Sputh, Faust & Chua 2001.

The main components of the model are:

- The Tuner, to enable reception of the broadcast frequency, to mix down the selected DAB ensemble to the Intermediate Frequency (IF) that connects to the channel decoder. In this case, an integrated amplifier is also present to increase the signal strength if necessary; as in the case of mobile reception.
- The DAB chipset, or channel decoder. This chipset demodulates and decodes the incoming DAB signal. If it receives a user request for a particular sub-channel from the microcontroller over the I²C bus, the DAB audio frames are streamed out from the Serial Output Data (SOD) pin to the MPEG (Motion Pictures Experts Group) decoder—sending the audio to the speaker.
- The I²C bus is a three-wire bus that provides serial communications between two chips in master and slave mode. Every slave chip on this bus has a unique address to allow the master to target data transfers at particular slaves along a common bus.
- The CPLD (Complex Programmable Logic Device) supplies data from the SOD clocked at 384 kHz in this model. It performs a serial-to-parallel conversion of the bit stream, sending an interrupt to the 8051 microcontroller in the USB (Universal Serial Bus) Interface after every 8 bits, slowing down the stream for the 8051 to handle the data.
- The USB Interface consists of three main parts—the Serial Interface Engine (SIE), the 8051 microcontroller, and the I²C Master. The SIE packs and extracts data in compliance with the USB protocol. The 8051 reads the incoming data over the USB by accessing registers within the SIE. This data is then passed on to the I²C Master which sends the data out to the I²C bus.
- The Personal Computer (PC) runs the main application that controls the DAB board. It decodes the FIC (Fast Information Channel) and Programme Associated Data (PAD), and presents a user interface to allow the user to select parameters like the DAB ensemble frequency and service sub-channels. The FIC contains metadata information on the audio and data services from a selected ensemble while the PAD, as mentioned above and else where, contains defined fields in a DAB audio frame that carries non-audio data.

This model is able to generate a continuous uninterrupted real time stream from the DAB channel decoder through to a client device, such as another PC. As there are multiple layers involved in the processing of data flowing through, there will be complications with synchronising trigger times, congestion, possible lost packets, and jitter and breaks in the audio output. This is reduced by a system of buffers assigned within the PC.

In a system such as the above, a radio producer/presenter creating content will have to note that the MPEG-1 Layer 2 standard separates audio data into frames of 24 ms, transmitting one frame every 24 ms. To achieve a continuous decoded audio output stream, the MPEG decoder has to receive one MPEG frame every 24 ms.

With the CPLD channelling data through at 384 kHz, that means that 384,000 bits are being transported in one second. Calculating this to 24 ms gives us 9,216 bits transmitted for every frame. At 128 kbps, we get 3,072 bits per frame. Based on a clock rate of 384 kHz, the time taken to transmit 3,072 bits per frame would be 8 ms. Given processing time, size of buffer and the data content, along with the decoding time of the audio content in the bit-stream, data and image screen refreshes takes the better part of 15 seconds. And so packet and image sizes are crucial to enabling the content to be displayed in a timely fashion, in sync where needed, and without interrupting the audio flow.

Webcasting is more straightforward as data and audio are fused together in a drag-and-drop manner using software similar to Windows Media Authoring. Creating images in a Windows environment is familiar to most people used to using word processors and draw/paint software. These images are automatically decoded and compressed when they are imported into an editing session in the media authoring software.

Compounded with the habits of radio listening, which remain largely an aural event, listeners are not compelled to purchase DAB receivers with monitors to enjoy their normal radio listening. And so, DAB monitors have remained an option and are not in great demand. The result is a greater range of DAB receivers sans the monitors. The product catalogue has now extended to include energy efficient handheld DAB receivers, where in the past, the DAB chipset drained the attached batteries within minutes due to the amount of processing that was involved. More domestic DAB receivers, designed for the home, have also surfaced since the publication of *Borderless Bandwidth: DNA of Digital*

Radio (Oei 2002). A list of DAB receiver products can be accessed at the World DAB Forum's website (http://www.worldDAB.org/).

5.6 MORE THAN A DECADE

Although developed in 1987, digital radio and Digital Audio Broadcasting (DAB) Eureka-147 only came to the forefront with some excitement in the mid-1990s. The first article on DAB Eureka-147, in Singapore, was by Dr Roland Tan in 1993 for the Audio Engineering Society. Six years later, in 1999, Singapore was the first in Southeast Asia to launch digital radio services using the DAB system. Germany had services running a few years prior to that, and broadcasters at the National Association of Broadcasters and the Broadcast Education Association conferences in the United States have been conferring about it for almost half a decade. England and the Netherlands produced digital broadcast services with much agony. Other countries remain cautious and are slowly providing similar services.

And yet, amongst all the excitement and initial flurry of the digital media blitz, wireless telecommunication services have overtaken the promise of digital broadcast media with cellular telephones that are mini-media and personal management organising centres. It is ironic that the wireless telephony service that was to revolutionise telecommunication services by being wireless and portable, thereby being the first "cellular telephone" in the 1920s, eventually became an information and entertainment medium for the masses—the radio. More ironical is the digital radio using systems like Digital Audio Broadcasting (DAB) Eureka-147 (developed to address the lack of spectrum space in radio frequencies, and possessing the potential in its now vast free-to-air digital bandwidth to include other data, visual and audio services along with the traditional radio transmission) has now been overshadowed by digital cellular telephones. Cellphones, eagerly embraced by consumers, deliver more information and entertainment (to the extent of even being a mini-digital camera) yet remain a telecommunication device.

Nevertheless, to reiterate, the potential in a digital broadcast environment described in *Borderless Bandwidth: DNA of Digital Radio* (Oei 2002), and as Hendy (2000) observes in the following is undeniable:

> Digital broadcasting not only creates the conditions for an expansion in the number of radio channels, it also moves the industry

technologically towards the multimedia future demanded by commercial imperatives. Radio will be produced and distributed by organizations with interests in other media, but also *consumed* by listeners using domestic technology that rolls together picture, data and audio services. (Hendy 2000, p. 56)

The recent advances in broadcast technologies have provided various means to transmit traditional radio services. As outlined in *Borderless Bandwidth: DNA of Digital Radio* (Oei 2002), interactivity in digital radio services is evident in web streaming, telecommunication services that offer radio transmissions and Internet surfing, and the ubiquity that is currently mobile telecommunications. However, as mentioned in the Introduction to this volume, the next generation cellular phones will be structured on Wide Orthogonal Frequency Division Multiplex (WOFDM), which is basically the DAB architecture developed initially for digital radio services.

5.7 DATA SERVICES AND MISSED OPPORTUNITIES

With the proliferation of advanced communications technology, radio listeners today are also web-surfers who communicate daily over the Internet and who are more than familiar with researching and information gathering over the "Web." This is the era of information users and contributors where radio listeners interact and are connected with information on demand. Brief descriptions of available services, discussed in *Borderless Bandwidth* (ibid.), and contemporary telecommunication examples clearly demonstrate the proliferation of on-demand information models already available to consumer-users.

> When virtually everything becomes a service, capitalism is transformed from a system based on exchanging goods to one based on accessing segments of experiences. (Rifkin 2000, p. 94)

Key to these services is the flow of information and the medium in which the consumer-user receives it. Castells (2000) in describing the "information technology paradigm" presents five characteristics. The first is that "information is its raw material," the second refers to the "pervasiveness of effects of new technologies" where information "directly shapes" society through new technological media. The third refers to the increasing complexity of the network in supporting "the creative power of such interaction" with the information. The fourth characteristic of the "IT paradigm" lies in its flexibility where "processes are reversible" and "organizations and institutions can be modified." The fifth characteristic has been the focus of this and my previous book (Oei 2002) in the context of radio broadcasting. This is the "convergence of specific technologies into a highly integrated system" where "separate technological trajectories become literally indistinguishable" (Castells 2000, pp. 70–72).

Castells succinctly adds a sentiment that has been central in *Borderless Bandwidth* (Oei 2002); that radio services will evolve beyond audio programming and that institutional radio will reorganise to support this. He said: "Data transmission becomes the predominant, universal form of communication. And data transmission is based on software instructions of coding and decoding" (Castells 2000, p 72). Unfortunately, it seems that institutional radio has been slow in meeting the challenge, evidenced by the development of mobile telecommunication services that have enhanced multimedia capabilities. Castells observed that "business control over the first stages of development of multimedia systems" is imperative (ibid., p. 397). That phase has since gone past broadcasters, not organised nor having the business structure to go beyond radio as an audio medium. And so broadcasters were unable to take quick advantage of the broad bandwidth and potential that digital radio suddenly offered.

The consumer market is now flooded with various FM and digital radio receivers, mini-disc players, MP3 players, and devices from service providers like Command Audio, that allow the listener to pre-programme for selected preferences in listening. Companies that provide news and stock services are able to update data and information and, with their permission, automatically download these into the customer's handheld devices like the PDA and even the cellular phone. The customer then has access to the latest news, information and data the next time access is made into the service. What, then, is the new face of the digital radio broadcaster?

CHAPTER 6

Conclusion

Borderless Bandwidth: DNA of Digital Radio (Oei 2002) was initially written to introduce the architecture of Eureka-147 DAB and its implications on the existing organisational structure of institutionalised radio. There had been a lack of literature covering digital audio broadcasting in 1998, although worldwide, excitement was mounting about the digital media revolution. It was evident at the time that the structure and paradigm of most radio organisations were ill-equipped to take advantage of the full potential of DAB. Radio stations, abuzz with digital fervour, streamed traditional FM-style programming through the digital bandwidth. This reminded me of lecturers who transferred and scanned reams of lecture worksheets and notes onto servers, while proudly announcing that they had an interactive online e-learning site. It also brings to mind educators who reproduced transparencies, used on overhead projectors from old lectures, on PowerPoint; although PowerPoint had the potential to create dynamic animated content accompanied by appropriate multimedia content. And so, *Borderless Bandwidth* (ibid.) explored the need to re-think, re-structure and re-focus the business and organisational paradigms of radio broadcasting. *Riding the Bandwidth: Producing for Digital Radio* extends that discussion into the content that flows through the digital bandwidth.

This book brings the reader back to the rationale and basics of radio broadcast production and presentation. The focus has intentionally been on methods and principles that aspiring broadcasters can adapt and build upon, rather than specific "how to" directions. These are tools that a broadcaster may also adapt to whatever technology that may emerge after digital broadcasting. As the potential of the broadcast media technology expands, so will broadcast services and the means to provide those services by broadcasters. It is inevitable that broadcast content and services will be enhanced, as consumers and users of digital media expect it.

Communities exist by sharing common meanings and common forms of communications. While this relationship seems obvious, it's often overlooked in discussions of communications, the implicit assumption being that communication is a phenonmenon in and of itself, independent of the social context it interprets and reproduces. Anthropologists argue that communications cannot be divorced from community and culture (Rifkin 2000, p. 139).

I have traced this relationship between the medium and the masses from Chapters One through to Five, showing how each influenced the other, causing both the medium, and the perception of the consumer–user, to adapt and evolve. And so, as the relentless digital technological march continues, it is imperative that traditional institutional radio provide the necessary inhouse education and work environment that encourages the creation of digital broadcast programme content and services for the masses through digital broadcast bandwidths; hence the title: *Riding the Bandwidth*. In summary, then, let us look at the focus behind preparing media students and traditional broadcasters for the digital world.

6.1 EDUCATING RADIO BROADCASTERS

Once considered a glorified wireless telegraph transmitter and receiver, the radio, known originally as "wireless telegraphy or wireless telephony" (Richardson 2001, p. 4; Douglas 1999, p. 9; Fang 1997, p. 89), has been relegated to being one of the many services received by the digital cellular telephone, and other digital media devices. Meanwhile, media educators have re-configured and re-organised courses to include modules on digital systems, compression formats, streaming technologies, and editing software to prepare media students for digital broadcasting on radio and the television.

Veteran radio broadcasters remain comfortable in their daily on-air shifts doing what they have done for decades. It has been said that as a career, radio is the medium with which you are able to grow old with because the listener is not able see you. Listeners just fall in love with the voice and the personality. On the other hand, digital technology has enabled listeners to be brought into the studio, beside the radio deejay as he or she spins popular songs, or presents the news. The interaction, connecting immediately, can now be both visual and auditory. How can two worlds reconcile in the same environment?

193

One of the most intriguing social aspects of learning is that, despite the metaphor of apprenticeship, the relationships involved in enculturation are not simply ones of novice and expert. Putting learners in contact with "the best in the field" has definite value. Peers turn out to be, however, an equally important resource (Brown & Duguid 2002, p. 221).

As an approach to learning, it is conceptually sound. Peer tutoring and industry attachments have benefitted students of all disciplines as real-world scenarios and functioning in the actual work environment provides tangible learning opportunities that the classroom cannot fully recreate. On the other hand, the above could also imply the reverse: that even if media students graduate with a host of skills in producing content-rich programming for digital delivery, and are ready to face the digital camera in the radio broadcast studio, it may be in vain if the broadcast environment, programmers and immediate supvisors (the "best in the field") insist on remaining lost in the world of FM programming.

While radio remains primarily an audio experience, the first transformations occurred in recent years as the digital revolution spawned diverse digital telecommunication devices to whet the consumers' appetite for information, novelty and entertainment. The danger with the influx, popularity and familiarity with digital media is the perception that media students and broadcasters must now only be educated with the latest software, hardware and techniques to optimise the digital domain. I agree that media students need to learn all there is to know about functioning within a digital production environment. However, the journey must begin with mastering the basic concepts of radio production and presentation. This includes understanding the process of radio as a medium of communication. Once the student is familiar with the nature of radio broadcasting, an attempt can be made to conceptualise content that is radio- or listener-friendly. The ability to create and produce the concept, to clearly transfer the thought onto paper and into some discernible structure, are essential to a producer-presenter. Methods of writing for the ear, editing, producing and presenting effectively for an aural medium that is transient (unless a listener records a programme and plays it repeatedly over again) are not simple. I have included an introduction to these in this book, using practical approaches to producing and presenting radio content that I have used in my own workshops, and in my broadcast career. These exercises work best under supervision, and the learning that occurs in the student must be coached and directed as no two students perceive information in the same way, nor will their output and performance be identical.

Media students may want to extend the study of the subject through many notable books available in the market; for instance by Melvin Mencher, Mervin Block, Michael Kaye, Andrew Popperwell, Martin Shingler, Cindy Wieringa and Robert McLeish, who go further into writing and producing for the radio. Foundational grounding in the skills mentioned above will then support the media student or broadcaster through the study and use of the vast array of available digital software and editing systems that promise to produce and deliver the best digital broadcast experience.

If we agree that technological advances produces the emergence of a "new society," it follows that despite historical influences, structural transformation is inevitable; made possibly by consumer–users who, through modified behaviour, adapt and assimilate new technologies into daily life. Castells, in *End of Millennium* (1998), notes:

> A new society emerges when and if a structural transformation can be observed in the relationships of production, in the relationships of power, and in the relationships of experience. These transformations lead to an equally substantial modification of social forms of space and time, and to the emergence of a new culture (Castells 1998, p. 340).

Castells adds that in order to enable a community of adaptable individuals, education is essential, as opposed to skills training.

> The concept of education must be distinguished from skills. Skills can be quickly made obsolete by technological and organizational change. Education (as distinct from the warehousing of children and students) is the process by which people, that is labor, acquire the capability constantly to redefine the necessary skills for a given task, and to access the sources for learning these skills. Whoever is educated, in the proper organizational environment, can reprogram him/herself toward the endlessly changing tasks of the production process (ibid., p. 341).

By extension then, educators, being custodians of knowledge and sometimes trend spotters and setters, are bound by their profession to produce responsible, knowledgeable and responsive media producers, presenters, programmers, consumers and users. The outcome of receiving an education is in the ability to understand the rationale behind processes, to be able to analyse, synthesise, expand beyond the known, and tap into the source of the skills required. To understand the process is to have the ability to adapt and respond to a constantly evolving environment.

And so, to attract and maintain a healthy listener base, a paradigm shift is needed in the radio production process that will build on already inherent production knowledge to meet the demands of the consumer–user who expects to interact with data and information. To understand these needs and to utilise available technology, producers will now have to think beyond producing merely aural experiences and extend the already familiar production process to feed the other senses as well.

6.2 SO WHAT NOW, THE WIRELESS?

Back in 1998, when I first introduced Eureka-147 DAB into the Advanced Radio Production module, Mass Communication students were excited with the prospect of the digital radio. Some despaired because they felt it was the demise of "traditional" radio. Consequently, there were similar responses with every batch of third-year radio students. We discussed the implications for the radio stations, the listeners and the business potential available in creating companies that would provide data content, design and information services to aggregate and enhance existing audio content. Those students had realised that there was a vast amount of content that had to be re-purposed and re-aggregated for digital radio transmission and digital archiving.

While business opportunities abound in digital broadcast media, radio stations, media conglomerates, and listeners, have almost become lukewarm about the prospect of a digital radio future, and of developing systems like Eureka-147 further. In fact, consumers are mostly excited about the latest digital cellular telephone or handheld multimedia devices and regard digital radio as simply just another audio service streamed through the Internet. Nevertheless, the broadcast media landscape is vastly different from a decade ago and will continue to evolve dramatically over the next decade. The ability to produce for multimedia transmission will be an important skill to possess even though consumer uptake for digital radios is ponderous. The reality is, we have grown to depend on the ubiquity of digital media services. To increase its competitive edge, institutional radio, through digital radio broadcasting, will expand and deliver enhanced digital broadcast services to its consumer-users. Taking the digital broadcast revolution beyond its novelty will determine the quality and relevance of digital radio content and services being developed, produced and streamed through the digital airwaves; riding on the immense potential present in the digital broadcast bandwidth.

Bibliography

Ang, Ien. 1991. *Desperately Seeking the Audience*. London: Routledge.

Ang, Ien. 1996. *Living Room Wars: Rethinking Media Audiences for a Postmodern World*. London: Routledge.

Ang Peng Hwa. 2000. Tension and Creativity: Singapore's Media in Transition. In *inform.educate.entertain@sg: Arts & Media in Singapore*. Singapore: Ministry of Information and the Arts, pp. 88–119.

Ang Peng Hwa, and Sankaran Ramanathan, eds. 2000. *Communication Education and Media Training Needs in ASEAN*. Singapore: Asian Media Information and Communication Centre and School of Communication Studies, Nanyang Technological University.

Arbitron Inc. 2001. *How Kids and Tweens Use and Respond to Radio*. Available online: http://www.arbitron.com/downloads/childrensradio_wi00.pdf

Arbitron Inc. 2002. *Radio Today 2001: How America Listens to Radio*. Available online: http://www.arbitron.com/downloads/radiotoday01.pdf

Arbitron Inc., and Edison Media Research. 2000. *Radio Station Web Site Content: An In-depth Look*. Available online: http://www.arbitron.com/downloads/radiostationwebstudy.pdf

Arbitron Inc., and Edison Media Research. 2002. *Internet 9: The Media and Entertainment World of Online Consumers*. Available online: http://www.arbitron.com/downloads/I9Presentation.pdf

Arbitron Inc., and Edison Media Research. 2003. *Internet and Multimedia 10: The Emerging Digital Consumer*. Available online: http://www.arbitron.com/downloads/Internet10Presentation.pdf

Bennis, Warren. 1997. Rethinking Leadership: Becoming a Leader of Leaders. In *Rethinking the Future: Rethinking Business, Principles, Competition, Control & Complexity, Leadership, Markets and the World*. Edited by Rowan Gibson. London: Nicholas Brealey Publishing, p. 152.

Blair, Robin. 1999. *Digital Techniques in Broadcasting Transmission*. Boston: Focal Press.

Block, Mervin, and Joe Durso Jr. 1998. *Writing News for TV and Radio*. Chicago: Bonus Books.

British Broadcasting Corporation. *History of the BBC*. Available online at http://www.bbc.co.uk/thenandnow/history/ (accessed 1 October 2002).

Brown, John Seely, and Paul Duguid. 2002. *The Social Life of Information*. Massachusetts: Harvard Business School Press.

Brown, Michael. 1998. Radio Magazines and the Development of Broadcasting: Radio Broadcast and Radio News, 1922–1930. In *Journal of Radio Studies* 5, no. 1. Washington DC: Broadcast Education Association, pp. 68–81.

Bucy, Erik P., ed. 2002. *Living in the Information Age: A New Media Reader*. California: Thomson Wadsworth.

Campbell, Richard. 2000. *Media and Culture: An Introduction to Mass Communication*. Second edition. Boston, New York: Bedford/St. Martins.

Castells, Manuel. 2000. *The Rise of the Network Society.* Massachusetts: Blackwell Publishers.

Castells, Manuel. 1998. *End of Millennium.* Massachusetts: Blackwell Publishers.

Castells, Manuel. 1997. *The Power of Identity.* Massachusetts: Blackwell Publishers.

Chaston, Ian. 2001. *E-Marketing Strategy.* Singapore: McGraw-Hill Publishing Co.

Chan Meng Khoong, ed. 1999. *IT2010: Beyond the Web Lifestyle.* Prentice Hall.

Chen Ai Yen. 1997. The Mass Media, 1819–1980. In *A History of Singapore.* Edited by Ernest Chew C. T. and Edwin Lee. Singapore: Oxford University Press, pp. 288–311.

Chowdhury, Subir, ed. 2000. *Management 21C: Someday We'll All Manage this Way.* London: Pearson Education.

Clark, Bruce H. 1997. Welcome to My Parlour... In *Internet Marketing: Readings and Online Resources.* Edited by Paul Richardson (2001). Singapore: McGraw-Hill Book Co., pp. 66–79.

Crane, Diana, Nobuko Kawashima, and Ken'ichi Kawasaki, eds. 2002. *Global Culture: Media, Arts, Policy, and Globalization.* New York: Routledge.

Crisell, Andrew. 1994. *Understanding Radio.* 2nd edition. London: Routledge.

Crook, Tim. 1999. *Radio Drama Theory and Practice.* London: Routledge.

Daniels, Tom D., Barry K. Spiker, and Michael J. Papa. 1997. *Perspectives on Organizational Communication.* 4th edition. Chicago: Brown & Benchmark Publishers.

Dickey, Lew. 1994. *The Franchise: Building Radio Brands.* Washington DC: National Association of Broadcasters.

Dizard Jr., Wilson. 1993. *Old Media New Media: Mass Communications in the Information Age.* New York: Addison-Wesley Publishing Co.

Douglas, Susan Jeanne. 1999. *Listening in: Radio and the American Imagination, from Amos 'n' Andy and Edward R. Murrow to Wolfman Jack and Howard Stern.* New York: Random House Inc.

Drucker, Peter F. 2002. *Management Challenges for the 21st Century.* Massachusetts: Butterworth-Heinemann.

Eureka 147 Project. 1997. *Eureka-147: Digital Audio Broadcasting.* Germany: Eureka 147 Project. Available online at http://www.worlddab.org/eureka.aspx (accessed August 1997).

Evans, Philip, and Thomas S. Wurster. 2000. *Blown to Bits: How the New Economics of Information Transforms Technology.* Massachusetts: Harvard Business School Press.

Fairclough, Norman. 1992. *Discourse and Social Change.* Cambridge: Polity Press.

Fairclough, Norman. 1995. *Media Discourse.* London: Arnold Publishers.

Fang, Irving E. 1997. *A History of Mass Communication: Six Information Revolutions.* Boston: Focal Press.

Fernandes, Allwyn. 1999. Managing Information and Media Relations in the New Media Age. In *Media Asia* 26, no. 3. Singapore: Asian Media Information and Communication Centre and School of Communication Studies, Nanyang Technological University, pp. 146–149.

Folkerts, Jean, Stephen Lacy, and Lucinda Davenport. 1998. *The Media in Your Life: An Introduction to Mass Communication*. Boston: Allyn and Bacon.

Fukuyama, Francis. 1999. *The Great Disruption: Human Nature and the Reconstitution of Social Order.* New York: The Free Press.

Garner, Joe, Walter Cronkite, and Bill Kurtis. 1998. *We Interrupt this Broadcast: Relive the Events that Stopped Our Lives ... from the Hindenburg to the Death of Princess Diana.* Illinois: Sourcebooks.

Gerber, Michael E. 1995. *The E-myth Revisited: Why Most Small Businesses Don't Work and What to Do About It.* New York: HarperBusiness.

Gibson, David. 1997. *The Art of Mixing: A Visual Guide to Recording, Mixing and Production.* California: Mix Books.

Gibson, Rowan. 1997. Rethinking Business. In *Rethinking the Future.* Edited by Rowan Gibson. London: Nicholas Brealey Publishing, p. 6.

Godin, Seth. 1999. *Permission Marketing: Turning Strangers into Friends and Friends into Customers*. New York: Simon & Schuster.

Goonasekera, Anura, and Eddie Kuo C. Y. 2000. Towards an Asian Theory of Communication? In *Asian Journal of Communication* 10, no. 2. Singapore: Asian Media Information and Communication Centre and School of Communication Studies, Nanyang Technological University.

Haeckel, Stephan H. 1998. About the Nature and Future of Interactive Marketing. In *Internet Marketing: Readings and Online Resources.* Edited by Paul Richardson (2001). Singapore: McGraw-Hill Book Co., pp. 13–22.

Hanson, Ward. 1998. The Original WWW: Web Lessons from the Early Days of Radio. In *Internet Marketing: Readings and Online Resources.* Edited by Paul Richardson (2001). Singapore: McGraw-Hill Book Co., pp. 3–12.

Harper, Christopher. 2002. *New Mass Media*. Boston: Houghton Mifflin Company.

Hauben, Michael. *History of ARPANET*. Available online at http://www.dei.isep.ipp.pt/docs/arpa.html (accessed 17 August 2001).

Hayes, Joy Elizabeth. 2000. Did Herbert Hoover Broadcast the First Fireside Chat? Rethinking the Origins of FDR's Radio Genius. In *Journal of Radio Studies* 7, no. 1. Washington DC: Broadcast Education Association, pp. 76–92.

Hendy, David. 2000. A Political Economy of Radio in the Digital Age. In *Journal of Radio Studies* 7, no. 1. Washington DC: Broadcast Education Association, pp. 213–234.

Hendy, David. 2000. *Radio in the Global Age*, Cambridge: Polity Press.

Hoeg, Wolfgang, and Thomas Lauterbach, eds. 2001. *Digital Audio Broadcasting, Principles and Applications.* Singapore: John Wiley & Sons.

Huey, John, ed. 1999. Businessman of the century. *Fortune*, vol. 140, no. 10.

Huey, John, ed. 1999, *Fortune*, vol. 140, no. 11, pp. 64–99, 102–112.

Infocomm Development Authority of Singapore. 2000. *Survey and Statistics on Information Technology Access and Usage in Singapore*. Available online at http://www.ida.gov.sg/Website/IDAContent.nsf/vSubCat/Infocomm+Facts+&+FiguresSurvey+Results?OpenDocument (accessed 27 September 2000).

Infocomm Development Authority of Singapore. 2002. *Broadband Usage in Singapore.* Available online at http://202.157.129.12/ida/fasttrack/html/archives/newsletter/20020722_surveys.html (accessed 25 July 2002).

Infocomm Development Authority of Singapore. 2002. *Connected Homes Programme.* Available online at http://www.ida.gov.sg/Website/IDAContent.nsf/vSubCat/Key+ProgrammesConnected+Homes+Programme+?OpenDocument (accessed 25 July 2002).

Infocomm Development Authority of Singapore. 2002. *General Information and Statistics.* Available online at http://www.ida.gov.sg/Website/IDAContent.nsf/dd1521f1e79ecf3bc825682f0045a340?OpenView (accessed 7 August 2002).

Jolaoso, Ronke. 1998. Digital Radio Broadcast Update. In *World DAB Forum Newsletter,* no. 8. London: WorldDAB Forum Project Office, pp. 4–5.

Jolaoso, Ronke. 1998. Digital Audio Broadcasting: Where Do We Stand Now? Paper presented at the *BroadcastAsia 98 Show Daily,* 5 June 1998, in Singapore. Singapore: Raffles Trade Press, pp. 18–20.

Kalakota, Ravi, and Marcia Robinson. 1999. *E-business: Roadmap for Success.* Massachusetts: Addison-Wesley Publishing Co.

Kaneb, Michael A. 2000. Forum. In *Journal of Radio Studies* 7, no. 1. Washington DC: Broadcast Education Association, pp. 1–7.

Kanter, Rosabeth Moss. 2001. *Evolve! Succeeding in the Digital Culture of Tomorrow.* Massachusetts: Harvard Business School Press.

Katz, Elihu, Michael Gurevitch, and Hadassah Haas. 1973. New Media Theory. In *Living in the Information Age: A New Media Reader.* 2002. Edited by Erik P. Bucy. California: Thomson Wadsworth.

Kau Ah Keng, Tan Soo Jiuan, and Jochen Wirtz. 1998. *Seven Faces of Singaporeans: Their Values, Aspirations, and Lifestyles.* Singapore: Pearson Education Asia.

Kaye, Michael, and Andrew Popperwell. 1995. *Making Radio: A Guide to Basic Radio Techniques.* Second edition. Bristol, UK: Broadcast Books.

Keith, Michael C. 2000. *The Radio Station.* Fifth edition. Boston: Focal Press.

Keith, Michael C. 2002. Casey Kasem: Reaching for the Stars. In *Journal of Radio Studies* 9, no. 1. Washington DC: Broadcast Education Association, pp. 92–96.

Keith, Michael C. website. Available online at http://www.michaelckeith.com/ (accessed 23 October 2000).

Koh, Gemma. 1995. Radio: The Way We Were. *Female,* October issue, Singapore edition, p. 135.

Korgaonkar, Pradeep K., and Lori D. Wolin. 1999. A Multivariate Analysis of Web Usage. In *Internet Marketing: Readings and Online Resources.* Edited by Paul Richardson (2001). Singapore: McGraw-Hill Book Co., pp. 80–100.

Landauer, Thomas K. 2002. The Productivity Puzzle. In *Living in the Information Age: A New Media Reader.* Edited by Erik P. Bucy. California: Thomson Wadsworth.

Lewis, Peter M., and Jerry Booth. 1990. *The Invisible Medium: Public, Commercial and Community Radio.* Washington DC: Howard University Press.

Liu, Gretchen. 1999. *Singapore: A Pictorial History 1819–2000.* Singapore: Archipelago Press and the National Heritage Board.

Loader, Brian D., ed. 1998. *Cyberspace Divide: Equality, Agency and Policy in the Information Society*. London: Routledge.

Lochte, Robert Henry. 2000. Invention and Innovation of Early Radio Technology. In *Journal of Radio Studies* 7, no. 1. Washington DC: Broadcast Education Association, pp. 93–115.

Low, Linda, ed. 1999. *Singapore: Towards A Developed Status*. Singapore: Centre for Advanced Studies, National University of Singapore and Oxford University Press.

Lury, Celia. 1996. *Consumer Culture*. Cambridge: Polity Press.

MacFarland, David T. 1997. *Future Radio Programming Strategies: Cultivating Listenership in the Digital Age*. New Jersey: Lawrence Erlbaum Associates, Inc.

Madanmohan, Rao, ed. 2002. *News Media and News Media: The Asia-Pacific Internet Handbook, Episode V*. Singapore: Eastern Universities Press.

Mahizhnan, Arun. 2001. Digital Divide: Will it Deepen or Diminish? In *Media Asia* 28, no. 2. Singapore: Asian Media Information and Communication Centre and School of Communication Studies, Nanyang Technological University.

Makimoto, Tsugio, and David Manners. 1997. *Digital Nomad*. Singapore: John Wiley & Sons.

Marconi Corporation plc. 2004. *Metropolitan-Vickers Ltd. (Metrovick) History*. Available online at http://www.marconi.com/html/about/metropolitanvickershistory.htm (accessed 1 February 2004).

McLeish, Robert. 1999. *Radio Production: A Manual for Broadcasters*. 4th edition. London: Focal Press.

McLuhan, Eric, and Frank Zingrone, eds. 1995. *Essential McLuhan*. New York: Basic Books.

McLuhan, Marshall. 1994. *Understanding Media: The Extensions of Man*. Massachusetts: The MIT Press.

McLuhan, Marshall, and Eric McLuhan. 1988. *Laws of Media: The New Science*. Toronto: University of Toronto Press.

McQuail, D., J. Blumler, and R. Brown. 1972. The Television Audience: A Revised Perspective. In *Sociology of Mass Communication*. Edited by Dennis McQuail. London: Longman.

McRae, Hamish. 1999. 20/20 Vision. *Fortune*, vol. 140, no. 10, p. 48.

Meister, John. 2001. *Overview of Computing History*. Available online at http://www.wagoneers.com/UNIX/computing-history.html (accessed 8 October 2002).

Mencher, Melvin. 1999. *Basic Media Writing*. 6th edition. Boston: McGraw-Hill College.

Miles, Peggy. 1998. *Internet World Guide to Webcasting: The Complete Guide to Broadcasting on the Web*. New York: John Wiley & Sons.

Miles, Peggy, and Dean Sakai, 2001, *Internet Age Broadcaster*. 2nd edition. Washington DC: National Association of Broadcasters.

Mukerjea, Dilip. 1998. *Braindancing: Brain-blazing Practical Techniques in Creativity for Immediate Application*. Singapore: The Brainware Press.

NAB Science and Technology Department. 1999. *A Broadcast Engineering Tutorial for Non-Engineers*. Washington DC: National Association of Broadcasters.

Nathan, Darran, Bernhard Sputh, Oliver Faust, and Chua Beng Koon. 2001. Software Architecture of a PC-based USB-DAB Receiver. Paper presented at the *DAB Short Course*, in Ngee Ann Polytechnic, Singapore.

Nathan, Darran, Bernhard Sputh, Oliver Faust, and Chua Beng Koon. 2002. Real-Time Decoding and Streaming of DAB Audio Frames by a User-Space Program Running on a Non-Real-Time OS. In *IEEE Transactions on Consumer Electronics* 48, issue 2. Institute of Electronic and Electrical Engineering, pp. 313–321.

Negronponte, Nicholas. 1995. *Being Digital*. New York: Vintage Books.

Norberg, Eric G. 1996. *Radio Programming: Tactics and Strategy*. Boston: Focal Press.

O'Connor, Joseph, and Ian McDermott. 1997. *The Art of Systems Thinking: Essential Skills for Creativity and Problem Solving*. London: Thorsons Publishers.

Oei, Rafael. 2002. *Borderless Bandwidth: DNA of Digital Radio*. Singapore: Times Academic Press.

Oon, Wilson. 2000. Applications & Potential Areas of Development for Digital Radio. Paper presented at the *Singapore DAB Forum*, 22 January 2000, in Singapore.

Oravec, Jo Ann. 2000. A Community of Iconoclasts: Art Bell, Talk Radio, and the Internet. In *Journal of Radio Studies* 7, no. 1. Washington DC: Broadcast Education Association, pp. 52–69.

Peacock, James. 2002. *Radio Ad Effectiveness Lab Research Compendium*. Peacock Research, Inc. (http://www.peacockresearch.com/) Report available online: http://www.radioadlab.org/library/RAEL_Compendium_firstedition.pdf

Pepper, Gerald L. 1995. *Communicating in Organizations*. New York: McGraw-Hill.

Powell, Larry, and Minabere Ibelema. 2000. Credibility of Radio News. In *Journal of Radio Studies* 7, no. 1. Washington DC: Broadcast Education Association, pp. 70–75.

Pugh, Derek S., David J. Hickson, and C. R. Hinings. 1971. *Writers on Organizations*. New York: Penguin Books.

Rabiner, Lawrence. 2002. Telecommunications, Media Technologies and Wireless: Three Keynote Lectures. Papers presented at the *Communication and Media Forum, Summer School Series*, 5–7 June 2002, in National University of Singapore and Nanyang Technological University, Singapore. Abstracts available online at http://www.comp.nus.edu.sg/~pris/summer_school/commedia.htm (accessed June 2004).

Radio Corporation of Singapore. 1999. *RCS Station Profiles*.

Radio Corporation of Singapore. 1999. *RCS Annual Report*.

Radio Corporation of Singapore. 1999. *RCS Audience Ratings*.

Radio Heatwave website. Available online at http://www.radioheatwave.cjb.net/ (accessed March 2003).

Radio Singapore. 1959. *Radio Singapore: How it All Began*. Singapore: Government Printing Office.

Rappa, Antonio L. 2002. *Modernity and Consumption: Theory, Politics, and the Public in Singapore and Malaysia*. New Jersey: World Scientific Publishing Co.

Rediffusion Singapore. 1995. *Rediffusion Corporate Brochure*.

Reese, David E., Mary E. Beadle, and Alan R. Stephenson. 2000. *Broadcast Announcing Worktext: Performing for Radio, Television and Cable*. London: Focal Press.

Richardson, Paul, ed. 2001. *Internet Marketing: Readings and Online Resources*. Singapore: McGraw-Hill Book Co.

Rifkin, Jeremy. 2001. *The Age of Access: How the Shift from Ownership to Access is Transforming Modern Life*. London: Penguin Books.

Rodman, George. 2001. *Making Sense of Media: An Introduction to Mass Communication*. Boston: Allyn and Bacon.

Sakai, Dean. 1999. *The Targeted Audience: Internet and Database Marketing Strategies for Broadcasters*. Washington DC: National Association of Broadcasters.

Samsung. 1999. Telecommunications Advertisement. *Fortune*, vol. 140, no. 10, pp. 16–17.

Serwer, Andy. 1999. The Prince of Tech Investors. *Fortune*, vol. 140, no. 11, p. 38.

Shingler, Martin. 2000. Some Recurring Features of European Avant-Garde Radio. In *Journal of Radio Studies* 7, no. 1. Washington DC: Broadcast Education Association, pp. 196–212.

Shingler, Martin, and Cindy Wieringa. 1998. *On Air: Methods and Meanings of Radio*. London: Arnold Publishers.

Siegel, David. 1999. *Futurize your Enterprise: Business Strategy in the Age of the E-customer*. New York: John Wiley & Sons.

Singapore Broadcasting Authority website. Available online at http://www.sba.gov.sg/sba/aboutus.jsp (accessed 3 June 2002).

Singapore Department of Statistics website. Available online at http://www.singstat.gov.sg/SVYFINDING/stats.html

Siow, James, ed. 1995. Radio Milestones. *Female*, October issue, Malaysia edition, pp. 135–138.

Stace, Doug, and Dexter Dunphy. 1997. *Beyond the Boundaries: Leading and Re-creating the Successful Enterprise*. New York: McGraw-Hill Education.

Stein, Janine. 1998. Digital TV: A Compressionable Age. *Cable and Satellite Asia*. London: FT Media & Telecoms, pp. 28–34.

Stewart, Thomas A. 1998. *Intellectual Capital: The New Wealth of Organizations*. London: Nicholas Brealey Publishing.

Straubhaar, Joseph D., and Robert LaRose. 2002. *Media Now: Communications Media in the Information Age*. 3rd edition. California: Thomson Wadsworth.

Street, Sean. 2000. BBC Sunday Policy and Audience Response 1930–1945. In *Journal of Radio Studies* 7, no. 1. Washington DC: Broadcast Education Association, pp. 161–179.

Talbot-smith, Michael. 1998. *Audio Explained*, London: Focal Press.

Talbot-smith, Michael. 1997. *Sound Assistance*. Second edition. London: Focal Press.

Talbot-smith, Michael. 1995. *Broadcast Sound Technology*. Second edition. London: Focal Press.

Tan, Roland K. C. 2000. Technology & Technicality: Characteristics of DAB. Paper presented at the *Singapore DAB Forum*, 22 January 2000, in Singapore.

Tan Yew Soon, and Soh Yew Peng. 1994. *The Development of Singapore's Modern Media Industry*. Singapore: Times Academic Press.

Tay, Dora. 1995. Editorial. *Accent*. Singapore: Accent Communications Pte Ltd.

Telecommunications Authority of Singapore. 1997. *Speech by Prime Minister Goh Chok Tong for the Opening Ceremony of Asia Telecom 97—Monday, 9 June 1997*. Available online at http://www.gov.sg/gvthome/min1.htm (accessed 30 August 1998).

Tham, Derek, and Dora Tay. 1995. With Radio You Could Be Anywhere. *Accent*, December issue. Singapore: Accent Communications Pte Ltd., pp. 20–21.

Tubbs, Stewart L., and Sylvia Moss. 1994. *Human Communication*. 7th edition. Singapore: McGraw-Hill College.

Wacker, Watts, and Jim Taylor. 2000. *The Visionary's Handbook: Nine Paradoxes that will Shape the Future of Your Business*. New York: HarperBusiness.

Wall, Tim. 2000. Policy, Pop, and the Public: The Discourse of Regulation in British Commercial Radio. In *Journal of Radio Studies* 7, no. 1. Washington DC: Broadcast Education Association, pp. 180–195.

WorldDAB Forum. 1998/99 Newsletters, London. Available online at http://www.worlddab.org/newsletter.aspx (accessed 2003).

Wright, Peter. 1996. *Managerial Leadership*. New York: Routledge.

Zyman, Sergio. 2000. *The End of Marketing as We Know It*. London: HarperBusiness.

Glossary

3G	Third generation handheld wireless telephones.
AIC	Auxiliary Information Channel: Part of the Main Service Channel, used to carry information, e.g., SI, redirected from the Fast Information Channel.
ARPANET	Advanced Research Projects Agency Network of the United States Department of Defense, formed in response to the Soviet Union's Sputnik in 1957; considered the major precursor to the Internet.
Audio frame	Frame of 24-millisecond duration which contains information of an ISO/IEC 11172-3 [3] Layer II encoded audio signal, corresponding to 1,152 consecutive audio samples at 48 kHz sampling frequency. It is the smallest part of the audio bit stream that is decodable on its own.
Bluetooth	Low-cost wireless communication system born in 1994; currently under development for wireless data delivery via mobile telephony. Operates in the 2.4 GHz range, using fast-frequency technology to avoid interference from other radio signals.
b/s	Bits per second, unit of data rate where 1 kb/s = 1,000 bits per second. *See also* kb/s, Mb/s.
CA	Conditional Access: Mechanism by which the user access to services can be restricted.
CDMA	Code Division Multiple Access: A spread-spectrum approach for the digital transmission of data/voice over radio frequencies. Sound bits are digitised and the data is split into data packets that are encoded with unique identification tags. All of the data/voice is sent over a spread range of radio frequencies. The cell phone or data device receives all of the data packets but only reassembles those packets with the correct code and transforms the broken-up bits of data into useful sound and data.
COFDM	Coded Orthogonal Frequency Division Multiplex: Transmission technique by which the complete ensemble, or multiplex, is transmitted via several hundred closely-spaced radio-frequency carriers that occupy a total bandwidth of approximately 1.5 MHz, also known as the frequency block.
Convolutional coding	Coding procedure that generates redundancy in the transmitted data stream in order to provide robust—as opposed to distorted—transmissions.
CPU	Central Processing Unit: Refers either to the principal microchip that the computer is built around—such as the Pentium or PowerPC chip—or the box that houses the main components of the computer.

CRC	Cyclic Redundancy Check: A CRC is a type of check value designed to catch most transmission errors. A decoder calculates the CRC for the received data and compares it to the CRC that the encoder calculated, which is appended to the data. A mismatch indicates that the data was corrupted in transit.
DAB	Digital Audio Broadcasting, frequently referring to the European standard Eureka 147.
DAB audio frame	Same as the audio frame but includes DAB audio-related information like the PAD.
DLS	Dynamic Label Segment: Supports a 128-character message. Supports displays from 1+16 or 2+16 characters, LCD screens, and PC monitors.
Doppler effect	An apparent shift in the received frequency of a source due to relative motion between source and receiver.
Dual-channel mode	Audio mode in which two independent programme contents are encoded within one audio bit stream. The coding process is the same as the stereo mode.
Ensemble	The transmitted signal, or multiplex. It contains programme and data services.
FIC	Fast Information Channel: Part of the transmission frame which contains the multiplex configuration information together with optional Service Information and data service components.
FIDC	Fast Information Data Channel: The dedicated part of the Fast Information Channel that is available for non-audio related data services, such as paging.
FIG	Fast Information Group.
Footprint	Coverage area of a satellite signal that can be focused to cover specific geographical areas.
FM	Frequency Modulation: Instantaneous variation of the frequency of a carrier wave in response to changes in the amplitude of a modulating signal.
GHz	GigaHertz, equivalent to 1,000 MHz. *See also* kHz, MHz.
GIF	Graphics Interchange Format: A common format for image files, especially suitable for images containing large areas of the same colour. *See also* JPEG.
GPS	Global Positioning System: Satellite-based navigation system to provide positional information.
HTML	Hypertext Markup Language: Computer language used to create hypertext documents, allowing connections from one document or Internet page to numerous others. *See also* XML.
IBOC DAB	In Band/On Channel Digital Audio Broadcasting: The American DAB system, keeps DAB close to existing FM bands, so preserves the power of existing networks and stations.

IEC	International Electrotechnical Commission: It was founded in 1906 and is currently based in Geneva, Switzerland. Its function is to coordinate, design, and publish international standards in fields related to electronics, including telecommunications.
IMT	International Mobile Telecommunications: IMT-2000 is also known as the "third generation mobile system" that aims to provide "anytime anywhere" mobile communication systems.
ISO	International Organization for Standardization: The world's largest developer of standards. It is a network of the national standards institutes of 148 countries, on the basis of one member per country, with a Central Secretariat in Geneva, Switzerland, that coordinates the system.
ITU	International Telecommunication Union: Global organisation that considers new developments in broadcasting technology and agrees on the technical standards of broadcast systems for radio and television.
ITU-R	International Telecommunication Union-Radiocommunication Bureau: It plays a vital role in the management of the radio-frequency spectrum and satellite orbits.
JPEG	Joint Photographics Expert Group: An ISO/IEC standard to digitally encode and compress still pictures. *See also* GIF.
kb/s	Kilobits per second, equivalent to 1,000 b/s. *See also* b/s, MB/s.
kHz	KiloHertz, 1,000 periods per second, the unit of frequency. *See also* GHz, MHz.
LCD	Liquid Crystal Display: A digital display that uses liquid crystal cells that change reflectivity in an applied electric field; used for portable computer displays and watches, etc.
Masking	Property of the human auditory system where an audio signal cannot be perceived in the presence of another audio signal.
Mb/s	Megabits per second, equivalent to 1,000 kb/s. *See also* b/s, kb/s.
MCI	Multiplex Configuration Information: Information that defines the configuration of the multiplex. This contains the current details about the services, service components and sub-channels and the links between these objects. This is normally carried in the FIC in order that a receiver may interpret this information in advance to decode the service components carried in the Main Service Channel. It also includes the identifier of the ensemble and a date and time marker.
MHz	Megahertz, equivalent to 1,000 kHz. *See also* kHz, GHz.
MMDS	MultiMedia Data Server.
MOT	Multimedia Object Transfer: Protocol used to support the transfer of useful data and multimedia objects, via DAB using all transport mechanisms provided. These include "stream mode", "packet mode", and "PAD" mode.

MP3	Third generation MPEG encoded audio.
MPEG	Moving Picture Experts Group: A standard ISO/IEC 11172-3 (MPEG 1 Audio Layer II) and ISO/IEC 13818-3 (MPEG 2 Audio Layer II) on source-coding systems/audio-compression formats to digitally encode and represent moving pictures and associated audio, making use of the phenomenon of Psycho-acoustic Masking. This system is also known as MUSICAM.
MSC	Main Service Channel: A channel that occupies the major part of the transmission frame and which carries all the digital service components that include audio and/or data.
Multiplexing	The process of interweaving two or more lower-speed data streams into a single high-speed radio-frequency channel for simultaneous transmission.
MUSICAM	Masking pattern Universal Sub-band Integrated Coding And Multiplexing: MPEG ISO-standardised audio-compression technique used in DAB.
Packet Mode	Mode of data transmission in which data is carried in addressable blocks called packets. This is similar to files or folders that have to be downloaded before the programme can be executed or the content viewed.
PAD	Programme Associated Data: Information that is transmitted together with the audio data. The PAD field is located at the end of the DAB audio frame.
PC	Personal Computer.
PCM	Pulse Code Modulation: Signal encoding through modulation of a carrier pulse width. A signal encoding technique used in digital audio and some switching power supplies.
PCMCIA	Personal Computer Memory Card International Association: A standard format for credit-card-size expansion cards, used to add features to laptop computers, handheld computers, and desktop computers.
RDI	Receiver Data Interface: An interface between DAB receivers and peripheral devices that may include computers, printers and so on.
RF	Radio Frequency: Frequency that is used for radio transmissions. Usually between 10 kHz and 300 GHz.
Service Label	Alphanumeric characters associated with a particular service and intended for display in a receiver.
SFN	Single Frequency Network: A network of DAB transmitters using the same radio frequency to achieve large area coverage.
SI	Service Information: Auxiliary information about services, such as service labels and programme type codes.
Stereo Mode	Audio mode where two channels forms a stereo pair (left and right) that is encoded within one bit stream. The coding process is the same as for the Dual Channel mode.

Stream Mode	Mode of data transmission within the Main Service Channel where data is carried transparently from source to destination.
Sub-band	A subdivision of the audio frequency range. In DAB, the audio-coding system uses 32 sub-bands of equal bandwidth.
Symbol	One isolated signalling waveform.
TMC	Traffic Message Channel: An additional service transmitted as a part of the FIC to provide digitally encoded traffic messages.
Transmission frame	The actual transmitted frame specific to the four transmission modes, conveying the Synchronisation Channel, the Fast Information Channel and the Main Service Channel.
UMTS	Universal Mobile Telecommunication System: A member of ITU's IMT-2000 global family of "third generation" (3G) mobile communications systems.
WAP	Wireless Application Protocol: A secure specification that allows users to access information via handheld wireless devices such as mobile phones, pagers, two-way radios, smart-phones and communicators.
XML	eXtensible Markup Language: Developed by the World Wide Web Consortium (W3C) to overcome the limitations of HTML. It allows the creation of customised tags, thus enabling the definition, transmission, validation, and interpretation of data between applications and between organisations.

Additional Resources

FURTHER READING

Block, Mervin. 1997. *Writing Broadcast News: Shorter, Sharper, Stronger*. Chicago, IL: Bonus Books.

Block, Mervin. 1994. *Broadcast Newswriting: The RTNDA Guide*. Chicago, IL: Bonus Books.

Kaye, Michael. 1995. *Best of "From Our Own Correspondent"*. Bristol, UK: Broadcast Books.

Mencher, Melvin. 2002. *News Reporting and Writing*. 9th edition. Columbus, OH: McGraw-Hill Co.

Mencher, Melvin. 1995. *Reporter's Checklist and Notebook*. Columbus, OH: McGraw-Hill Co.

WEBSITES

Mervin Block personal website
(http://www.mervinblock.com/)
Radio College (project of the Association of Independents in Radio)
(http://www.radiocollege.org/)

ONLINE BOOKSTORES

BestBookBuys.com
(http://www.bestwebbuys.com/Radio-General-books.html)
Computer Book Centre
(http://www.compbook.com.sg/)
Powells.com
(http://www.powells.com/subsection/CommunicationsTVRadioProduction.html)

DIGITAL AUDIO BROADCASTING (DAB)

Dambacher, P. 1996. *Digital Broadcating*, The Institution of Electrical Engineers (IEE), London,UK.

Digital Radio Tech (http://www.digitalradiotech.co.uk/cofdm.htm).

Stott, J. H. 1997. *Explaining some of the magic of COFDM*, 20th International Television Symposium 1997, Montreux, Switzerland. Available online: (http://www.bbc.co.uk/rd/pubs/papers/paper_15/paper_15.html).

Tan, R. K. C. 1998. "Eureka-147 Digital Audio Broadcasting", *Sound Works Magazine*, Jan/Feb issue, pp. 22–26.

Tan, R. K. C. 1999. "Going Digital: The Prospects of Starting DAB in the Asia-Pacific Region", *Sound Works Magazine*, Apr issue, pp. 17–19.

World DAB Forum, an international non-governmental organisation whose objective is to promote, harmonise and co-ordinate the implementation of DAB Digital Radio services based on the Eureka 147 DAB system (http://www.worlddab.org/).

DIGITAL SIGNAL PROCESSING (DSP)

DeFatta, D. J., Lucas, J. G., and Hodgkiss, W. S. 1988. *Digital Signal Processing: A System Design Approach.* John Wiley & Sons.

Rabiner, L. R., and Gold, B. 1975. *Theory and Application of Digital Signal Processing*, Prentice Hall, Inc.

WIRELESS MOBILE COMMUNICATIONS

History of GSM (http://www.gsmworld.com/about/history/index.shtml).

"Bluetooth Technology" (http://www.bluetooth.com/).

"An Introduction to Bluetooth" (http://www.wirelessdevnet.com/channels/bluetooth/features/bluetooth.html).

"An Introduction to WAP" (http://www.wirelessdevnet.com/channels/wap/training/wapoverview.html).

"An Introduction to GPRS" (http://www.gsmworld.com/technology/gprs/intro.shtml).

Index

213

FM. *See* Frequency Modulation
FM stereo radio, 58–61, 186
Folkerts, Jean, 22
'format clock,' 75–6
format radio, 50–4, 57, 74–6. *See
also* 'Top 40' radio format
Fortune poll, 39
4G, xvi, xvii
fourth generation wireless
technology. *See* 4G
Free Press, The, 46–7
Freed, Alan, 52–3
Frequency Modulation, 186

Galvin brothers, 29
GE. *See* General Electric
General Electric, 17–18, 22, 89
Gerbner, George, 83
Germany, 189
*Global Culture: Media Arts, Policy and
Globalization* (Crane, Kawashima
and Kawasaki), 65
global media market, 89
'global village,' 12
Godfrey, Arthur, 33–4
governance, 41
gratification theory, 67–70
Gulf War (1991), 12
'gun microphone,' 18
Gurevitch, Michael, 68
Gutenberg, Johannes, 8

Haas, Hadassah, 68
Hanson, Ward, 13, 19
Harris, Oren, 52
Hauptmann, Bruno, 37
Havas, 38
header core, 181
header extension, 181–2
headphones, 18
Hendy, David, 62, 65–6, 72, 77, 82,
104, 107, 132, 136, 139, 189–90
Henry, Joseph, 12
Herrold, Charles, 30

Hertz, Heinrich, 13
hierarchical narratives, 136–9
Hindenburg crash, 39
*History of Mass Communication: Six
Information Revolutions, A* [Fang],
7
History of Singapore, A [Chen], 5
Hitler, Adolf, 39
Hoeg, Wolfgang, 129, 181, 183
Hong Kong
Internet use, 101–2
personal computers, 102
*How Kids and Tweens Use and Respond
to Radio* (Arbitron), 64
HTML, 169, 181, 183

I²C bus, 187
I²C Master, 187
ICC. *See* Imperial Communications
Committee
IDA. *See* Infocomm Development
Authority of Singapore
*IEEE Transactions on Consumer
Electronics*, 184
IF. *See* Intermediate Frequency
Imperial Communications
Committee, 24–5
Independent Television. *See* ITV
Infocomm Development Authority
of Singapore, 64, 92
'Information Highway,' 9
'information technology paradigm,'
87
INS. *See* International News
Services
*Intellectual Capital: The New Wealth
of Organizations* (Stewart, T A),
65
interactivity between radio and
listeners
chat rooms, 81
digital innovations, 83–90,
167, 190–1, 193
email, 81

217

Asian Media Information and Communication (AMIC) Series

The Asian Media Information and Communication Series is a co-publication series with AMIC Centre, located at Singapore's Nanyang Technological University's School of Communication and Information.

Community Broadcasting: Concept and Practice in the Philippines
by Felix Librero
ISBN 981 210 328 7

Cultural Rights in a Global World
edited by Anura Goonasekera, Cess Hamelink and Venkat Iyer
ISBN 981 210 235 3

Media in a Terrorized World: Reflections in the Wake of 911
edited by S Venkatraman
ISBN 981 210 234 5

News Media and New Media: The Asia-Pacific Internet Handbook (Episode V)
edited by Madanmohan Rao
ISBN 981 210 232 9

Rhetoric and Reality: The Internet Challenge for Democracy in Asia
edited by Indrajit Bannerjee
ISBN 981 210 231 0

Strengthening Women's Voices: Building Women Communications for Environmental Conservation
by Mildred Moscoso
ISBN 981 210 236 1

For information on pricing and availability, please log on to
www.marshallcavendish.com/academic

CyberPR Series – From Main Street to Cyber Street: Changes in the Practice of Communication
by Basskaran Nair

Today the paradigm for communications is being defined by new technology, particularly the advent of the Internet. This CyberPR series explores how mainstream communication practices are changing significantly to factor in the new technologies; the practice of communication must take a sharp turn from Main Street to Cyber Street in terms of understanding the new tools, techniques and strategies.

Basskaran Nair is Associate Professor (Adjunct), Information and Communications Management Programme, Faculty of Arts and Social Sciences, National University of Singapore. He was equity partner in international financial public relation relations firms and has held senior positions in companies like CapitaLand Limited and DBS Bank. He was also accorded the Best PR Professional Award by the Institute of Public Relations, Singapore and was past president of East West Center Alumni (Singapore), a US think-tank.

Vol. 1 – Investor Relations
ISBN 981 210 224 8
Vol. 2 – Government Relations
ISBN 981 210 225 6
Vol. 3 – Issues Management
ISBN 981 210 226 4
Vol. 4 – Marketing Communication
ISBN 981 210 237 X

Vol. 5 – Employee Communication
ISBN 981 210 228 0
Vol. 6 – Community Relations
ISBN 981 210 229 9
Vol. 7 – Media Relations
ISBN 981 210 227 2

Other Titles in Communication and Media Studies

Borderless Bandwidth: DNA of Digital Radio
by Rafael Oei
ISBN 981 210 201 9

Latent Images: Film in Singapore
by Jan Uhde and Yvonne Ng Uhde
ISBN 019 588 714 X

For information on pricing and availability, please log on to
www.marshallcavendish.com/academic